1600
9938

Kurt Koffka

Kurt Koffka

an unwitting self-portrait

Molly Harrower

preface by Mary Henle

A University of Florida Book
University Presses of Florida
Gainesville

Library of Congress Cataloging in Publication Data

Harrower, Molly, 1906–
    Kurt Koffka, an unwitting self-portrait.

    "A University of Florida book."
    Bibliography: p.
    Includes index.
    1. Koffka, Kurt, 1886–1941.   2. Harrower, Molly,
1906– .   3. Psychologists—Correspondence.
4. Gestalt psychology.   I. Koffka, Kurt, 1886–1941.
II. Title.
BF109.K59H37   1983   150'.92'4   83–10455
ISBN 0–8130–0760–7

    University Presses of Florida is the central agency for scholarly publishing of the State of Florida's university system. Its offices are located at 15 NW 15th Street, Gainesville, FL 32603.
    Works published by University Presses of Florida are evaluated and selected for publication, after being reviewed by referees both within and outside of the state's university system, by a faculty editorial committee of any one of Florida's nine public universities: Florida A&M University (Tallahassee), Florida Atlantic University (Boca Raton), Florida International University (Miami), Florida State University (Tallahassee), University of Central Florida (Orlando), University of Florida (Gainesville), University of North Florida (Jacksonville), University of South Florida (Tampa), University of West Florida (Pensacola).

contents

list of illustrations

foreword

Publication of the correspondence between Kurt Koffka and Molly Harrower, 1928–41, is most gratifying. Very few people knew about these letters until the 1960s, when Molly Harrower showed a sample of them to historically conscious friends. They wisely urged her to make the entire collection available to scholars and also suggested that a wider audience would find this record of an intellectual friendship to be illuminating for the history of ideas. She responded by publishing one detailed discussion between the correspondents on the then new Rorschach technique of personality assessment ("Koffka's Rorschach Experiment," *Journal of Personality Assessment* 35, 1971), by participating in symposia on Gestalt psychology, and by giving addresses on Koffka's place in the Gestalt movement. These contributions provided a glimpse of the range of subjects that the letters cover and strengthened the demands for more comprehensive material to be made available.

These published documents allow Koffka and Harrower to speak again on matters of importance to them over a much wider range than before. Their publication coincides with the preparation of various biographies of the cofounders of Gestalt psychology, Max Wertheimer and Wolfgang Köhler. Historians are finding it profitable to reexamine the ideas of the inaugural members of the Gestalt movement.

Koffka was born in Berlin in 1886. His father was an attorney, and the family has been described as financially secure. Before attending the University of Berlin he spent a year at the University of Edinburgh, an experience that perhaps made his later decision to leave Germany to live in the United States less difficult than it was for some of his colleagues. He attended the University of Berlin from 1904 to 1908, when he received his Ph.D. in psychology. A series of academic appointments followed. In 1910 he was at Frankfort and there began the close association with Wertheimer and Köhler. From 1911 until 1924 he was at the University of Giessen. During World War I, he was associated with a clinic at Giessen that treated aphasia as well as other varieties of intracranial pathology.

In 1924 Koffka came to the United States and, after 1927, was associated with Smith College until his death in 1941 at the age of fifty-five. He published his most important book, *The Principles of Gestalt Psychology*, in 1935, about the mid-point of the correspondence contained in this volume.

Molly Harrower was born in 1906 in South Africa of Scottish parents and grew up and was educated in England. She came to the United States in 1928 on a fellowship to be assistant to Koffka at the newly established Gestalt research laboratory at Smith College. She received her Ph.D. in experimental psychology from Smith College in 1934.

During the years covered by the letters she became a widely respected figure in her own right, an expert on projective techniques. Particularly pertinent to the development of the correspondence was the Rockefeller Medical Foundation fellowship that she received in 1937, thereby becoming one of the first experimental psychologists to move into a field now known as neuropsychology. This move, in turn, led to Koffka's renewed interest in the clinical field and his appointment to Oxford in 1939.

Harrower is professor emeritus in the Department of Clinical Psychology at the University of Florida, where she was recently awarded an honorary degree.

Both correspondents are remarkably sensitive to the subtleties of language. Harrower is a published poet and has written on the use of poetry in psychotherapy. Koffka, using English as a second language, evidences a sensitivity shared by many who, in coming to a new language, have been confronted with both its facility and difficulty. Koffka and Harrower came to the United States as educated adults and observed the American scene with the penetrating perspective of adapting strangers. Their correspondence is about the psychological and intellectual world, articulately expressed with the frankness of informality. It assesses the American scene and its influence upon them.

Molly Harrower is uniquely qualified to serve as the editor of these letters. She is personally familiar with the events that are recorded. She has more sophisticated knowledge than any other person about the passages that are most pertinent for the past and the enrichment of the present.

John A. Popplestone
Archives of the History
of American Psychology

preface

This book that I have the pleasure of introducing is significant for a number of reasons: It is set in an important and lively period in American intellectual history; it deals with a significant movement in psychology, Gestalt psychology; it features a central figure in that movement, Kurt Koffka; and it constitutes an experiment in autobiography/biography. Each of these aspects of the book deserves our attention.

Most of the letters on which this *Unwitting Self-Portrait* is based are from the period just before and after January 30, 1933. On that date Adolph Hitler came to power in Germany, and there soon followed an exodus of German intellectuals. Some of them—natural scientists, social scientists, artists, writers—came to the United States. Although their numbers were small—pitiably small compared with present practices of granting asylum to victims of totalitarian oppression—their distinction was great, and their influence on the American intellectual scene far exceeded their numbers. The Germans were soon joined by Austrian, Italian, French, and other émigré scholars and writers.

The newcomers influenced and were influenced by their American colleagues. In psychology and the social sciences, for example, the Europeans were impressed by, and adopted, the standards of evidence of their American counterparts, while the Americans became interested—if not wholly engaged—in the theoretical issues that concerned the émigrés. The tension between a broader outlook and interest in a more coherent picture, on the one hand, and precise investigation of small problems, on the other, led to mutual education and lively and productive discussion.

Among the ideas which the German émigrés brought to America were those of Gestalt psychology. These ideas, which first arose around 1910, were not totally unknown to American psychologists before the years 1933–35, by which time all the major representatives of this movement were in the United States. A number of young American psychologists had studied at the Psychological Institute of the University of Berlin, whose director was Wolfgang Köhler, and where Max Wertheimer lectured until 1929; they, together with Koffka, were the founders of Gestalt psychology. In addition, both Koffka and Köhler had been visiting professors in this country during the academic year 1924–25, and Koffka again in 1926–27, before he took up permanent residence in America, at Smith College, in 1927. Koffka had written the first article in English on perception from the point of view of Gestalt psychology in 1922; and both he and Köhler had been publishing in English, and had had works translated into English, before the period with which this book is concerned.

Still, the presence in the United States of Wertheimer, Köhler, and Koffka made a strong impression on American psychologists. All three lectured widely; they were listened to with respect but were often the center of controversy. For Gestalt psychology can be described as no less than a revolution in psychological thought. It challenged the very foundations of the traditional psychologies, which it found to be unable to deal with essential human characteristics. There was no place for meaningfulness or for value in the prevailing scientific psychologies, both in Germany and in America, and the order of psychological and corresponding biological events was seen as artificially imposed by constraining conditions.

When the Gestalt psychologists came to America, they found that the dominant psychology was no longer the structuralism of Wundt and Titchener, but behaviorism. They also found that the same kinds of criticism which they had leveled against structuralist conceptions applied also to behavioristic ones. Both structuralists and behaviorists, because they wished to establish the scientific status of a new discipline, took nineteenth century physics as their model. They adopted the atomism and mechanism of that science as they viewed it. The failures of the traditional approaches, the Gestalt psychologists thought, arose not out of the use of the scientific method, as some had said, but out of a misconception of that method. Gestalt psychology took as its model the newer conceptions of field physics.

Rejecting atomistic analysis of consciousness into sensory elements, as well as the analysis of behavior into similarly artificial units, the Gestalt psychologists started with experience as it presents itself directly to observation. Such experience shows no elements, rather segregated wholes that cannot be understood as aggregates of predetermined small units. Indeed, in the clearest cases, it is the whole which determines the functions and properties of parts. In such cases, analysis must be "from above," from whole to natural parts, rather than "from below," the traditional analysis into supposed elements.

Thus Gestalt psychologists begin with phenomenology, the direct and, as far as possible, unbiased report of experience. The next step is demonstration and experiment, perhaps qualitative at first, before quantitative experimentation is undertaken. In this way the Gestalt psychologists try to keep in touch with the phenomena they are investigating. This approach contrasts with that of many American psychologists (both in the 1930s and now), who rush into quantitative investigation often of minor problems, thus running the risk of losing sight of major issues.

The Gestalt approach was applied at first mainly to perception, where it quite simply transformed the field. The emphasis now is on the study of phenomenal objects, not on analysis into abstract elements. No American perceptionist today can escape the heritage of Gestalt psychology, though some may be unaware of the debt.

Very early, Gestalt psychologists were breaking new ground in the psychology of thinking, which had hitherto been dominated by associationistic conceptions. There followed work on learning, remembering, and forgetting. Gestalt psychologists showed that not even associative learning, a common laboratory task, can be explained by associationism, but is to be subsumed under Gestalt principles.

How were the new findings to be explained? It had previously been assumed that the remarkably orderly processes of perception were to be accounted for by the orderly arrangement of neurons in the nervous system. With regard to other psychological functions, too, a machine-like order of the histology of the cerebral cortex was likewise held to be responsible. Gestalt psychologists applied their field theoretical approach to the nervous system and explained orderly psychological processes by corresponding dynamic interactions in the cortex.

The implications of Gestalt psychology beyond the traditional problems of experimental psychology soon became clear. It found a central place for value, traditionally neglected by psychology, and showed the compatibility of value with natural science. In addition, new approaches to social psychology, motivation, the perception of persons, the expression of personality, and other areas were offered. Beyond psychology, Gestalt thinkers became interested in problems of aesthetics, truth, logic, other problems of philosophy, anthropology, brain physiology. Some of the implications of Gestalt psychology for education have begun to be worked out; others remain as a challenge. It is not surprising that philosophers, art historians, and scholars in other fields have become interested in Gestalt psychology.

Despite the stir it created in American psychology in the 1930s and 1940s, Gestalt psychology never became dominant. Uprooted from one intellectual tradition, it seemed somehow alien in its new scientific surroundings. It was carried on in the United States by its founders and by a small group of co-workers. Aside from its major impact on perception, and to a lesser extent on the psychology of thinking, it was (and continues to be) imperfectly understood in this country, despite the vigorous efforts of its proponents to correct misunderstandings. In one important respect, however, the situation in psychology is now changing. Cognitive psychologists who have no relation to Gestalt theory are beginning to investigate Gestalt problems, though not yet by Gestalt methods.

But these problems will in time force their investigators to use appropriate methods, and it is to be hoped that a new, improved, and expanded Gestalt psychology will one day emerge through the combined efforts of its founders and their co-workers and the new generation of psychologists who have been forced by the necessities of their own work to a new consideration of Gestalt problems.

In this changed atmosphere, the appearance of Kurt Koffka's *Self-Portrait* is particularly appropriate. In his letters we see Koffka's whole-hearted commitment to Gestalt psychology and his concern with its implications for problems beyond psychology proper. We see his elation when an audience has understood his message and his patient efforts to correct misapprehensions. And we see the letters written against a background of devoted writing and continuing research.

What is Koffka's special place in Gestalt psychology? His record of experimental work, particularly in visual perception, is distinguished and of lasting value. His role in introducing Gestalt psychology to America has already been discussed. He took his part in the polemical efforts to which Gestalt psychologists found themselves obliged to devote so much time. Koffka will be chiefly remembered, however, for his great book, *Principles of Gestalt Psychology*, which attempts to set forth systematically the principles of this psychology and to show that they can encompass the full range of experimental psychology of the time, not merely the work of the advocates of Gestalt psychology. The extension of these principles to little worked areas of psychology and to problems beyond its borders is part of the work of the systematist as Koffka saw it.

We have taken a brief look at Koffka's contributions to science as well as at the psychology he represented. What kind of person was this interesting thinker? In this volume, Dr. Harrower employs an unusual, perhaps unique, method of showing us. She has selected, excerpted, and organized letters from her thirteen-year correspondence with Koffka, a correspondence which was at first sporadic but became a continuing dialogue between 1931 and 1941, the year of Koffka's death. Under Dr. Harrower's skillful guidance we learn Koffka's views on a variety of issues, his values, his enthusiasms, a good deal about a vivid and complex personality. The book is indeed an unwitting self-portrait, but since this portrait would not have emerged without the organization and insights of its editor, I prefer to think of it as an experiment in autobiography/biography.

Mary Henle
New School for Social Research

introduction

In my attempt to create a word portrait of Kurt Koffka I must play two distinct roles. On the one hand, the material on which this book is based comes from more than 2,000 letters which he and I exchanged over a thirteen-year period. On the other hand, from the perspective of the present day, I must play the part of an editor, supplying what is needed by way of explanations, selecting appropriate topics from the unwieldy mass of handwritten pages, and passing judgment on which portions of my own letters need to be included in order to understand what Koffka wrote. To sharpen this distinction I have referred to myself as MH, or Harrower, at those points in the narrative where my letters are introduced.

Some details about these letters and how they have been handled as research material over the past five years may be helpful. By actual count there were 2,166 letters exchanged, 1,084 from Koffka, 1,082 to him. From the start I had kept Koffka's letters in large folders year by year. Since they were all written on 8 × 11 standard sheets they could easily be kept in order. Koffka had kept my letters in their envelopes, a bulky arrangement but, as it turned out, of great value, since the postmark recorded the date of mailing to which he had added the date of arrival. This orderliness proved of importance since I had failed to put a date on any of them!

Strictly speaking, the correspondence covers the years between 1928 and 1941. Except for a few notes written in the first two years, however, the letters themselves do not begin until 1930. I had come from England to work with Koffka in his research laboratory at Smith College in 1928. As a junior member of our international group, my work involved Koffka's experiments rather than a project of my own.†

In 1930, I was offered a position as instructor in psychology at Wells College for a year. However, as soon as I had left the research laboratory, innumerable questions arose for Koffka as to the whereabouts of protocols and calculations and how to construct the apparatus needed for our work, and since it was also my task to edit our manuscript and produce idiomatic English, my absence necessitated much correspondence. At that time we were involved in writing the articles subsequently published as "Color and Organization, Parts 1 and 2" (Koffka and Harrower 1931).

A comparable situation, when frequent correspondence was necessary, arose in 1932–33 when, owing to the sudden death of Victoria Hazlitt, a psychology professor at London University, I was appointed senior lecturer for a year to fill her place. At this time Koffka was working on *The Principles of Gestalt Psychology* (Koffka 1935b), and all 750 pages of this manuscript journeyed back and forth across the Atlantic for comments and editing.

Out of these letter exchanges there emerged an almost day-by-day account of the experiences of each of the correspondents. When in 1934 I set forth equipped with a Ph.D. from Smith College, the correspondence not only continued but swelled into nearly 6,000 handwritten pages, from which Koffka's self-portrait can be culled.

Koffka's letters came chiefly from Smith College, where, after heading a research laboratory for five years, he taught undergraduate students. He also wrote from as far afield as Russia and Uzbekistan during a brief research trip, from Germany on vaca-

---

†Psychologists working with Koffka at the Northampton laboratory during the late 1920s and early 1930s included Alexander Mintz (Russia), I Huang (China), Fritz Heider (Austria) and his wife, Grace Moore Heider (U.S.A.), Eugenia Hanfmann (Estonia), Tamara Dembo (Germany), and, for shorter periods of time, from England, Julian Blackburn and Margo Harvey.

tion, and from Oxford, England, where he spent an important year.

I wrote from various locales, including London during my year of teaching; from New Jersey, where I was director of students at New Jersey College for Women (now Douglass College); from Montreal, where I broke from academic psychology and entered the clinical field at the Neurological Institute with Wilder Penfield;* and from Spain, where I was unexpectedly overwhelmed by the Spanish Civil War.

Unfortunately, the printed versions of these letters lose much that is of interest to the eye of a psychologist interested in graphology and even to the eye of a naïve observer. The unvarying size of the paper used by Koffka, his systematic spacing, and the uniform and closely packed lines of his handwriting are in marked contrast to my off-the-cuff contributions, where any available piece of stationery was utilized and, as likely as not, poems or drawings punctuated the text.

In 1941 at Koffka's death, I as his executor retrieved all the scientific material from his laboratory and office, among which were my letters to Koffka. I spent considerable time ordering his papers, lecture notes, and general correspondence and saw through the press the one completed manuscript, "The Place of a Psychologist among Scientists" (Koffka, 1954). All this material was then turned over to the Archives of the History of American Psychology.

I have listed these items from the research laboratory in an article, "A Note on the Koffka Papers" (Harrower 1971a), reproduced in part in Appendix D. The original letters from both correspondents are now in plastic sheaths and are also destined for the archives.

My letters to Koffka and his to me I felt required a distance and perspective. I needed leisure to reread and assess them, but it was simply nonexistent in the intervening years of a busy professional and married life. It was not until 1975, when I reached emeritus

---

*An asterisk by a name indicates inclusion in the glossary of names at the end of the book.

These two letters reflect the writers' different use of material and spacing. Koffka packed words on his page, using the margin for additional ideas. The spaces between his lines are small, as are those between the words themselves. He always had a wide left-hand margin and a much smaller one on the right. Harrower's spacing, both between lines and words, is much wider. The pages do not appear crowded or suggest pressure, even when the content reflects constant activity.

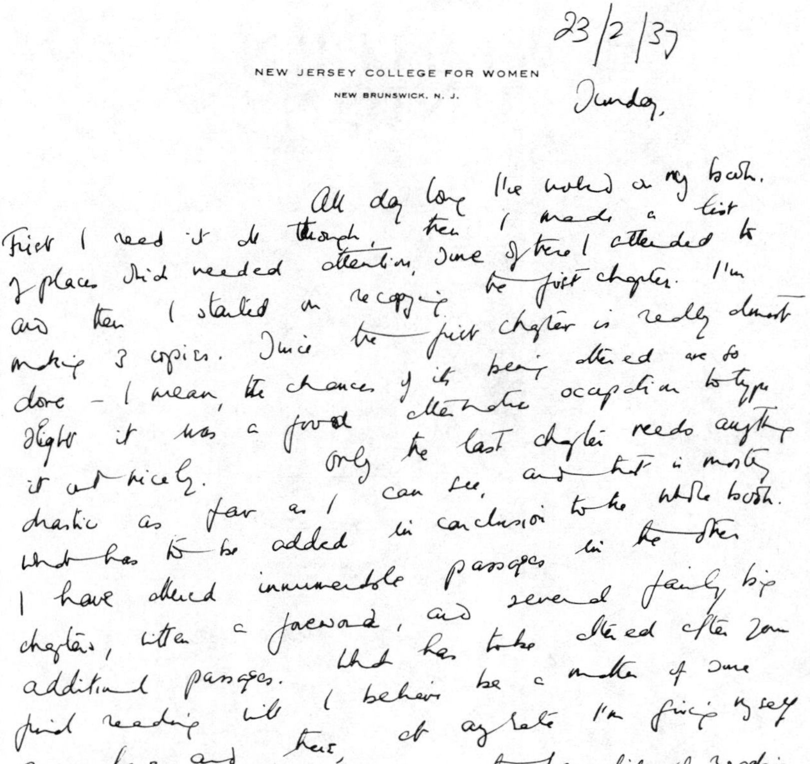

23/2/37
Sunday,

[handwritten letter, largely illegible]

All day long I've worked on my book. First I read it all through, then I made a list of places which needed attention. Some of these I attended to and then I started on recopying the first chapter. I'm making 3 copies. Since the first chapter is really almost done — I mean, the chances of its being altered are so slight it was a good alternative occupation to type it out nicely. Only the last chapter needs anything drastic as far as I can see, and that is mostly what has to be added in conclusion to the whole book. I have altered innumerable passages in the other chapters, with a foreward, and several fairly big additional passages. That has to be altered after some final reading will I believe be a matter of some pages here and there, at any rate I'm giving myself the benefit of this and yet the benefit of reading a nice copy! However, it will take time: a regular typist's speed is only 6 pages an hour and while I am fast rather than absolutely accurate, I can't do much more than that.

Koffka's approach to letter writing was a systematic one. He wrote in the same place, at his desk in the laboratory, and at about the same time of day, in the late afternoon an hour or so before leaving. He always used the same large writing pad that he used to record his experimental findings. He wrote with a favorite fountain pen, which he refused to lend to anyone. This practice, however, was not unusual in the thirties. Fountain pens were very personal possessions and had carefully chosen nibs, suitable for one's own handwriting.

CLASS OF SERVICE DESIRED	
DOMESTIC	CABLE
TELEGRAM	FULL RATE
DAY LETTER	DEFERRED
NIGHT MESSAGE	NIGHT LETTER
NIGHT LETTER	SHIP RADIOGRAM

Patrons should check class of service desired; otherwise message will be transmitted as a full-rate communication.

WESTERN UNION

R. B. WHITE
PRESIDENT

NEWCOMB CARLTON
CHAIRMAN OF THE BOARD

J. C. WILLEVER
FIRST VICE-PRESIDENT

CHECK

ACCT'G INFMN.

TIME FILED

Send the following message, subject to the terms on back hereof, which are hereby agreed to

19____

To _____ Excuse this, but there is nothing

Street and No. ____ else to write on down here into

Place ____ Rockefeller Center. I have just

seen Lambert. Prepared long distanced him

asking for money for Hebb — Lambert refused

and suggested a National Research Council — Since

this may not go through there is a possibility

that P.K. may be in an awkward position!

Lambert agrees that I should go to Berlin,

Morehead, but until I am a fellow they cannot

finance me — So that pretty bad for me,

but I still believe its necessary to go.

Sender's address
for reference

**WESTERN UNION GIFT ORDERS ARE APPROPRIATE GIFTS
FOR ALL OCCASIONS.**

Sender's telephone
number

He has given me some essential literature, and also feels that routine operations it 2 hold be invaluable.

He is now working on full line cases - & is doing exactly what I had planned to do, adapt some of the good tests so as to show up certain things more clearly. (Washington showed me what was

needed in this direction) He felt it to Lambert if I need it to urge him initial training period. He even thinks he can supply a graduate student to work in Washington

I am now dining alone, and in style of a delightful restaurant. Henri on 45th Street. Just off 5th so I hope he can gather in March 6th when your have

After leaving the relatively leisurely tempo of the research laboratory, Harrower plunged into full-time activities as a faculty member and director of students, then into the pressures of clinical situations in Montreal. She wrote when opportunity arose, using any writing material that was available—a telegraph form or a very small notebook might serve the purpose. Most of her long letters were typed. There were frequently two mail deliveries a day, guaranteeing the arrival of letters overnight. Thus many of the letters are diarylike, forming a continuous record of daily living.

status at the University of Florida and was freer to order my own time, that I started to review them after this long interval.

The first months were spent in actually interfacing the letters so that there was now one total, uninterrupted document. Two separately ordered sequences had to be brought together. When this step had been completed, I read for the first time what had suddenly become a living correspondence, a seemingly endless exchange of experiences, views, and ideas.

The next year I decided to provide guidelines through this massive material for myself and future research workers, mainly by underlining in different colors the various themes which ran through the years. At this time, all proper names mentioned throughout the correspondence were listed month by month, and separate lists of the dates of letters were made for Wolfgang Köhler,* Max Wertheimer,* Kurt Lewin,* and some important others.

The following year I achieved a one-page summary of ideas and topics for each of the 144 months involved in the correspondence, and my last major undertaking was to embark on a shortened typewritten manuscript reducing the mountain of handwritten pages to an 1,800-page typed version.

It is from this more manageable version that I have attempted to produce a picture of Koffka in his own words. It might, I suppose, be called his unwitting self-portrait. In most instances the material has been organized so that quotations from his letters concerning various topics have been brought together.

I include as an appendix a biographical account adapted from the obituary that I wrote at the time of Koffka's death (Harrower-Erickson 1942). I feel it is important for the reader to be able to place him in a historical setting. I have chosen this account rather than write another; the material was carefully researched in 1941, and I doubt if I could be equally accurate today.

The initial chapter of the current volume deals with Koffka as a psychologist, indicating, for instance, his place in the Gestalt triangle as I now see it. There follow direct quotations from his letters describing his relationships to Köhler and Wertheimer at different times, and his off-the-cuff comments on the writing of *The Principles of Gestalt Psychology*.

The next chapters begin to reveal Koffka the man. "The Private Koffka" reflects his tastes in music, drama, and literature, as well as the qualities in human beings that he endorsed or disliked. The quotations from the chapter "The Public Koffka" show his role as a club member and his role in the American Psychological Association and catch some of his political orientation. This chapter also reflects aspects of his personality which made public lecturing and undergraduate teaching difficult but which brought him great success with groups of graduate students and young faculty members. Here we also see Koffka's need to reach out to outstanding thinkers in other fields.

"Koffka as Mentor" portrays his concern for the intellectual development of his young correspondent. In "Koffka as Colleague" the excerpts reflect the development of the correspondents' relationship toward one of equals, partners in ideas and interests.

"The Russian Expedition" recounts Koffka's impressions and reactions to his research adventure in Russia and Uzbekistan, undertaken at the invitation of Alexander Luria in 1932. "Reactions to the Gathering Clouds of War" includes quotations from both correspondents' letters relating to the ominous encroachment of World War II.

The final two chapters deal with Koffka in Oxford. The first explores the year's professional challenges; the second includes letters almost in their entirety to give a more rounded picture of Koffka's Oxford life.

koffka as psychologist

Contribution to the Gestalt Idea

If one sets up a triangle with Wertheimer at the apex and Köhler and Koffka along the baseline, one sees Wertheimer's position as the originator of the Gestalt idea and sees him supported by Köhler and Koffka, each in his own unique way.

How can one describe the components of Koffka's support system to the Gestalt idea?

First, I would list a personal loyalty, with a concomitant feeling of responsibility to protect and further an idea which he valued, both intellectually and with an almost religious feeling. It is important to point out that this loyalty of Koffka's and his true appreciation of the idea were totally untouched by any need to claim kudos for himself in terms of basic Gestalt contributions. This innate modesty was viewed with particular sympathy by Koffka's British colleagues because it enabled them to learn more easily from him than from the other two contributors. Indirectly this same manner did much to break down arbitrary barriers. In 1923, at the First International Congress of psychologists in Oxford after World War I, "He is one of us," reported psychology professor Beatrice Edgell* of the University of London.

Second, I would see among Koffka's supporting contributions his view of himself as a needed systematizer. He felt strongly that there was a need for a thorough, cohesive Gestalt system that attempted to cover all areas and did not bypass unsolved problems. The result was *The Principles of Gestalt Psychology*, the product of a three-year dedication of Koffka's life and working hours. This work has remained the only systematic and thorough assessment of Gestalt theory.

Third, I would point to Koffka's acceptance of the task of dealing with, and answering systematically, serious arguments and criticisms leveled at Gestalt theory. His reply to McDougall* (Koffka 1938) is a case in point, but he answered with equally meticulous detail argumentative letters written to him personally, provided he felt that they had been put forward in good faith and had arisen from genuine misunderstandings of Gestalt literature. He did not enter into emotional polemics and he delighted when light dawned.

Finally, I would cite as an example of Koffka's support system and his ways of furthering the whole Gestalt idea his discussions by mail with outstanding thinkers in other fields and other countries. For example, a forty-page typewritten letter to the noted astronomer Sir Arthur Eddington* led Eddington to modify some of his thinking, admitting the relevance of a Gestalt argument to his own field (see Appendix E). There was also correspondence to the author of Holism, Jan Christiaan Smuts,* whose philosophical treatise on the nature of the world had a wide influence on philosophical thought in Europe.

Most striking, however, was Koffka's impact on medical and neurological thinking in Oxford during the years 1938–40. At that time Koffka had been appointed a member of the newly founded Nuffield Institute for Brain Surgery in Oxford and was invited to become a fellow of one of the prestigious colleges in the university. By immersing himself in the clinical situation of the hospital, he began to formulate his ideas in such a way that the Gestalt concept began to filter into medical thinking. His lectures were published in the important English medical journal, the *Lancet*, and he was working on a book, *Psychology for Neurologists*, at the time of his death.

In summary, Koffka was an active, wholehearted appreciator of an important idea. He was a relentless systematizer—as in the

Principles—refusing to let unthought-through areas escape. He was a careful watchdog, preventing misleading criticism, a correspondent with some of the major thinkers in science and philosophy, and a far greater creative contributor to Gestalt theory than he ever gave himself credit for.

So much for Gestalt psychology per se. But how did Koffka envisage and relate to his two colleagues on a more personal basis? In this regard the letters allow Koffka to speak for himself over the years.

Koffka Relates to Köhler

There are 135 references to Köhler in the letters between 1930 and 1940. During these years Koffka shows a consistent acceptance of, and pleasure in, Köhler's dominant position in the Gestalt fraternity. Within this framework one can trace several themes.

For instance, Köhler's approval of the task Koffka had set for himself, that of the systematic presenter of the important Gestalt ideas, was valued highly.

> Köhler congratulated me very much on my paper in the *Psychologies of 1930* [Koffka 1930]. He thinks it is one of the best things I've ever written. [8 July 1930, Northampton]†

> Many good talks with Köhler. He agrees with my Ego Theory completely [see Koffka 1935b, 319–42]. It did not even seem to be new to him. He finds it as necessary a conclusion as I did, which gave me great satisfaction. He enjoyed his stay, he is an amazing person. [15 June 1933]

The extent to which Köhler was appreciated by American colleagues was also Koffka's concern. It became a responsibility to further this where possible:

---

†Unless another locale is specified with the bracketed date, that excerpt is from a letter written by Koffka from Northampton, Massachusetts.

Koffka and Köhler at the International Congress of Psychology in 1929 at Yale. Harrower took the photo.

Have you, by the way read the review of Köhler's *Gestalt Psychology* in the *British Journal* [*of Psychology*] by Oeser [British psychologist]? I think it is very stupid. One feels the bias of the reviewer who has been a student of Jaensch's [German psychologist Erich Jaensch*]. Probably arguing about it won't serve any purpose. The more fruitful theory will survive, others will be gradually abandoned and forgotten. Nevertheless I'll ask Köhler to write something for the British Journal since it seems to me that British public understands Gestalt Theory very badly although a good many people seem at the moment rather interested. But I doubt whether Köhler will do anything. [22 October 1930]

And two years later after having attended an International Conference in Copenhagen:

One more word about Copenhagen, I made great friends with young Oeser, you know the Cambridge man who wrote that rather nasty review of Köhler's book. Eventually he had a long talk with Köhler, and everything was patched up. I am certain that he will never again write against Gestalt Theory, not because of personal reasons, but because he was much impressed by things I told him and by Köhler's paper. [Copenhagen, 29 August 1932]

Special recognition of Köhler, and a quality of genuine integrity, delighted Koffka:

Köhler showed me a passage in Woodworth's [Columbia University psychologist Robert Woodworth*] contribution to the *Psychologies of 1930*, in which Woodworth proves himself a gallant gentleman. You remember that Woodworth, as many others, has made the mistake to think and write that according to Gestalt Theory the outside gestalten get into the mind in a perfectly mysterious way. Now, after having read Köhler's new book, he admits not only that his interpretation was wrong but also that in no place in his previous publications had Köhler

written anything to justify the error. Isn't that a splendid thing
to do! [Europe, 8 July 1930]

Koffka had great difficulty in allowing himself to recognize the
extent to which he was hurt by Köhler's long silences and by
Köhler's failure to communicate with him on matters he considered vital. In this letter this problem between them first found
expression:

Did I tell you about the German Psychological Society? I am
not sure, therefore I'll tell you the story briefly. The regular
biannual meeting was to have taken place at Dresden in the
beginning of the month, [William] Stern* being the president
of the society and [probably Gustav] Kafka the chairman of the
local committee. I received a program, quite interesting in
parts, but containing a significant innovation: church services,
protestant and catholic, for the members. A little later I had a
note saying that owing to the political situation the meeting
had been indefinitely postponed. Shortly afterward I received a
longer official communique that the full committee had met at
Berlin where Messrs. Stern, [David] Katz, and Kafka had resigned. [Erich] Jaensch, Klemm [unidentified], and Reiffert
[unidentified] had been elected in their places, and the members of the new committee present at the meeting had unan-
imously elected Krueger [developmental psychologist Felix
Krueger] president of the society. The meeting would be held
in Leipzig on October 15th! Nice, isn't it? I shall do nothing—
much as I want to send in my resignation from the society—
before I hear from Köhler, lest I injure their position. But of
course Köhler does not write! [18 April 1933]

By far the most interesting letters relate to the role Köhler was
playing against the background of the encroachment of Nazi influence into academic circles. The first of these reflected perplexity as to what underlay Köhler's motivation in praising the new
regime. This perplexity was felt not only by Koffka but by the research team that worked with him at that time. Grace Heider re-

members vividly Koffka's excitement and concern over Köhler's article.

The article (Köhler's) is extremely well written, if anything could have any affect at all it would be this. Cautious, and yet brave appeal. What startled me is the introduction, in which he praises the achievement of the New [Nazi] Regime in rather glowing terms, I do not know whether this is just politics in order to give more weight to his defense of liberals, and Jews, or whether it represents his own opinion. Heider [Northampton lab psychologist Fritz Heider] showed us yesterday a clipping from a German newspaper with the names of those professors at a number of universities, who, till a final decision, have been given leave of absence. Wertheimer is of course among them. Frau Köhler wrote that Wertheimer is outside Germany at the moment. [10 May 1933]

A month later Koffka wrote:

Turning to the second part of the *New York Times* I found on its front page a headlined column wireless from the Bremen about Köhler's coming to Chicago. Quite an interview, cautious but in no way a wholehearted acceptance of the present regime. At this moment he is already ashore, I expect a telegram from him at any moment. I'm terribly curious what he will have to say. [7 June 1933]

When Köhler finally arrived in Northampton, face-to-face discussions began to clear up the misunderstandings: "I had a short note from Köhler yesterday, arriving on the same boat as he did himself. He will be here, for a very short time, either tomorrow or Sunday" [13 June 1933]. A few days later: "Köhler has been here since Saturday and will stay till tomorrow evening. It was tremendously interesting. I learned a lot about Germany without changing my ultimate judgment about it. He, Köhler is a very courageous man, much more than one could know" [15 June 1933].

It was not until the following year, however, that long discussions took place which were reported in the letters:

Frau Köhler arrived delayed by a snowstorm in Boston. She told lots of interesting things. They are absolutely anti-Nazi. Köhler has three times sent in his resignation without ever receiving any answer. Quite evidently the German government wants to play the same game with him which the Italian government played with Borgese [Italian literature professor Giuseppe Borgese]. Köhler is tremendously busy. His lectures which will be published are called Beyond Psychology. I am terribly curious to know what he says. [15 October 1934]

Now from here. Köhler's visit was absolutely magnificent. We had marvelous talks on psychology, physics and Germany. To begin with the last: I have changed my personal outlook a great deal after what he told me. I do not longer believe, as I did more or less, that a majority of Germans enjoy the Hitler regime. I see now utter chaos, the disunity, party strife, and chief and worst of all, the demoralizing influence which the regime exerts on the people. Köhler is furious with the slack attitude of American intellectuals—we had grand talks about tolerance in this connection. You may speak about this very freely provided you do not mention Köhler's name; as a matter of fact it would be good if you could influence public opinion in N.J.C. [New Jersey College for Women] in this direction. The present tolerance kills the efforts of all the decent people in Germany. They who want to be pro-German are really the worst enemies of the best German people. Köhler's own behavior is simply beyond praise. He does speak out to the man in power, and at the same time he does it diplomatically so that his actions have as much effect as they possibly can. I'll tell you more about it when we meet. To summarize: One cannot be sufficiently anti-Nazi! They are the enemies of all true morality, which they consider intellectualistic prejudice. Sneaking underhand creatures they are.

You can imagine how exciting all this was. But what he told

me about his work in physics was not a whit less exciting. Of
this the result will, I hope, be visible early next year. And they
will, if he succeeds in making the last few steps, be truly stupendous. I know that I was right all along that he is a truly
great man, a man who simply cannot be missed! We also had
many excellent talks on psychology. He is so brimful of ideas,
a rare combination of the experimentalist and the theorist.
[13 November 1934]

Köhler talked a great deal and marvelously well of his work
in physics. It is not quite finished yet. He is so rundown at the
moment from the continued effort that he cannot complete it
very quickly. Besides he is, alone on third class, sailing for Europe on the Ile de France next Saturday. He wants to look after
his financial affairs in Germany and at the same time visit the
Kultur Ministerium. Harvard has offered him nothing and
does not seem likely to do so. Why? Nobody seems to know.
However, he has got an invitation for two quarters at the University of Chicago where he will begin his activities, one-hour
seminar and research work at the end of March. During the
summer he will be in Iowa. Last night we all went to Allport's
[Harvard psychologist Gordon Allport*] house for a reception
given in the honor of [William] Stern. The Sterns will come
here on Friday and stay till Monday. . . . After this brief report
of my doings I turn to your letters. [5 February 1935]

During the years 1935–36, Köhler was involved in Koffka's life
in two different ways. Koffka had by then been told by President
William Neilson* of Smith College that the research laboratory
would not be continued after the end of its prescribed five-year
term. While this was not unexpected, it amounted to the fact that
Koffka would be without a position thereafter. Köhler therefore
became a colleague who was told of this situation, and who had
influence. If for no other reason than the furtherance of Gestalt
theory in America, he would be eager to see Koffka established in
a position where his influence would be felt.

At the same time, Koffka's major work, *The Principles of Ge-*

stalt Psychology, was published. It had been dedicated to "Wolfgang Köhler and Max Wertheimer in Gratitude for their Friendship and Inspiration," and perhaps even more than needing its success in general to guarantee a future position, Koffka wanted the good opinion of his two friends and colleagues.

These events introduced two new elements into the relationship. In the first place, Koffka was loath to use Köhler's influence to get a position. In the second place, he was depressed at the failure of both Köhler and Wertheimer to acknowledge the book with its immense amount of systematic Gestalt-oriented work. Thus while Koffka never questioned Köhler's role as a truly great scientist, an emotional overtone, a personal strain was expressed in the letters. One such example of the new situation unfolded in several letters:

[KK] I am a bit fed up with my bad luck, I mean the quite unnecessary initial delay in the printing of my book in England. For I have heard of several big positions that have been filled. First came a letter from Mrs. Köhler saying that the president of Swarthmore had been in Cambridge and had talked to Köhler. Apparently he wants to establish an entirely new psychological institute there and has offered that position to Köhler, but Köhler does not seem interested because the salary is not big enough for him to support his other family [by his first marriage]. [28 March 1935]

[MH] Everyone thinks you are ideally settled at Smith. Robert MacLeod* [Swarthmore psychology professor], I know, thinks so. Probably they do not think that you want to move. But that is not the point, unless you tell Köhler that you are interested in Swarthmore in the event of his not wanting it, then I think there cannot be anything to your friendship, and I would frankly despair of your ever getting another position. It's the most natural thing in the world for Köhler to suggest you, provided he does not want it, and knows that you do. What would hold you back in that? Write Köhler a letter at least to suggest you. [29 March 1935]

[KK] Perhaps I am altogether more or less a failure. I say this frankly and calmly, and quite honestly, even the fact that nobody considers me for the new position seems to prove my point. I am quite willing to take the general opinion about my abilities as the true one. And the general opinion may not be very high. And perhaps my book may fall flat. And perhaps Köhler does not think me fit for the Swarthmore position. I would accept that judgment, and therefore would never have considered writing to him about it. However, I think I shall do it now, after what you said, and take the risk. First, however, I must finish the Index, I think the publication of the book is the main thing. [30 March 1935]

[MH] What have these years done to you that you speak so of yourself! It seems to me that you need a strong dose of Me! That's why I shout at you, in a panic, lest you miss what might be perfection. You must not be angry. [3 April 1935]

But Koffka still delayed:

Of course you are quite right about my inertia. I shall write to Köhler today, or tomorrow. I am very curious what he will answer. Don't be too angry with me please, in a way I deserve your ire and therefore I shall do all I can to dissipate it. I don't quite know myself why I have such strong inhibitions about asking for something for myself, but there they are. However, I shall overcome them. I have already planned the text of my request in my head, so writing will be comparatively easy. [9 April 1935]

This morning I had a new letter from Köhler, very important! He likes Swarthmore tremendously, and has decided to accept it, if no more lucrative post is offered to him. If his last attempt to stay in Germany fails, this means that he will go to Germany only for the winter. If then he finds it impossible to stay he will go to Swarthmore, although $6,000 is really far too little for his financial obligations. Aydelotte [Swarthmore College president Frank Aydelotte] will wait for his decision till

February next. At the same time Köhler has spoken very plainly about me to both Aydelotte and [Robert] MacLeod. If my book is a success this delay may be entirely to the good, don't you think. . . .

I must write to Köhler whom I want to consult about the summer and then prepare my plans. [4 May 1935]

The second element introduced into the relationship was Koffka's depression and anxiety at the failure of Köhler and Wertheimer to acknowledge his book. Each week through May and June 1935 he wrote sadly such comments as "Of course I have not heard from Köhler yet," and "Not letter from Köhler yet," and "Alas, no letter from Köhler" [17, 31 May, 26 June 1935].

As the year progressed and *The Principles of Gestalt Psychology* became known and appreciated, the tension with Köhler lessened. There was in the wind an invitation from Edward Tolman* for Koffka to become professor of psychology at Berkeley.

A report from [Gordon] Allport said that the only thing wrong with it was that it should have been called the Principles of Psychology. Of course this is indirect, and may be grossly distorted. Then, at last, a very long and cordial letter from Köhler, I'll bring it along. . . . Köhler writes that after having attended the Midwestern Division of APA [American Psychological Association] that the interest in the book is much greater than he ever expected and greater in the middle west than in the east. On May 10th several people had already read it. He adds that the book could not be more fitting for the present situation. Then in a rather cryptic remark he congratulates me about Berkeley, and says that he was particularly pleased to hear about it. He had felt that I would have felt obliged to accept, very reluctantly the call from another university which cannot be compared with the University of California. [21 June 1935]

My two days were well worthwhile. A good drive down on Sunday, 4 hrs. 20 min. A fine time. In it a long discussion on traces, in which Köhler and I explained and defended our views which were identical to a point, to Wertheimer, who now I believe, accepts them.† The Forschung [The *Psychologische Forschung*, the Gestalt journal] business is strange. I shall tell you about it, for to understand it you must know all the details, and it would take too much time to write them. However, there is as yet no question of the Forschung being stopped. [5 November 1935]

I came back into real winter, an icy blast which is turning the snow into ice. I found a letter from Köhler explaining his delay in writing. He had been busy writing to Germany about the taxes he has to pay in leaving the country. A very complicated and urgent task. He is expecting me next Tuesday. [19 February 1936]

By 1937 events in Germany again claimed attention:

This morning a letter from Köhler with rather exciting news which has to be kept secret for the time being. For the first time the powers in Germany interfere with the editorial policy of the Forschung, and that in a way which makes it impossible for Köhler to remain an editor. Consequently, he will see through the volume that is just being set up and then resign, giving notice of his intention at once. He hopes that by seeing this volume through the press he can induce the publishers to stop publication of the Forschung after his resignation, rather than to put in another editor. Well, another chapter will be closed. How much enthusiasm when we first discussed the idea and how much achievement during the following years. I honestly think that the Forschung has a fine record. Remember, all this is as yet strictly confidential. [4 June 1937]

At the time of the publication of Köhler's *The Place of Value in a World of Facts* in 1938, Koffka described it as the "event of the week": "It is absolutely magnificent. A fascinating book, not

---

†The word *trace*, when used by psychologists, refers to the residue of a given experience which remains in the brain and allows us to recall the event or experience. The Gestalt psychologists were constantly reevaluating their ideas as to the exact nature of this common but miraculous achievement of human beings.

strictly technical, although it deals with many technical points in different sciences, but not quite easy. A marvelous chapter on the adaptiveness of the organism, of fundamental importance to biologists" [19 November 1938]. Later, in Oxford, Koffka enjoyed sharing the book with colleagues: "Yesterday afternoon I read the first chapter of Köhler's *Place of Value* (1938) to Lady Zimmern [wife of Sir Alfred Zimmern] who jumped and screamed with enthusiasm! I knew she would like it and she was extremely grateful" [21 January 1940]. And by the next week Koffka was able to extend the impact the book would make: "Vice President Paton [Herbert Paton of Corpus Christi College, Oxford] . . . asked me whether I could give some philosophical lectures in Corpus during the next term. I accepted, of course, but turned it into a seminar on Köhler's book on *Value*. He seemed very pleased" [22 January 1940].

Köhler had also been enthusiastic about Koffka; for example: "Köhler said my lecture in Bryn Mawr was 'ausgezeichnet' ['marvelous'] and pointed to the very long applause as proof of its impression" [18 April 1939].

In one of the last references Koffka made to Köhler in this correspondence, he was able to state happily that Köhler was becoming more and more part of the American scene in areas other than psychology:

> I can tell you that the religious group was delighted with Köhler. Köhler had told me of a Dr. Christian, a member of the Department of Religion here at Smith, who had been an outstanding person in the discussion. Well, I saw Christian and we had a nice chat. He told me of the excellent impression Köhler had made. They had heard that he would be rather stiff in discussions, but they had found the very opposite. Very rarely he said had an outsider fitted so well into their group. [13 September 1940]

Koffka Relates to Wertheimer

There are almost a hundred references to Wertheimer* in the correspondence. In a letter in 1930, Koffka expressed a wholehearted appreciation of him as a creative scientist, who has had a profound influence on his life.†

It began with Wertheimer and Köhler in Frankfort, with me as a third. We liked each other personally, had the same kind of enthusiasm, the same background, we saw each other daily discussing almost everything under the sun. When Wertheimer explained to me the story, the germ of his new idea, I was ready to receive it and let it grow, in well prepared soil. Believe me, I was overwhelmed by the intrinsic beauty and fruitfulness of Wertheimer's new approach, and that I therefore wanted to share the gift I had received with all other psychologists thinking that, in my then still youthful naivity that they, having been caught by the same problems which bothered me at the time, would be equally glad to have a new gate open to them.

Köhler went to Teneriffe, and did his work there, became fascinated by the beauty of the facts which were accessible on this new road. We didn't start a "movement," we hoped to get rid of a number of problems that had been debated for a long time without any apparent progress.

Continuing in somewhat the same vein, Koffka envisaged Wertheimer's idea as a "leap" forward and as illustrating true scientific advance:

My idea of scientific progress is this: certain problems arise at certain times and in various places, and several people have new ideas in the strictest sense of the word. Metaphorically speaking, each of them makes a small leap, very often, these leaps are not high enough, and fail to raise the general level of science, which goes on as if these leaps had never been made. . . . Sometimes it happens that somebody—Wertheimer—succeeds in making the leap high enough, then the

† Koffka repeated this explanation, originally part of a discussion with Harrower, in a letter to Edward G. Boring.*

scientific situation is really changed. Then the historian can always find other leaps going in the same direction, construct a picture of continuity, which, however, is post factum, and as I see it, inadequate. [22 April 1930]

Koffka felt the same basic responsiblity where Wertheimer was concerned as he had with Köhler, namely, to further the understanding of his articles or lectures, particularly with a view to English-speaking audiences. When Willis Ellis was translating some of Wertheimer's work (Ellis 1938), Koffka wanted at all costs to keep the record straight: "I read the summary Ellis had written of Wertheimer's lecture and found I'm sorry to say, a great many mistakes. We discussed these mistakes at length, he taking my criticisms in the best of spirits" [13 February 1933].

Again in the same vein, when a poorly trained psychologist who knew Koffka personally undertook a review of a book dealing with Wertheimer and Gestalt theory, he wrote in exasperation: "It's a disgrace that [X] be given a book like that for review. Can't you see to it that she does no harm? She simply cannot say that Gestalt psychologists disagree amongst themselves for she knows nothing about it. How could she? Perhaps if you would tell her from me it might help. She has misunderstood everything. I'm afraid it's a hopeless case" [8 November 1932].

At the personal level, however, Koffka found Wertheimer difficult to relate to. At one point, Wertheimer had written to Koffka asking him, when he was in Berlin that summer, to come to Frankfort to help him with business arrangements. But Koffka, receiving no further word after many months, wrote: "On Sunday I must proceed to Frankfort to visit Wertheimer. Although I have not had a single line from him perhaps he does not want to see me. I don't understand his silence" [8 July 1930].

Koffka's instinctive reaction was that certain situations "require" that people keep in touch: lack of communication could only mean that the situation had changed. Over the years he really suffered when his colleagues failed to conform to his expectations. It took Koffka a long time to realize that he and Wertheimer envisaged interpersonal relationships very differently.

Koffka would never have dreamed of keeping the "other fellow" uninformed of joint plans. However, when Wertheimer was tardy in his reply to the gift of *The Principles of Gestalt Psychology*, for some reason Koffka accepted this more easily than he had Köhler's silence.

By 1933, far more ominous occurrences had obscured all personal trivia. Wertheimer and Kurt Lewin* were among the psychologists who had lost their positions in Germany. Koffka hastened to do what he could. "[Edwin] Boring* has circularized the American psychologists about [Kurt] Lewin, who made a very great impression here. But he says at the end of his letter, 'I just do not see what America can do for Lewin and Wertheimer.' Of course, for all I know, Köhler's position may be badly shaken. It is too horrible for words" [2 May 1933]. Harrower, lecturing in London University that year, was called on to help to obtain positions for them. She contacted Professor Morris Ginsburg,* the leading British sociologist and social psychologist, and wrote: "At Ginsburg's request I sent you a cable the meaning of which I hope will be clear, since he cannot get a direct statement from either Lewin or Wertheimer he wants your statement concerning their dismissal and will then use this as a basis for his appeal either to Jewish Relief Societies, or the London School of Economics" [19 May 1933]. With the inevitable delays of transatlantic correspondence Koffka replied:

The Ginsburg news is splendid, I do not think that you will find the same spirit of personal sacrifice in any country except England. I hope the statements I sent about Wertheimer and Lewin are all right. Although I probably went too far in their qualifications. . . . (later) Yesterday in the *New York Times* it stated that the London School of Economics has already invited four German professors. It is absolutely marvellous. Is Wertheimer or Lewin among them? [27 May 1933]

By early 1935, Wertheimer was safely established in the United States with a home in New Rochelle and a position at the New School for Social Research. Koffka was able to invite him to give lectures at Smith; Harrower, making independent contacts, was invited to the Wertheimer home: "I had a grand weekend. I adored the Wertheimer children and wife. She is simply lovely. It was all alive and vital and happy like the nursery in my own childhood at its best" [18 February 1935, New Brunswick, N.J.].

The lecture at Smith was of course successful and brought in its wake an unexpected offer for Harrower, at that time on the faculty of Douglass College, part of Rutgers University. Koffka wrote:

Just a few lines. Wertheimer's talk in seminar last night was excellent, and very successful. It fitted our general year of discussion very well. And another thing he told me on the drive from Springfield, very confidential, [American psychologist] Lawrence Frank has made very close contact with him. The General Education Board is going to undertake a psychological survey of High Schools, and wants Wertheimer to cooperate in this venture in a leading role. Wertheimer asked if he could appoint some of the actual research workers and was told that he could. Now he told me that the only person that he could think of was "die Harrower." I told him that as far as I know you would not be willing to give up your present job. Apart from everything else the Board would appoint the person only for the period of the investigation, without guaranteeing their future. Therefore, he thought that you might take a leave of absence, and also thinks that in consideration of the great importance of the work, the collaborator would have a very good chance of getting other positions afterwards. I am writing this to you, because, although I feel sure that I know your mind, I do not feel justified in taking the decision out of your hands. I shall not tell Wertheimer that I am writing to you, because Frank asked him to keep the whole thing secret and not to speak of it to prospective candidates. . . . Wertheimer wants you particularly because you combine the two necessary requirements for the job, scientific equipment and interest in people, and the ability to deal with them. He knows nobody else who represents this combination. [26 April 1935]

The relative proximity of New York to Northampton facilitated visits, and in the next year Koffka had to face up to the fact that Wertheimer's life style was very different from his own. After visiting twice in September 1936, he wrote:

On Sunday night we had supper with a former German Member of Parliament, a Democrat, at Sinclair Lewis' [American Nobel prize author] house in Bronxville. A charming house, an excellent supper and a discussion of Communism and Fascism which must have resounded over hill and dale. Did they shriek! Wertheimer being the most excited of all. They were all very nice people, and there was no ill feeling when I left but it was quite alien to me and not pleasant. [15 September 1936]

Tuesday evening at the Wertheimers was quite exciting. Courant (mathematician formerly at Gottingen, now at NYU) came and brought Professor and Mrs. Levi-Civita from Rome. He is one of the world's renowned mathematicians, a lovely man, small, old and with a courtesy that is born from a humble heart and love of people. His wife, much younger, is a real lady, very attractive, but they had to leave rather early and witnessed only the beginning of a tremendously interesting political discussion which was held on an amazingly high level. The beginning of the party was rather difficult. Mrs. Wertheimer was upstairs all the time, and Wertheimer himself disappeared constantly whenever new guests arrived, so that I had to do the receiving of to me perfectly unknown people. And even when they eventually came down, their concern with the guests' comfort put all the burden of placing them on me. [25 September 1936]

In 1938 when a controversy developed between Wertheimer and fellow Gestalt psychologist Kurt Goldstein,* Koffka felt free to take Goldstein's side. Trying to explain the difficulty, Koffka wrote: "Wertheimer has the feeling, objectively totally unjustified, that Goldstein has treated him and Gestalt Theory unfairly in his book [Goldstein 1939]. And that a man like Tillich [German philosopher Paul Tillich] would not have acted thus. Therefore he has a moral grudge. You can imagine that I did my level best to change this attitude and I think I succeeded a little" [17 January 1938]. And when Harrower, working with Goldstein at that time, attempted to bring about some reconciliation, Koffka wrote: "I'm glad you played the role of the angel of peace between Goldstein and Wertheimer, and that you are going out again to New Rochelle to see Wertheimer" [17 November 1937].

In 1940, Koffka could assess Wertheimer's current writing objectively and felt no need to endorse it all:

The days with Wertheimer were pleasant and interesting. We had lots of time for discussion. His book seems to be almost finished, and I really believe now it will be printed. I read the greater part of one chapter. It is fascinating and interesting. But whether this mode of presentation, his general style, his mixture of the scientist, the prophet and the reformer will have the effect he wants to produce I don't know. I can take it because I know him but if I came across such a book, by an author unknown to me, I might resent it. I gave a few hints but the matter is far more general. [29 August 1940]

In 1941, Koffka commented on a class of Wertheimer's on the psychology of art and music which he attended: "Very suggestive but terribly unsystematic" [31 March 1941].

Koffka and *The Principles of Gestalt Psychology*

What light do the letters throw on Koffka as the author of *The Principles of Gestalt Psychology*? The first pages of the book, written in a letter of 14 July 1932, under unusual conditions in a strange locale, took a most unlikely direction. Koffka, taking part in Russian neuropsychologist Alexander Luria's* expedition to study the Uzbek culture, was laid low with relapsing fever in Fargana, Uzbekistan. He finally met the only English-speaking person in the area, the wife of a Jewish Russian scholar:

I really owe her some gratitude. At first she disappointed me terribly. I looked forward to borrowing English books from her. But not a single one did she have, but she gave me a good suggestion: "If you can't read books, you must write one." And so, between malaria days, or even on them when the fever had subsided, I wrote what is to be a first chapter of a book on Psychology for such students and laymen as have a real interest in the subject without wanting to specialize in it, a book, by the way, that never will be written although I hope to finish its first chapter. And that is to justify why I want my readers to learn psychology and why my particular kind of psychology. I think you will like what I have done. [14 July 1932]

By February of the following year a few chapters had been written, and he asked a question about the direction of the rest:

I have been thinking a good deal about my book. What kind of a book it will appear to be, to whom it will appeal and so on. It certainly is not a textbook, but I believe quite honestly that without such a book no real Gestalt textbook can be written. And then it entered my mind that when the book is out, we two should write a textbook together. What do you think of that? You have experience with young students and know how to catch their interest and how far to tax their powers. Think it over, I would love to do it. Koffka and Harrower is already a familiar combination, let it become more so.

I'm just trying to write in my book about the laws which determine the figure-ground reorganization, which field parts will have become figures, which ground. And then I remembered that the best experiment done in this field was begun by M. R. Harrower, who told me about it last summer. . . . I need the results badly! I want to have them in my book. I also want to check up the ideas which I have on the subject with these results. [7 February 1933]

The letters to Harrower, then lecturing at the University of London, contained a running comment on what Koffka had dealt with in his thinking and writing.

I'm doing something rather amusing in my book just now: correlating the fovea as the "figure sense," with Rubin's law that the enclosed area will become figure, the enclosing one ground. If fovea is a "figure sense," the periphery a "ground sense," then all the differences between fovea and peripheral vision are intelligible; acuity, color. [17 February 1933]

I've done a lot of writing. The whole theory of reflexes as far as it will be treated in the book. I'm on page three fourteen and I have to omit about thirty pages at the end of the last chapter. So I have actually written thirty pages less than that. Still it is quite a lot. [7 March 1933]

I have just introduced the ego given in Köhler's theory and I am now faced with two closely interconnected questions. One, granted that my hand is organized in the field in the same way as my pen, my pad, etc. etc., why is it experienced as *my* hand? And not just a "familiar hand" or "Koffka's hand." Two, more generally, what forces produce the reorganization of the ego as a special part of the total field? Neither of these questions have, as far as I know, ever been raised. I have a few rather incomplete and possibly inadequate ideas about this answer. Do you know any place in the literature where these questions are being discussed? I frankly do not. I'm not sure they will interest you. They may have a great importance, might be of great significance for social psychology by their bearing on the problem of "property" among other things. What do you think? [9 March 1933]

I enclose the syllabus of my fifth chapter. It is incomplete as you will see. The sixth chapter is called Action and is well un-derway. Thirty-seven pages written. Tomorrow my last class before spring vacation. That shows how we are approaching the end of the academic year. [17 March 1933]

Very soon I hope to be able to send you the third chapter and perhaps even the fourth will make its appearance before the year is out. The fourth will give you a better idea of what the main part of the book will be like than the first two. Because it begins the actual and concrete study of organization. Whereas the third is more or less theoretical. Although doing the spade-work for all that is to come. I feel convinced that in all these earlier chapters, at least chapters two and three, a good deal of condensation could be done. You will help me with that. [18 March 1933]

I need you terribly badly for discussing my new ideas which I can share with nobody. I have just introduced a new term "the executive" meaning by that all the different means at the disposal of the organism to relieve stresses or tensions. It is a wider concept than Lewin's "motorik" [see Koffka 1935b, p. 342]. It embraces thoughts and attitudes as well as actual movements. The former being means of relieving tensions as much as the latter. And I am trying to discover the connection between the executive [see Koffka 1935b, pp. 342–67] and the Ego. I know that there are problems which would interest you about which your advice would be invaluable. I hope we can do something about it in the summer. But even so you see that my depression has not prevented me from doing some real work involving hard thinking and a bit of imagination that I possess. [23 March 1933]

I am preparing my notes. I had a new idea which probably has been in incubation stage for several days and which I must let you know though I have to be so brief that you probably won't understand it. One, the phenomenal Ego and the phenomenal environment are a segregated field part. Two, when Ego disappears from the phenomenal world or consciousness ceases altogether, the need tensions within the Ego system survive. Therefore, the real, psychophysical Ego is not identical with the phenomenal Ego, but it is permanent. This persistence of the Ego is not memory in the usual sense, but comparable to the persistence of the real organism in the real environment. This makes a theory of personality possible. Four, if the Ego as a segregated system persists independently of consciousness, then the environment from which it is segregated must also persist independently of consciousness. Otherwise there would be nothing to segregate and unify the Ego system. Therefore an entirely new theory of memory is necessary. I already had ideas number one and number three. I have just found number four. Is it crazy or really good? Do you understand what it means and do you see the implications? I can't say that I see them very clearly yet. But I'll leave that till I come to my chapter on memory which should thereby become quite interesting. [24 March 1933]

I'm at a very difficult point in my book: The relation of the executive (which I explained in a previous letter) to the Ego. The relation of the needs and the demand-characters has to be discussed. Physiognomic characters must be introduced. Questions of energy-supply taken up. In short, it is a lot of work which requires concentrated thinking so much the better that now I am in a position to throw myself into it without having to make an effort to keep my thoughts on my work and therefore I shall start right now. [24 March 1933]

I have written three pages, chiefly on esthetic problems. I am now introducing the demand-characters and that gave me an opportunity of branching off into esthetics.

We (Willis Ellis) had a great discussion last night about my new theory of memory. It begins to clear a bit and to expand. Its possibilities seem enormous. Perhaps my Harvard notes may give you an idea, therefore only a few words more. [31 March 1933]

Sometime later, working on a different part of the book he wrote again:

I have finished anisotropy,† quite a different treatment from the one you know, but I should have given a great deal to have

---

† Of *anisotropy* of space, Koffka (1935b, 275–76) wrote: "The space we see around us has different properties in different directions. For example an object

had your [Ph.D.] examination paper to help me. That part I did not do half as well as you under the strain of your exam. Altogether I have done 8 pages beyond the bit that you got, and about half a page of which is to be inserted into your installment. Now comes motion, I wish it were all done. . . . Gibson [James J. Gibson, Smith psychology professor] has just left me, he wanted to discuss my theory of framework, after having read some of my Chapter 5. I should go on writing on motion, but I want to thank you for your awfully good experiments, well planned, clear results so far. More subjects will make them clearer.

I worked a good deal last night, reading and thinking about the movement section, I started to write this morning, but have not achieved much, two pages. However, by the end of the week, most of it will be done, and that means practically the whole of the fifth chapter.

Yesterday a record day, I worked for a bit in the evening and wrote altogether ten pages, my bag today is 6. So that I have already 25 MSS pages which are not yet typed. I have finished Brown [J. F. Brown, a psychologist who wrote on Gestalt-related problems] and I believe I have done a good job. The arguments are certainly not easy, you will swear at them! But I believe my presentation is as simple as possible, and really quite lucid, if one takes the trouble to think through the argu-

---

ascending vertically will appear to be travelling faster than one travelling horizontally at the same speed." In his theory of *framework*, Koffka expresses one of his many experimental attempts to demonstrate Gestalt principles in the field of perception. Depending on the "framework" or "ground," two small, identical figures will be experienced as different shapes.

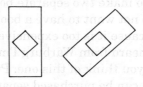

ment. I hope that this is just not author's vanity, or elation after having achieved something. The end of Chapter five is now near. Just a brief treatment of Ternus v. Schiller [presumably a current controversy regarding perception issues], and the new Metzger [Wolfgang Metzger, a German psychologist studying perception] paper. All closely related. The statement of the problem has already been prepared, in an earlier part, so I foresee no difficulty. Movement has really gone much more easily than I expected, although many of my arguments are new in form and substance. [7 and 8 August 1934]

Rejoice with me! The fifth chapter is finished. I just wrote the last line. And after I have finished this letter, I'll read it through and put it into the section titles so that tomorrow it can be copied. . . . I am terribly thrilled about the progress of your work. Will you send me your MS [Harrower 1936] or shall I read it while you read mine? We surely must discuss it thoroughly.

(Later) I am now revising the first chapter. The difficulty is what to leave in, and what to destroy. But I am getting on. [13 August 1934]

As the work neared completion, the publisher unexpectedly suggested that Koffka make a short book out of his manuscript in addition to the longer version. Koffka was concerned at this sudden possible change of plans, and Harrower reacted to his concern.

[KK] May I now ask you to do something for me? You'll understand that I am rather worried about what I was told of Warburg's [Harcourt Brace staff member] reaction. It is of course impossible to make two separate books out of one! On the other hand I do not want to have a book produced which nobody will buy because it is too expensive. Therefore, although I have not heard from Warburg I'm looking over possibilities. What do you think of this one: Publish the book in two volumes which can be purchased separately but with a special title for each volume. It would not really be satisfactory, involving duplication of bibliography and index and leaving fragments in the hands of the readers, but perhaps it might work. I enclose a Table of Contents of the two only possible divisions. The second is, as you will see, a little more symmetrical as far as the number of pages go, particularly if one bears in mind that the pages of the earlier part of the book are slightly fuller than those in the later, and that of the 112 figures, 90 occur in the first seven chapters. All I want you to do is to ponder the matter a little and possibly suggest sub-titles for the two volumes. I shall be tremendously grateful for your help or any suggestions that you might make. [28 September 1934]

[MH] For Heaven's sake don't let them force you to do anything you won't want. Stick to what is best for you, say you'll get another publisher if your wishes are not carried out! Don't give in, it is desperately important that the book goes through so that everyone can see what you have contributed in its fullest and most complete aspect. [29 September 1934, New Brunswick, N.J.]

[MH] You will see by my Saturday letter that I had already thought about you and the publisher. I infinitely prefer the first division for this reason. You are so often thought of in terms of perception, and only in those terms, that I would like the people reading the first book to have a taste of what is coming in the second. Therefore, I suggest:

Volume 1   Chapters one through nine
Volume 2   Chapters ten through fifteen†

You see, I think there is almost more new and original in Vol-

---

† Chapters 1 through 7 of *the Principles of Gestalt Psychology* deal with what Koffka called the environmental field, essentially *perceptual* experiences and problems. From chapter 8 on Koffka turns to action, namely the ego, the executive, adjusted behavior, attitudes, emotions and the will. Following this are chapters on memory, learning, society and personality. A division of chapter 7 would have left the proposed Volume I without any indication of where Koffka's thought was taking him in areas other than perception with which most of his published work had already dealt. Harrower was anxious that Volume I should contain more that was new.

ume 2, and I want that appreciated. Please consult me before you do anything final; there might be another solution. I believe that the general title and two subsidiary ones is a very good idea. [30 September 1934, New Brunswick, N.J.]

In compiling the bibliography, Koffka was pleased to note that his book dealt with current publications:

This morning I finished the typing of the bibliography, a little more than 16 pages. I made a sort of statistic that shows how modern the book is. I'll reproduce it here. The figures meaning the number of items listed for the respective periods of time.

Before 1880	'80–'89	'90–'99		
6	3	4		

1900–'10	'10–'19	'20–'24	'25–'29	'30–'34
12	29	70	92	101

There is a tremendous jump after 1919, before that I added 10 years, after only 5, yet the numbers leap up. I shall send the bibliography to England today. [15 September 1934]

As the work progressed, Koffka's confidence in it waxed and waned:

I got some encouragement for my book. Dembo [Northampton lab psychologist Tamara Dembo] had sometime ago asked me to let her read my section, as yet but introductory, about the law of Prägnanz. I had left it after seminar on the table and she had read it the same evening. Well, she told me, that she had found it by far the clearest presentation she had ever come across, so that is something, what I want to do with the book is, of course, to make matters clear. [7 January 1933]

I feel rather satisfied, unfortunately that is no proof of its value since I usually have that feeling while I am working. The test will come a year later. [19 January 1933]

I feel hectic, I feel nervous with fear that I shan't get through so that I cannot sleep at night. [3 July 1934]

The Principles of Gestalt Psychology, when published in 1935, was well received. It was taken very seriously by reviewers. It was too tightly reasoned and too relentlessly thorough ever to be easy reading, but it was acknowledged by all as a major work. Koffka treasured personal letters which some of his colleagues wrote him and kept a special file containing those from Leonard Carmichael, Robert Thouless, Herbert Langfeld, Beatrice Edgell, George Humphrey, Alexander Luria, William McDougall, and Gordon Allport.

George Humphrey's* letter, for example, pleased him: "I had a charming letter from George Humphrey and quote one sentence, 'It (my book) is a massive and at the same time subtle piece of work which will be read when most of what is written today has been long forgotten.' This is nice, though of course I do not agree" (3 December 1936). On another occasion Koffka wrote, "A letter from Luria this morning. He has received my book and looked through it. 'Es ist gleich zuschen, dass es ein grossartiges Werk ist.' (It's easy to see that this is really an outstanding work.) Very generous of him" (20 January 1936).

Koffka spoke of his letter from McDougall*: "In my correspondence when I got back this morning was a letter from McDougall. 'I have at last found time to read almost all of your great book. I found in it very much to admire and to agree with. I shall not indulge in any further comment because I am writing some comments for publication which will be more systematic than anything that can be found in a letter'" (27 February 1936).

Gordon Allport* wrote a long letter. "One of my ego-stresses demands that I write this note. No answer is 'required' by the situation. I simply want to tell you that I took along on my vacation a most excellent and important book, probably the most significant treatise in mental science published thus far in the XXth century. It is called, 'Principles of Gestalt Psychology'—but so expertly is it done and so broad in scope and so persuasive that it might with justice have been entitled simply, 'The Principles of Psychology.'

Previous systematists did not qualify their theories, but claimed universal and unexceptionable applicability for them. And yet they had less right to do so than you, for you have built a completer, more consistent and undoubtedly more enduring structure than they" (Harrower 1971a:151–52).

the private koffka

Thomas Carlyle is supposed to have said that similarities in tastes and sentiments, with difference in opinion, make for an excellent meeting of the minds. Koffka had his own way of saying this, calling it "mental nearness," a term which he had once heard used by Raymond Dodge,* a psychologist at Yale in the 1920s, and had always liked and remembered.

Certainly Koffka and Harrower enjoyed a wide range of common experiences. Their tastes coincided in music, literature, and human qualities to which they gave high priority. They were both animal lovers and relished the outdoors, mountain-climbing, and sports. Perhaps most important it was possible for each to express the most basic needs and beliefs in the written exchange.

Music

In the 1930s the radio provided important musical experiences and was thought of by the letter writers as a common concert hall. They alerted each other to upcoming programs and assumed that the other would listen. There were opportunities in each one's academic setting for outstanding professional performances which could be enjoyed and subsequently discussed. Koffka wrote of these to Harrower over the years.

Koffka's enthusiasm for mountain climbing was unbounded. He climbed in the Swiss and Italian Alps every summer. Harrower, also a climber, made two ascents with him.

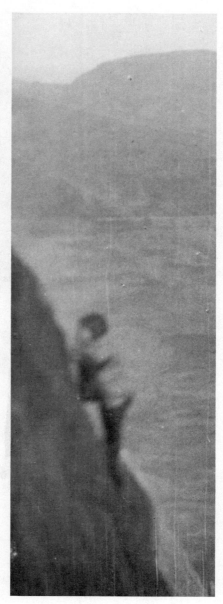

Harrower wins the singles tournament.

Four enthusiasts for deck tennis returning from Europe on the SS Minnewaska in 1933. Natalie Clothier (wife of the president of Rutgers University) holds the coit.

Lovely radio music yesterday, a violin sonata by Cesar Franck in the morning, then the radio Musical Hall did some good things. About 5:30 the C Major Piano Concerto by Beethoven, and from 8 to 9 the General Motors concert. . . . I am now at last reading a biography of Beethoven. I had it among my books, the German work published by Bondi. I do not think that it is first rate in every respect but it gives a lot of tremendously interesting material and builds up the personality rather well. [8 October 1934]

Did you hear the Ninth symphony? It was marvelous. As a matter of fact when the third movement began, I had to cover my face lest I should show too much of my emotion. And all the time during the heroic and victorious first movement, during the gay and boisterous, yet always graceful and dignified second, and during that pathetic third which expresses without a sickly lament the tragedy and suffering of the world, I thought of you and how sometime we shall sit together to listen to this music which belongs to the few greatest creations of humanity and is, despite Goethe, in my mind the greatest contribution of the German spirit to world culture. [18 November 1935]

Then the Perole Quartet and the lovely second movement from Schubert C major symphony, by the Music Hall of the Air. The third piano concerto in the afternoon, how it reminded me of the week before. [Koffka and Harrower had been together in New York City.] Marion De Rondo's concert in the evening was excellent. She plays now with so much warmth and expression. She looked again beautiful. There was a rapture in her face, an intensity, a devotion to something beyond her that was to my eyes a great experience to behold. No longer any mask to shut the soul off from the external world. I was for some minutes seized by a poignant and almost physically painful longing that pierced like a sharp dagger. . . . Next Sunday Toscanini, instead of playing Verdi's Requiem, will perform Beethoven's 8th and 9th. That I shall not miss. [2 March 1936]

Fidelio was grand. Still I like and liked the 3rd overture
played between the two last scenes, better than anything else.
The noble solution of the terrific tension carried by the strains
of the final theme, which follows directly the trumpet signal, is
almost divine. That music that could have been written by no
one but Beethoven. Then yesterday's two symphonies! The joy-
ousness and lovely simplicity of the 8th and the catholicity
of the 9th which epitomizes everything great in human life.
"Freudig wie ein Held zum siegen" ["Joyful as a hero returning
from victory"]. [9 March 1936]

Yesterday was a great day of music. First at 10:30 a Schubert
Quartet from Cleveland, then the Perole with Opus 131 which
you probably heard too. Then at 12:30 a Haydn symphony. . . .
The evening concert was just grand. I know no other music
that excites me so much as the first movement of the Kreutzer
sonata, under its influence I could do almost anything. It was
beautifully played, except in that the first movement I should
have preferred the piano part to have been played more bru-
tally, with a harder touch. When I told that to the pianist, who
had played the piano part, not as criticism, but my reaction to
the movement as such, he said that he had never felt that way
about it. That explains, probably why he does not play it "my"
way. Then Op 111 only two movements and yet one of the greatest. The second is the Arietta, a lovely slow theme with varia-
tions. And finally the Trio in B flat Op 97. Absolutely grand.
[16 March 1936]

I hope you heard the 7th Symphony yesterday. I liked it, particularly the third movement; it suits my sense of its propor-
tions to have the two alternating parts strongly contrasted and
the grand theme played with solemnity and gravity. Other
conductors treat it much more lightly, and much can surely be
said in favor of that interpretation; but I prefer the way Cheves
did it.

Later in the afternoon I read the Yeoman of the Guard—
some beautiful poetry in it—and finally got the gramophone

and played my Mikado and Iolanthe records on it. [15 February 1937]

Did you hear the second symphony? I did. And did you listen to the overture of Offenbach's Orpheus in Hades, a great favorite of mine, sparkling like champagne! [23 March 1937]

Last night a truly great event. I don't think that ever in my life I have heard a singer like Marian Anderson. A voice so rich in color and beauty, so full of expression and so absolutely musical. Her rendering of Schubert's Ave Maria was simply sublime. [14 April 1937]

Yesterday I had a huge orgy of music and I hope that you were enjoying some of it at the same time. In the morning I had the Walburg-Brown and the Perole String Quartets. The first playing Mozart, the second Schuman. At two, Trial by Jury and then at three the last Philharmonic Concert with Bach, Beethoven and Brahms. I am sure you heard the fifth. In the evening the Northampton String Quartet gave a recital. Two Beethoven quartets op. 18 No. 2 and op. 59 No. 3, a magnificent one with a grand fugue in the last movement. A marvelous concert. [19 April 1937]

The concert last night, [Ross] a pianist from Cornell, played a program he is going to play in New York on Monday afternoon in Town Hall. Mozart C Major, violin sonata, a beautiful program. The Bach Chaconne, Beethoven piano sonata No. 8 and Brahms violin sonata. Very well done, although I'm not quite sure what the New York critics will say. Ross definitely does not seem to have enough power for the Chaconne. Still it is wonderful to listen to such music in a house instead of a concert hall. [6 November 1937]

I am sure you heard Toscanini play the Pastoral Symphony on Saturday. What a different piece it was from the one we heard in New York. Absolutely beautiful and now one of my

favorites. I thought of you during the Eroica yesterday afternoon, and tried to send a message at the beginning of the last
movement, but I am sure I was not concentrating properly because the music broke through all the time. [10 January 1938]

This evening I am going to a faculty musicale, but I am determined at all costs to leave early because Toscanini will actually be heard here playing the 9th! . . . Just heard Serkin in
the Emperor Concerto, do you remember 2 years ago? [7 February 1938]

Hindemith: contrary to expectations it was not a lecture at
all but a concert. He played four of his works. A sonata for
Viola d'amore, a sonata for viola, the ordinary one, solo one for
piano, and finally one for viola and piano. One understands little if one is as little prepared as I am or has so little musical
ability, nevertheless I got the impression of a real composer,
and liked some parts very much. [11 March 1938]

Of the various things I did during the week the finest was a
concert by Myra Hess in the Town Hall. A magnificent pro-
gramme magnificently executed. Scarlatti, Bach, the Appa-
sionata, Schumann and Chopin. [10 March 1940, Oxford]

And another event you will want to hear about is the coming
of the D'Oyle Carte [opera company] who started a 3 weeks'
engagement on Monday. I went into a debauch and bought
three tickets, seeing Iolanthe, the Mikado and Yeoman of the
Guard. . . . I cannot tell you how much I enjoyed it all. [12 May
1940, Oxford]

Some excellent music last Sunday. Mozart's G minor symphony, Beethoven's 8th and a concerto for two pianos by Bach
with two excellent soloists. [8 March 1941]

The music festival of Smith College, from Palaestrina to
Bach, held last weekend was magnificent. Smith at its very
best. You should have heard the orchestra under Josten [Smith

music professor Werner Josten] play the second Brandenburg Concerto! [1 May 1941]

So glad you heard Beethoven's Fifth. It lifts me on a wave, I cannot help being drawn down into that magnificent spirit of heroic motion, heroic calm, heroic frolick, and heroic victory. When it was over Frau Köhler said "except for the very last quartets Beethoven's music does not touch me at all. It stays outside. I remain a mere listener. It tells me nothing." You see people are different. And that we are not different with regards to Beethoven makes me very happy. Beethoven touches something in me that I think is quite vital, belongs to the most central provinces of my personality, and I know the same is true of you. [15 October 1934]

Also involved with music, Harrower often recommended books:

By the way, I got for my birthday a very good book which I am sure you would like: *Essays in Musical Analysis* by Donald Tovey, of Edinburgh. I have got Volume 1, the *Symphonies*. It is published by the Oxford University Press. I think you would get a lot more out of it than I do, as you know so much more about music, so if you have a chance of getting it, do. [11 February 1941, Montreal]

Books

In much the same way the correspondents listened to music and delighted in sharing it, they exchanged books, quoting passages and recording their opinions. The excerpts are mostly from Koffka's letters, with occasionl remarks from Harrower.

[KK] I have just finished an English novel published in 1917 by St. John G. Ervine, "Changing Winds," very good. The main hero is a young Ulsterman whose three best friends are English. They are marvelous friends, two are being killed and one feels that the other two will eventually be killed also. The Irishman is just going to marry the sister of one of the two dead friends and a little later to enlist. All this is painted on the background of the Irish English relationship; Nationalism with its positive and negative values and some splendid people in it. Hardly a single person that is really unpleasant and amazing that such a book was published during the war. No hatred of Germans in it. [15 September 1934]

[MH] I have just read Vera Britain's [Brittain] *Honourable Estate* [1936]. There are some passages about different kinds of love that I want to copy. It is strange that she cannot get away from the motive of loving a young gallant soldier completely, and then finally marrying a person (Denis) of quite different temperament and finding both kinds of happiness valuable. Only after their wedding had she fully realized the contrast which would confront her between the earlier union, springing spontaneously from passion, and a marriage based upon tender affection and mutual respect. The memory of desperate love made adjustment more difficult she knows. Passion had been, for its brief duration, violent and abandoned, while affection was considerate and infinitely patient, yet the rapture in that passion had made everything easy and unpremeditated, whereas the relationship between herself and Denis involved a conscious cooperation which demanded as much from intelligence as from instinct. [20 January 1937, New Brunswick]

[KK] Thanks for the very interesting quotation from Vera Britain. [21 January 1937]

I have just read Dorothy Sayers' *Gaudy Night* [1935]. Tremendously good. Have you read it? If not, you should. If you like, I can bring it along on the 26th. It is really worth reading, a tense novel with a very definite problem that concerns you quite intimately, with heart and brain. [13 April 1936]

I have nearly finished *Hatters Castle* [A. J. Cronin, 1931], but I am quite afraid to approach the end. It is one of the most relentless tragedies, the helplessness of the poor sisters, the degradation which Brodie has produced in his entire family, in which Mary alone has completely escaped. A gruesome tale, a great book. [19 September 1932]

Angel Pavements [J. B. Priestley's *Angel Pavement*, 1930] I have finished. It held me to the last. How one knows those people, and how, through them, one knows ever so many more. How one feels the pulse of our time beat in one, and in a large section of our society. It is Dickensonian in a way. Less humor than Dickens, on the other hand, probably more conscientiousness, I mean a greater effort to be fair all round, to distribute light and shadow more evenly than Dickens did. But if one wants to compare Priestley and Dickens, then what a change in the general atmosphere! This is almost the most astounding side of this comparison. And will strike posterity most. [8 November 1930]

Thanks for your letter and the books. I have read *H. M. Pulham Esq.* [John P. Marquand, 1941] and after the first few chapters which seemed to me too much of a caricature, I liked it very much indeed. I adore the girl, Merwin Myles, and I like Harry's sister Mary. The whole thing is really terribly sad. A somewhat refined *Babbit*, more impressive for being more refined. I am keeping the Churchill speeches for a fitting mood, and I shall certainly look at the summary of German War Psychology. I read not long ago the article in the Psychological Bulletin dealing with the same subject though of course in a much briefer form. [18 August 1941, Wakefield, R.I.]

[MH] I hope things are going well for you down by the sea: has it been hot? Have you read *Berlin Diary* [William L. Shirer, 1941]? I think it is tremendously interesting. A book called *This Above All*, by Eric Knight [1941] has been tremendously well spoken about, but I was somewhat disappointed, or perhaps it is just that one cannot appreciate what these people have lived through. [8 July 1941, Montreal]

[KK] Nothing from here. I read your two books with intense pleasure. The *Berlin Diary* particularly after the outbreak of war, is fascinating. *This Above All* I simply adored. I thought it a beautiful book, probably the finest war novel I have ever read. I suppose it is best to keep the books for you till you can come and take them. [4 August 1941, Wakefield, R.I.]

I am now reading *Bonfire* [Dorothy Canfield Fisher, 1933]. I am amazed at the wealth of human character in the book. Including cats and dogs. And the power by which the specific character of a whole people, Vermont Villagers, is brought out. Old Miss Gussie the deaf one is lovely. The conflict that tears at the roots of this society is brought out in a manner superior to Miss [Mary Ellen] Chase's *Mary Peters* [1934]. One sees more its intrinsic necessity, which is stronger and more important than the external factors, economic changes, influx of summer people, etc. Altogether you see the group at work in this book, and the group-individual relationships. I am very grateful that you recommended that book to me.

(Later) I have finished *Bonfire*. When I wrote to you last about it, the exciting part had only just begun. The attempted murder of Anson and Lixlee. From then on, till fairly near the end, the tension increases steadily, and for a time the individual fate of the leading persons overshadows the life of the group. I was tremendously touched, most strongly of course, by the marvelous relationship between Fred Kirby and Anna. The beauty of their coming, and belonging together has a poignancy and depth that has moved me to the quick. . . . I think it is quite intentional that of all the people in the book, only those two can develop such a bond, which unites the inmost core of their personalities and makes the best in each still better, greater, than it was. A beautiful pattern to model one's life by. The way in which Anson is treated shows, in my opinion, also great insight into human nature and human values. Anson remains a failure in spite of all that Anna and his splendid young wife, are doing for him. Artistically, the least successful character is, in my mind, Lixlee. At heart, except perhaps in

the first chapter, taken in by her, I never could feel that magnetic force that she was supposed to possess. Too soon I saw her
as just a guttersnipe. But Anson's agonies of jealousy are excel-
lently brought out. [6 October 1934]

Having stayed in Vermont with Dorothy Canfield, Harrower
commented: "So glad you liked *Bonfire*. You know of course that
Dorothy Canfield is herself deaf."

By accident Koffka came across a writer with a great reputation in England but little known in the States and found him a
sympathetic author.

Have you ever heard of Mark Rutherford, or William Hale
White (his real name) he died in 1914. I am reading a book
called the *Groombridge Diary*, by a D. Hale White [actually
Dorothy V. White, 1924], a woman who was 31 years old when
she met White who was 73. The whole diary turns about him
and since the woman bears his name I gather they became
married. I liked reading in it, it strikes something of a chord
which resounds in my own soul; please tell me whether you
know anything about the book or the diary. According to the
Cambridge History of Literature the man has a high standing.
. . . I read a little more in the *Groombridge Diary*. Amazing
the love letters which the old man writes. He must have been a
fine person. She gives no excerpts from her own letters. She
plays cricket and has boys' Sunday School classes, Church of
England. He was expelled from New College as a young man,
and served in the Admiralty for many years. You would like
the book.
. . . I'm almost through with the *Groombridge Diary*. They
are married at last. The reason why it is finally done is very
curious and paltry: Summer approaches and she ought to spend
part of her holiday with her family. Not wanting to leave White
alone she marries him. She comments herself on the inade-
quacy of this explanation which nevertheless may be perfectly
true for such is life.
. . . I have finished the *Groombridge Diary*. W. Hale White is

dead, he died before they were married two full years. There are very few entries during these years. They were always together and blissfully happy. In the last pages of the book she tries to recapture his personality for herself. He was 45 years older than she, 81 when he died. [8 August 1934]

Harrower replied: "I asked my mother about Mark Rutherford. He is a well-known literary figure. She delights in him and his writing. Ask her about him sometime when you write to her" [15 August 1934, Nova Scotia].

Movies

Trading views of movies did not figure as so important as exchanging books and listening to music, but some of Koffka's comments indicate his tastes. The first excerpt is historically interesting. In the 1930s good movie production was sufficiently new as to evoke the comment about good facial expression.

I saw *Mutiny on the Bounty* last night. A good film, but not one of the really great ones. Lawton [Charles Laughton] is excellent, Clark Gable very good. And I liked particularly that young newly married boy who is pressed into service. But the Tahiti scenes are weak, rather Hollywoodish, I think. Magnificent the first unfurling of sails. [December 1935]

In the evening I saw *David Copperfield*. I was a bit disappointed, the book so much greater than the film. Nevertheless, there were many good scenes. The boy played awfully well. Betsy was not quite good enough, too exaggerated in the beginning and not quite big enough in the end. It cannot really be done. The figures are all quite legendary, tremendous as heroes of Greek mythology and the movie cannot succeed in giving that impression. However, I am glad I saw it. [December 1935]

Escape Me Never is a magnificent film. Some parts even more impressive than the play, others not quite so good. But the advantage of the film is that wherever you sit you are near enough to see facial expressions as though you were in the front row of the stalls. I was very deeply moved. [Elizabeth] Bergner is absolutely great and the rest of the cast supports her well. [28 January 1936]

I went last night to the movies: *The Informer.* . . . it is without exaggeration perhaps the best play I have ever seen on the movies. It easily belongs in the best three. I should love to see it again with you! It is real art. Absolutely magnificent acting, first rate photography and a gripping plot. [Later] I am so glad you liked *The Informer*. It stands in a class different from that of the average pictures. [4 March 1936]

In the evening a movie: Marlene Dietrich and Gary Cooper in *Desire*. A very good picture of the regular Hollywood type, but nothing above that. Still, worth seeing. [29 April 1936]

Tonight . . . the Russian picture *Three Women* shown once before last year when I did not see it, one very long scene in this picture is probably the best thing that I have ever seen on the screen, a scene in a large pub, full of all types of workers, a chaos of different minds and moods, and then four children sing a revolutionary song, which they have been taught. At first the crowd goes on with its noise, but gradually they listen. Then under the leadership of a revolutionary they take the song up. Their faces change. They become one united group. Then the police comes and a hush falls over the crowd. And then the leader rises again, stamps the floor with his stick and begins to sing and the whole crowd and the children break out into a surge of fervid almost sacred song. It is impossible to describe the impressions because the idea is carried in terms of visual art. You see all these strange faces, beautiful, brutal, wasted, disillusioned, young, hardly developed. Absolutely magnificent. [1 December 1937]

Human Qualities

The qualities in a person which Koffka most admired can be seen best from a series of thumbnail sketches which occur in his letters. The examples are drawn from persons in different walks of life, from a king to a seller of combs, but they seem to carry a consistent picture.

The first thing that comes to mind is the death of King George. I heard it last night. A good man has closed his eyes, a simple man and a loyal one. I was deeply affected, and the thought of this event stayed in my mind all through the evening. He will go down in history as a token that the simple human virtues find their recognition; that people cannot help loving a king who does his life's work lovingly, modestly and without conceit or selfishness. King George has perhaps created a new type of kingliness, the one type that has its justification in our time. I do not belong, as you do, to that great family of the British Commonwealth, but I feel at this occasion as though I did.

The new king [Edward VIII]! What did he feel when the crown descended on his head? What difficult readjustment in life. I wish him all possible success and happiness. I have seen no paper as yet and I don't know what has happened. But I know that a new king may mean very much to the world at large. [21 January 1936]

I saw a little man with a short white beard and striking blue eyes, sort of standing around and had just about passed him when he asked me would I buy a comb from an old saddler. Motorcars had come in and abolished the need for harness so here he was an old man. How old? Seventy-three. The combs, pocket combs, were only 6 pence so of course I bought one and he gave me the full assurance of an expert craftsman that it was a good hard one and would not break. So I said to him, after having slipped the comb into my pocket, that I thought he had done me a real service by selling it to me. And then he said, with a wonderful expression on his old face: "That was a very kind remark, sir!"

It will sound quite trivial when you read it, but for a moment, it made me quite happy. I had at that instant established a human relationship of perfect equality between him and me. [12 November 1939]

You ask me about the man with whom I am having breakfast in New York. He is a Mr. Trenefels [unidentified], a friend of Kohn's [Hans Kohn, Smith professor of history and political science], a German industrialist, who because of his Jewish wife and on general ethical grounds has come over here to start a new life, although it will mean the loss of practically his whole fortune. A splendid kind of person, really well educated and as full of moral fervor as Borgese [Smith Italian literature professor Giuseppe Borgese], while being a good deal more objective and less self-centered than our grand Sicilian friend. [21 September 1938]

An interesting evening yesterday. A former Viennese doctor spoke, who has just come to this country after nine months in a concentration camp. The natural and unimpassioned way in which this man talked about that experience was one of the most impressive things I have ever heard. It is, of course, horrible beyond description. [1 May 1939]

Yesterday afternoon I had tea with charming old Wallenbery [unidentified] (78 years old), a man who six years ago received the Erb medal [for scientific achievements] in Germany. He is the nicest, kindest, wisest old man you can imagine. And he feels so cut off because though he reads English fluently he does not succeed despite great efforts to understand or speak it. [10 March 1940, Oxford]

Yesterday I met the Lindberghs, both very delightful people, and absolutely unspoiled. She very shy and introvert, he simple, modest, keen and knowing what he is talking about. They have almost a negative publicity complex. He did not leave the President's house for fear of being recognized and mobbed. [2 February 1931]

It would seem that modesty, unpretentiousness, and integrity were the common denominators in the qualities Koffka admired. Other human qualities, however, he made no bones about disliking. One was lack of loyalty. When he heard a colleague make fun of a student, telling a good story at a friend's expense, he wrote:

She read a very amusing sketch of a graduate seminar. Clever and awfully well written. She talked about it almost the entire evening and I feel that her love for good stories dominates, at the expense of other and more noble emotions. Of course, she only said nice things about the girl, and yet her slightly amused and facetious attitude about this person who is not just an ordinary student, but a serious personality, hurt me not a little. I can't stand this lack of loyalty. [7 January 1933]

Koffka despised the purely negative critical spirit. Speaking of some English philosophers he said:

The spirit of these philosophers is abominable. I should not have minded to be thought a fool by the whole audience, had I been there. I would have given them a piece of my mind, they lay down the rules of the game they like to play "that is self-evident" and then they show their ingenuity and cleverness on their chessboard and despite the onlooker who points out to them that their game is just a game, and that the real questions are outside their scope. [15 November 1932]

False idealism also came under attack:

I do not accept it as an excuse, that some of these young Nazis are highly idealistic. What an idealism! which is at bottom self-glorification. You are right that personal difficulties, even if they are very serious, should be treated as molehills compared to these huge problems of mankind. But also wrong; in one of the Russian's post revolutionary novels, there appears a man who devotes his life to the party, he is honored and obeyed by the party, achieves a great deal for his community, but as a person is a perfect swine. In spite of all his social ties, he does not know what a true human relationship is. And of what value is a person's love for mankind, even if it entails real sacrifice, if that person is unable to love, or even respect any single human being. Mankind, it seems to me, may so easily become a mere idol, without flesh and blood. In Germany they call it the State, and their fanaticism appears to me as the worst kind of idolatry. How can you love mankind if you do not love some one human being? [11 April 1933]

Insofar as a lecture reflected the lecturer's human qualities, Koffka reacted pro or con.

I was asked to supper and then to hear Dorothy Thompson,* Mrs. Sinclair Lewis, speak in the Forum on Germany, and heard an extraordinarily good lecture. [She had been a corre-spondent in Vienna and Berlin in the 1920s.] Rich in content, marvellously well informed, and full of insight into the various forces at work. The lecture lasted till 9.45 and discussion after-wards protracted the meeting till 10.30.

Orton [Smith economics professor William Aylott Orton] asked us to his house to meet her, again it was very interest-ing, a good journalist reporter is really an invaluable person. Particularly if he or she has such an open and intelligent mind as Mrs. Sinclair Lewis. . . . Mrs. Orton said at the lecture that Mrs. Lewis reminded her of you. I could not agree. She lacked the power of clear concentration which you possess to such a high degree. If she had condensed her lecture a little bit more it might have been more effective, and that is what you would have done. Besides, words come more easily to you than to her, who sometimes had to stop, and search, only to come up with a rather banal term, still the lecture was good. It was the best speech on Germany that I have heard. [15 October 1934]

Laski [English political scientist Harold Laski*] was splendid. One of the finest lectures I have listened to and afterwards he told interesting stories of political events in England. He took part in the Indian Round Table Conference, and in the Imperial Conference. Also, he does act as go-between between the different party leaders. He is an excellent raconteur. [25 May 1931]

Last night Nadya Boulanger lectured here, the modern French teacher of music who has trained a great number of modern composers, most of them younger Americans. She is a superb person. You feel the master, as soon as she opens her mouth. Of all the lectures I have heard she reminded me most of Wertheimer, although she is different from him in many ways. It was a real experience to listen to her speaking and playing. [2 May 1938]

I forgot to tell you about [American editor and writer] Max Eastman*. . . . He spoke about modernistic poetry and the future. It was a very good lecture indeed. He made his positive and negative points with great vigor and finally advanced the theory that modernistic poetry was the outcome of the fact that psychology had now also entered the ranks of the sciences so that the poet was no longer needed to give information about the soul, just as the development of natural sciences had turned poetry from nature poems. Therefore poetry would more and more concentrate in expressing "pure experience." In the discussion I made a rather long speech in which I argued in a very friendly way, against the theoretical conclusions. In the first place I could not see that the great poets would write their poems differently because of the new psychology, and in the second that strictly pure experience was incommunicable into the communicable. To this he agreed, my first point he did not understand, and failed to see it even after [Lawrence] Stapleton had elaborated it in a very clever speech containing some very good ideas.

Altogether it was very entertaining and I had a great liking for the man. [22 January 1931]

A colorful personality, provided it included a good mind, was a genuine delight to Koffka. In the first excerpt, he wrote of Irish poet George W. Russell, whose pseudonym was A. E.

You have surely seen pictures of the man, rather tall, very heavy, with a big head and an enormous beard. Somewhat resembling Titchener [English psychologist Edward B. Titchener]. . . . Also reminded me of Schiller [English philosopher Ferdinand Schiller]. His lecture was one of the most beautiful lectures I have ever listened to. Here comes the poet, the center of a militant literary movement, the critic, the humorist and the man. How he chatted about [Standish J.] O'Grady, himself, Yeats, Alice Milligan, George Moore, G. B. S. [George Bernard Shaw], James Joyce and ever so many others [all Irish writers], was unequalled by anything I have heard before. And what a group. What imagination, what devotion to fantasy! How you would have loved it. It was a visit of a really great man, in whom antics and worship, roving imagination and critical realism, poetry and humor have formed a wonderful unity. [16 January 1931]

. . . Yesterday a lecture by Julian Benda [French philosopher Julien Benda*]. It was marvelous. What a fine and charming person, sitting at the desk and giving his "causerie" on the dilemma of divinism and humanism, the first representing the belief in the absolute value of reason and justice, the second standing for only relative values; the first being the foundation of democracy, the second of fascism and communism. It was all so beautifully done, so simply and so modestly. I was so enthusiastic that afterwards I telephoned Guilloton [Smith professor of French] and told him how much I had enjoyed it. He was so pleased with my reaction that he suggested the possibility of my meeting Benda sometime today. I hope I shall, because he attracted me tremendously. [13 April 1937]

Dogs

The letters contain many references to dogs, both writers being
unable to heed Kipling's advice: "Brothers and sisters I beg you
beware of giving your heart to a dog to tear." Koffka's dachshund,
Rolle, whom he brought with him from Germany, had his complete devotion and tender loving care. His favorite photograph of
himself was one with Rolle in his arms. Rolle had died before the
correspondence began, but letters about dogs were by no means
confined to individual ones. For instance, Koffka wrote a theoretical paper on dogs to give to his club:

I am to speak on Monday at the Club and instead of using
one of the things I did this year, like Wertheimer's seminar or
the Chicago lecture, I decided to do something quite different
and talk about dogs. I got the suggestion from an offprint
which Sarris [unidentified] sent me. Do you remember him, the
Greek from Paris? I have got a good deal of material and when
I have organized it, it may interest the Club. [26 February
1938]

Club went very well. Poor attendance; only 7 members but
they all liked it and were interested. Of course there was no
proper discussion, instead more or less silly dog stories, horse
stories, etc.
Tomorrow night a party at which I shall appear as a dog (i.e.
going as what I want to be). A dressmaker is making a sort of
dog costume for me. There is such a funny discrepancy between
the program which states "All inhibitions taboo"! and the people, most of them old and stodgy. [28 February 1938]

It was a great day when a puppy appeared on the scene.

Just now, during the few minutes I have before lunch, I shall
tell you of the main event here: The arrival of Jolly (a Dachshund puppy). We got him on Saturday evening after having
seen him in the afternoon. He is absolutely beautiful and as

*Koffka, aged twelve. He rarely spoke of his childhood; when he did it
was about his beloved dachshunds.*

Harrower, aged twelve, with Mac.

Koffka and Rolle, who accompanied him daily to his laboratory in Germany.

nice a pup—4 months old—as you can imagine. With the other
dogs of the Jostens [Werner Josten, Smith music professor] he
had been most cheeky and brave but, after all, he is such a
young thing, and therefore he was afraid of everything in our
apartment. Each new room held new terrors and then there is
so little to do when one is not allowed to chew at master's shoes
or socks or coat buttons.

He has however very quickly become attached to me and absolutely "dogs" my steps. He chewed all sorts of things here in
the lab and was twice sick—not much, probably swallowed
some sort of stuff. His face is serious and intelligent with the
never quite vanishing sadness of the creature that wants to understand and communicate more than it can. I am sure you
would love him. I wish you could see him now in his infancy,
with his head too large for his body and his lovely soft paws.
He came with a veritable trousseau, including an elegant basket for the night and his license and a smart collar and leash.
. . . One of Jolly's brothers from the same litter has been
given to President Roosevelt's private secretary who takes him
to all cabinet meetings which he, not being housebroken, does
his best to enliven. [28 September 1936]

Harrower responded with a poem to celebrate the occasion.

> I think I see you, in my mind's eye, Jolly
> I think I feel the warm silk of your skin
> Your big soft paws have padded on my floor,
> Your eyes have asked me "May I then come In . . .
> In . . . In . . . In . . . somewhere:" for you do not know
> Just what to ask for, or just where to go.
>
> I think I know you Jolly, think I see
> How strange the world of dogdom looks today.
> The old life dwindles and becomes a dream
> You cross a threshold now, you cross to stay
> The big bright sun of Master climbs the sky
> This is the light you'll live for, for this die.

You step into our world, a world so strange
Criss-cross complexities, drives, hopes and fear.
But, single minded pick the scent of love
Follow forever on those footsteps dear
Curl yourself in the corner of his heart
of Master's very life become a part.

So for your great adventure, little dog,
For that great game of loving which you play
I send you greetings: here come, sniff my shoe
This is the smell of someone who will stay.
Give me that big soft paw into my hand. . . .
Master, and this dog lover, understand.
    [30 September 1936, New Brunswick]

[KK] Jolly's letter yesterday must have shown you how I adored your poem. You have a wonderful insight into a dog's soul and you express it marvelously.

. . . I fetched Jolly who was tremendously attracted and impressed by Eric and Boris (Comment: 2 huge dogs). In the course of the evening Jolly tried again and again to play with Eric. It was a sight to see him torn between mortal fear, invincible curiosity and friendliness.

. . . Later some films were shown. Jolly sat on my lap quietly as I thought asleep. But in one of the pictures several boys walked by gesticulating whereupon he barked so violently that the other two dogs who had left the room, rushed back also furiously barking, and quite disappointed when they found no cause. Jolly must have watched very closely for he growled and barked several times more, the last time at a huge horse. [6 October 1936]

Alas, dogs are subject to distemper. Jolly luckily survived: "No real change in Jolly. You can't imagine how touching it is to see a heap of blankets and a wagging tail; this is the regular sight any time I come home—he even wagged his tail when the vet came today. His eyes, however, seem brighter, more shiny" [9 December 1936].

Harrower recounted an unusual dachshund story:

I had dinner with the family of one of my students. . . . the most interesting thing of all was the Dachshund Peter, a most beautiful dog. They told me this nice story (he is only 8 months and not fully developed yet, he sleeps in a basket about 3 times his size). He is only allowed to eat bones in his basket which is kept in the kitchen. One day they were in the living room and heard him eating his bones in the dining room. The girl came through, smacked him mildly and took him and his bone back to the basket. Shortly afterwards they again heard gnawing of the bone in the dining room and again the girl went through, smacked him and took him back plus the bone to his basket. Sometime later again he was heard in the dining room and this time the father said it's obvious that you people can't handle dogs and went through to the dining room to find that the dog had dragged his huge basket through from the kitchen, got it under the dining room table and was in it eating his bone! And just as you've always said, whereas the first two times he had expected to be smacked, this time of course he couldn't be smacked because there he sat wagging his tail. A marvelous dog and the people were so nice to him. [31 October 1935, New Brunswick]

[KK] The Dachshund is just incredibly clever. If the observation is really reliable—and I have no reason to doubt it except just professional skepticism—it proves such an analysis of the situation: It is not the room that is important but the basket; the basket is movable—therefore. . . . Very few dogs, I believe, would be able to do such clever thinking and acting. The fact that he objected to being punished reveals true understanding of what he had done. What an amazing insight into a situation so alien to his canine make-up. Perhaps the best dog story I know. [1 November 1935]

Harrower reported on her dogs:

Writing to you is the only thing I am capable of at this moment. I am waiting to help give Peter a dose of morphine which will be his last. He is terribly ill and for several days we have done everthing we can. Intravenous, injections of fluid, sulphur drugs. He was at the vets but got worse. It is unutterably pathetic to see the way he will let anything be done to him if I hold him. There is no need to go into it. You know! He wrings my heart out. This illness of his has shown me the real meaning of why people say women can't have a job and a home. Everything goes by the board for me if I can help a sick person, dog or human. And I cannot but believe that this incredibly strong emotion that I feel at his dependence on me, would not stand me in good stead with children. I feel as if I had glimpsed the normal family relationship in all its force and beauty. [20 June 1939, Montreal]

Wendy ran around burying bones because this was the first time she had found earth soft enough to play with. She saw a rabbit and sat and watched it most politely and then got out of its way as it lolloped off. [14 July 1939, Nova Scotia]

Wendy has just jumped on the bed, having developed a perfect "double standard" reaction: no beds when master is around, beds when mistress is alone! She is becoming the most beautiful dog, with a classic spaniel head: but she remains full of interesting contradictions in character. She is wholesalely friendly and yet essentially gentle and almost deferential. She never takes affection for granted and is overcome with gratitude even though she is petted all the time. She has never been smacked, but sometimes when her harness is put on she will shiver with fright or something, and hold a posture into which she has been put for as long as five minutes without moving. [2 January 1940, Montreal]

Wendy has just come in looking rather sheepish. She has for the last few mornings "sung" to the radio at exactly the same hour, when alone in the room with the music just preceding the news. It is a very high note, much higher than her bark. When we creep in she always stops, and looks apologetic. Once we saw her through the crack of the door. It's like a monotone on a bugle. I suppose it's a hound's cry. [13 March 1940, Montreal]

Reaction to Illness

Koffka's attitude toward his heart attacks was one of continued optimism and belief in his eventual recovery, even up to a few days before his death. He was able to make accurate observations on the attacks and was interested in recording them despite subjective distress. Eager to deny psychogenic causes, he tended to underestimate normal stresses as contributing factors.

The first genuine heart attack occurred in late 1936, and the symptoms were described over the phone rather than in a letter. Koffka was put to bed for a month and the descriptions of his condition began in this instance as he was returning to normal life.

A word about myself. I drove to Holyoke yesterday to see Nathan [Koffka's physician] and got an angina attack on the street, walking from the final parking place to Nathan's. In a way I was quite pleased because this would give him an opportunity of seeing me at my worst. Well, my pulse was absolutely perfect and so were my heart tones. As soon as I was in the office, that is within no more than two minutes, the pressure disappeared and I was quite all right. The symptoms were entirely I am sure, the result of the digitalis which I had taken. [2 February 1937]

I have just returned from Springfield and am now going to give you a full report. Dr. Nathan rang up to tell me two things: one that the report of the new blood test had come in but the Hinton test was unsatisfactory owing to the condition

in which the blood arrived at the doctor's lab so after a fortnight or so he is going to have to make a third test to clear
things up completely. But so far as it goes the news is good.

Two, at my last visit Nathan had already told me that he
wanted to have a fluoroscope done in order to inspect the aorta.
This on general principles but also because the spirochete frequently produces an aneurism of the aorta. He had meanwhile
made an appointment with a colleague for this morning at 10.
The inspection revealed a distinct, but regular widening of the
aorta but with no trace of an aneurism. Such widening is not at
all uncommon in a man of my age but of course it is not normal. Nonetheless the doctors both declared over and over that
it was nothing serious but no more tennis and no more real
climbing. They also made me swallow stuff specially prepared
to study the relation of the heart and esophagus but this was
absolutely and unmistakably normal. Altogether it seems as
satisfactory as can be expected. [15 February 1937]

Obviously in answer to Harrower's queries, he replied:

I am afraid that an artery, once distended, will never be re-
stored to its normal shape. These are irreversible changes, as
irreversible as time itself. I'm a bit depressed about the whole
thing, because in spite of all my care, I do not feel any kind of
improvement. Ordinarily I am, of course, quite all right. But I
am so very easily fatigued and I am never sure that I may not
have an attack; these are never bad and yet they are very disturbing. Please believe me: they are not psychogenic. They
come unexpectedly, they do not serve any purpose, are not a
flight from responsibility. In themselves they are not particularly bad, but as tokens they are rather depressing. In another
week I shall see Nathan again and I shall discuss all this with
him. [23 February 1937]

Apparently these issues were not brought up with the doctor:
"There is nothing to tell about my visit to Nathan. He found me

looking very well and considers that an important symptom. He took more blood and will telephone the results on Friday" [3 March 1937].

A few weeks later Koffka attended a meeting of the Experimentalists, a group of experimental psychologists to which he was devoted. It was a special meeting for him since it was held at Smith and he was the chairman. The Warren medal Koffka mentioned in the letter was awarded annually by the Experimentalists to a distinguished fellow member. From this account it would seem that the strain and excitement of the meeting contributed to an attack.

Well it is all over, and I believe well over. It was the best attended meeting we had, the reports were of the highest quality and everything went smoothly. Mrs. Curti [Margaret Curti,* child psychologist at Smith] being a delightful and most efficient hostess. Everybody seemed greatly pleased with Smith College hospitality and it seems that [my] performance of the Chairman's duties were widely recognized. Carmichael [Brown psychology professor Leonard Carmichael*] told me that I was the ideal Chairman, and [Edwin G.] Boring* quite effusive after the business meeting in his comments on my efficiency. For all that it was a strain, a strain that became steadily greater; for it was the Chairman's task to call on the members for reports; he is responsible that every member is given a chance for speaking and having his contribution discussed and he has only a very limited time at his disposal. However, 10 minutes before the first taxi was ordered everybody had had his say and I could close the meeting as planned yesterday.

The really exciting bit was the dinner, i.e. the award of the Warren Medal to Lashley [Harvard professor of neuropsychology Karl S. Lashley*]. When it was done and Lashley made a very fine speech of thanks—he seemed deeply moved but I had a slight attack; however it passed very quickly and I enjoyed with everybody else Miss Nicolson's [Smith dean Marjorie Nicolson]* highly amusing speech. [27 March 1937]

The medical report, however, continued to be encouraging: "My visit to Nathan was very successful. He finds me definitely improved and has even modified his former absolute veto on tennis, he now says that it may not be final. Also I must not consider myself an ill person. But, he found my hemoglobin had not improved and gave me an iron prescription" [31 March 1937].

Two years later, a few days after arriving in Oxford to work with Sir Hugh Cairns,* the first of a series of more serious heart attacks began. That attack is described in detail in chapter 9, "Koffka in Oxford," and despite it Koffka completed a successful year of work in Oxford. A year and a half later, however, back in Northampton, he had a final series of attacks in the summer of 1941.

I have not written before because the news I have for you is such that it does not lose by delay. But, unpleasant though it is and beastly for me for the time being it is nothing that you should be disturbed about. To be brief: My heart started its old trouble, and on the orders of a first-rate specialist I am now, and have been for the last eight days, in the hospital where I have to spend six weeks in bed and a seventh to make the transition to normal life. Nobody can tell, so all doctors assure me, what has caused this new attack, but they also tell me that after six weeks' rest new capillaries will have formed to supply that small part of the heart muscle with blood, that is now handicapped by a partial occlusion of some coronary vessel. They say that it is like a fractured leg which heals and is then as strong as it was before. It is unpleasant only for me who looked forward to a vacation and has now to spend it in a small hospital room. [17 July 1941, Wakefield, R.I.]

. . . Nothing to report here except that I am making good progress. The doctor declared my heart to be in good condition at his examination this morning. But it is such a bore. I have finished the essay I was writing for that book [Koffka 1954] and I shall now begin working on the third chapter of my new book

[*A Psychology for Neurologists*, never published]. [Wakefield, R.I., 24 July 1941]

Alas I have to stay in bed for another three weeks and somebody is to be near me all the time. Not a nice story. I was very cautious, but on Friday when all I had done was to walk to the lab, I did not feel too well, settled down to sleep, felt uncomfortable, felt nauseated. Nothing I could do helped. My pulse went down to 40. I dragged myself to the phone where I had all the symptoms of fainting without actually going quite off. Damned unpleasant. A little later Nathan came. By that time I had practically recovered except that my pulse was about 54. What had happened was a partial block of the conducting, not the vascular system. Nathan thinks it is possible that I had another slight thrombosis and therefore wants me to stay in bed throughout the month.

This means beginning classes two weeks late. You can imagine how I like that! I have the feeling moreover that this rest cure is exaggerated, I am feeling fine again. But terribly irritated and bad tempered.

. . . Don't get alarmed. I know the tone of this letter may not sound too normal but I am getting along very well. Pulse is back to 72, strong and regular. I wish I would give you more cheerful news but perhaps you as a semi-medical will be pleased to hear of the enforced rest. . . . Incidentally the heart attack had no assignable cause. It came in the evening of a quiet and unexciting day. [9 September 1941]

My news: Nathan saw me yesterday, a great improvement. My blood pressure has risen to 115 which is perfectly normal for me. Nevertheless Nathan wants to be overcautious and I have to fight him tooth and nail to come to some sort of compromise: I am not to leave the house before November the 1st but I may teach my classes up here during the last two weeks of October. I have to stay in bed until the middle of the month and he makes me take phenobarbitol regularly, so I am not too bright or energetic at any time, and cannot think of working on the book. I even refused to write a reply to a stupid anti-Gestalt article which Langfeld [*Psychological Review* editor Herbert Langfeld*] is publishing in the Review. But I needed to see some books and articles to do a proper job and did not feel that I could do it without undue excitement. [27 September 1941]

This respite lasted till the end of October and Koffka was excited to get back to a reduced schedule:

I sent you a letter after my first class. Since then I have had two more with the same excellent results, a pulse rate of 73 after two hours of teaching. So I shall stay here another week, the girls coming up for their classes after which I shall move into a ground floor apartment and start going to the Lab on the following day. I shall, however, continue to be very careful for a long time because I do not want a repetition of the attack I had on my return from Rhode Island. [21 October 1941]

The last letter, written a few days before he died on 22 November:

Alas I am back where I was before I wrote my last letter. For a while I went to the Lab to teach and typed my article but on Wednesday evening I had an attack of angina which I reported to Nathan who forbade me to hold any class either in the Lab or at home. He came the following morning and forbade me to leave the house till Christmas. So I am again spending most of my time in bed *but I want to get well!* [14 November 1941]

the public koffka

Koffka was not a good public lecturer in the United States. When he spoke to a general audience, he made the same mistake again and again: in his anxiety not to talk down to an audience, he ended up by demanding of the untrained listener the kind of tight reasoning even his colleagues found difficult at times. Because it would have made him appear to himself in some way superior, he refused to believe his presentations were too scholarly and difficult to follow.

One of Koffka's intellectual strengths was his capacity to see beneath the obvious statement of a problem, his distrust of superficial understanding; but he did not see that the majority of audiences did not want to be so challenged. They expected more dramatic presentations from an important speaker.

A watchdog for the success or failure of Koffka's public presentations, Harrower urged him many times and in different ways to modify this image which was being created.

I have to speak on your lecture to the Psychology Club [at New Jersey College for Women] on Monday. It was too difficult for almost everyone! So do be careful when you give it again. I went to a group of scientists at the Agricultural College for lunch yesterday and we discussed the lecture very well there. But all agreed it is not a public lecture. I hate to depress you, if I do, and probably you will never learn how little can be under-

74

stood without some background and perhaps you ought *not* to learn! I really don't know. On the other hand, I am happy to say that my friends certainly responded to you as a person when they met you for dinner. Miss B [Director of Students Alice Brown] said you stood for her "integrity and spirit, and that even if you are not an idealist in Philosophy, you are a confirmed idealist in life, three characteristics bound to make your life difficult." [8 December 1934, New Brunswick, N.J.]

Koffka was not a good teacher of undergraduates. He expected students to read on their own, without assignments, as in the British and Continental universities. He expected a level of sophistication in studying that was not evidenced. He admired the self-confidence and poise of the American undergraduate outside the classroom, but the lack of basic scholarship always startled him. Two letters written in 1932 reflect some of his problems.

The first unpleasant experience in my class, last Friday when I appointed a reporter, a girl, the last senior, said that although it would be her turn tomorrow, she could not undertake it since she would be absent. So today the first junior gave a report, a long exhaustive and as good as imaginable. Then I again appointed the senior girl; at the end of hour I observed already how she was continually dabbing her eyes with a handkerchief. And at the close she said that she could not report, she did not understand it and I must appoint somebody else. Two students volunteered at once, a junior whom I chose. The girl remained behind, she was in an awful condition, she wanted to drop the course and leave college. She did not believe anybody else understood it. A good report meant nothing but the ability to take notes. Of course that is all nonsense, the girls ask intelligent questions, and even if a good report were nothing but the result of quick note taking you can't take proper notes and select from them a report without understanding them. I told the girl to see me in my office hours, but it was all in vain. I suppose it can't be helped. [19 October 1932]

Now to the last point, the complaint of my students, it was awfully decent of you to tell me in the way in which you did. I have no difficulty in discussion of the matter for myself, but I find it much more difficult to explain to you. Thinking over the events of the class I can only remember one occasion and that but very vaguely, when I turned down a discussion. I even forget which student it was and that was long ago. Now, long ago the students were just beginning to learn Gestalt Theory. I don't see any gain in discussing their "opinions" as long as they don't know more about what they are discussing and don't even consider the little they might have known. After all a junior or senior who's had six or seven weeks of a course is not entitled to have her "opinion" considered as equally valuable as the conviction which their teacher has reached, after twenty years of work in that particular field. If they don't feel that, they are just stupid. I have given them several opportunities for free discussion after each chapter. The next will come soon and then I shall try to make them speak out. For by now I have introduced enough controversial matter for them to take sides. But at the earlier date it would have been a sheer waste of time and time is very precious. I really believe students should learn that "opinions" are worthless, they must have well supported arguments, not just beliefs and prejudices. I consider that one of the aims of my course. I shall never turn down a good argument, but I shall also expect that they first make an effort to understand the arguments which they get from me. I have always felt that I was on good terms with the class and I shall not let these complaints change my attitude in the slightest. One of my aims is to convince them that psychology is not a jumble of different opinions. [20 December 1932]

On the other hand, Koffka was excellent with graduates and young faculty members. An invitation from Edwin G. Boring* at Harvard led to this kind of experience:

Boring has written a number of very nice letters about my visit. I shall talk about the Ego and present some of my new ideas for discussion. I hope the colloquium will be successful. The topic is so very different from what Boring is interested in or even thinks psychology is. On the other hand, if Harry Murray* and his group attend, they would be interested. Of course they may all find my ideas perfectly crazy. I'm terribly sorry that you are not here now. It would give me much greater confidence if I had your reaction first. You will find a change in this respect. I rely much more on your judgment than I ever did before although you will admit I often enough took your advice but now you are a full fledged colleague, a psychologist of standing, one of the coming "men," and it is always wise to be on the right side of the new generation! When you come back we shall cooperate as never before. We should be able to produce a really good textbook together and other books afterwards. Harrower-Koffka are to become so familiar that psychologists will think it is a double name. [24 March 1933]

I went up to Boring's office, had a cordial reception and chatted with him till 4:20, then the colloquium. Although they had not announced my visit, the room was packed. I spoke, as Boring had asked me to, exactly forty-five minutes on the notes which I enclose. Then another forty-five minutes discussion in which faculty and graduate students took part. I cannot say at all what the general impression was. Then dinner with Boring at the faculty club. I talked first about the Uzbekistan expedition, then we had another long and rather good discussion in which [John Gilbert] Beebe-Center and [C. C.] Pratt defended a very conservative position while two of the younger men, Volkmann and Chapman, were wonderfully progressive, both agreeing to my notion of the phenomenal space behind, one of them suggesting spontaneously that there was space also behind opaque objects. I enjoyed this discussion very much and I believe the others did too. Boring also asked me about my book and when I had explained to him what I was aiming at, he said, "But that will be read by a lot of people." A rather queer remark to make. I answered, "Well it's not finished yet and I shall be glad if it is done by Christmas," or something like that. But I suppose that they really would like that kind of book, which does not mean they will like my book. [31 March 1933]

During a six-week summer school in 1939 with graduate students at Ohio State University, Koffka again found the kind of challenge and rapport that he dearly loved. Among his Columbus experiences described in the letters are some directly concerned with his students and others pertaining to his growing clinical interest and to his impending departure for Oxford to work with the neurosurgeon Sir Hugh Cairns.* Harrower at this time was working with Wilder Penfield* at the Montreal Neurological Institute and lecturing on psychology over the radio for the Canadian Broadcasting Company.

[KK] My room here is adequate and gives all the privacy I want. When it is too hot, I can spend as much time in my lab as I want. I met Burtt [Ohio State faculty member] this morning, who showed me the ropes. A tremendous campus, very well laid out. Tomorrow I begin my classes. They are scheduled as "daily" but I was told that most people give an extra assignment instead of the Saturday class. It will take a few days before I get my stride. I'll have to work quite a bit reading and writing to get my Bryn Mawr lectures ready for publication. Will you be willing to revise them when they are typed? Please do not say yes if you are too busy but I could not help asking you to do once more what you have done through so many years. [19 June 1939, Columbus]

Here it is hot and humid but apart from that, quite nice. Apparently I am very successful with the graduate students and assistants. I had a grand time with them on Wednesday evening after seminar when I went with my nice assistant to the house where he and a number of graduate students are living. Originally it had been the intention to listen to the Louis-Galento fight, but here we are on Eastern Standard time and my seminar lasts until 9:30 so we all went over when we got through. I stayed till after midnight and talked a lot. My assistant told me when he drove me home that this over-sophisticated group was so devoted to me that they would accept my word if I had said that black was white. However exaggerated this might be, it shows that they like me and get something out of my being here. [30 June 1939, Columbus]

The last three days here have been simply ghastly. The combination of heat and humidity drags me down. At the same time I was out every evening. People here are really very nice and I had a number of good discussions with younger and older men. I also mixed a good deal with the students, and through them meet other professors.

On the two next Thursdays I have to speak: next Thursday rather informally at the Club of the Advanced Psychology students, a week later at a National Honorary Educational Society I am to give a university lecture.

Last night I got a cable from Philpott, secretary of the Psychology section of the British [Psychological] Association, in which he chooses "The Ego and Its World" for my Dundee lecture and asks for a two hundred word abstract in return. I wrote it this morning but alas, I cannot submit it to the wise and critical eyes of my old and constant helper.

The administration here is not very generous about a salary. The check for the whole amount won't be ready before the very last day.

. . . I have started writing up the Bryn Mawr lectures (Koffka 1940) but I have made little progress because in this climate I'm unable to do much more than the absolutely necessary work.

Your name is well-known to the graduate students here. They asked me what had become of you and were much interested. [8 July 1939, Columbus]

[MH] Thanks so much for your letter. I am sorry for the heat and humidity but really glad that you are getting stimulating and interesting discussions. That's what I hated about Smith for you for so long, the lack of really good students.

. . . I am just off to a broadcast rehearsal. I hope to make a
series out of a modified *Psychologist at Work* [Harrower 1937].
That may help for next year. I am working at home most of
these days on the articles. It's slow but very interesting. It is
really the ideas that I gave at the Bryn Mawr meeting. But
amplified and developed.

. . . I'm really glad you are getting so much done and giving
so many lectures and getting real appreciation. I only hope you
can get into your stride in Oxford, honestly, you don't know
how I pray that international complications will hold off so you
can enjoy that year. For you will enjoy it, given half a chance.
[10 July 1939, Montreal]

[KK] I hope the psychology broadcast series will be arranged
and prove a success. It should boost the sales of your book. I
shall mention the book to my class who need something easier.
My course is much too difficult for the majority, I was led
astray by the brilliant graduate students who are auditing it
and who ask questions and made all sorts of fruitful
suggestions.

. . . Last night at dinner at a Fraternity House. The members
of the staff had come with their wives, lots of graduate students, so that it was quite a large meeting. Then someone
spoke for half an hour on occupational prospects of psychologists, a talk not distinguished by a superfluity of tact; I imagine he must have stepped on many people's toes. Then I spoke
for less than forty minutes on Uzbekistan and Ego-World relationships and tried to make it as much as possible a causerie,
avoiding all heavy guns. It seems to have been successful.

Work on Bryn Mawr lectures is progressing slowly. I am now
pretty certain that it won't be finished before I leave.

The work at the university is almost over, then only one
other full week and three days before I sail.

. . . How splendid about your radio talk. I suppose you get
fan mail! Does it pay well?

. . . I hope my lecture tonight will come off all right. It will
be a fairly large and very mixed audience I expect. The janitor

in this place, a colored man, told me that he would try and come. He said "I know nothing about psychology but I love it!"

All good luck to you. I know that I need not worry about you. You always come out on top, and you always will. Not because of the famous "silver spoon" but because you are you. [14 July 1939, Columbus]

I wish I could have heard, and could hear next autumn, your psychology broadcasts! But I am glad for you that you have got them, for they help to pay expenses. Also my congratulations to your fellowship in the Rorschach Institute. Some day I should take real lessons from you. Meantime I shall remember your results, and when I get frontal lobe cases, shall try other tests based on your Rorschach findings.

Well everything is over here. My activity was successful to the end. The graduate students and assistants told me that for years they had not had such an intellectual stimulus, and my Gestalt class gave me a very long and loud applause at the end of the last lecture, a demonstration which people say is not at all the custom here.

Last night I went places with the assistants and their wives. There were 18 altogether. For the first time in years, I danced again, but I had only one really good partner, a girl lighter than a feather. She has had training in physical education and does recreational therapy work at the State hospital here. I got home at 2 a.m. But that was early compared with the party at the house of the parents of my most brilliant student. All newspaper people frightfully amusing and really very nice. I got home at 3:30. [26 July 1939, Columbus]

[MH] Trying to fill the hour before broadcasting, always difficult!

. . . I am tremendously pleased that Ohio was such a success: I always felt it would be, and was delighted that you would have a new environment. On the strength of this please don't go to Oxford apologizing for your existence! There, if anywhere, you ought to be able to speak freely without finding that you were above people's heads. I think you could make a very positive contribution to their experimental institute, far moreso than the other two people who are listed with you. I was surprised to get a letter from someone in London, asking for the cards for use with patients, in my British Journal article [Harrower 1939] which just came out. Quick work! I may have them printed from the institute here and issued as the Harrower cards. It's about time I made some dent somewhere, psychologically, after working all these years. Shall I send you a series? Would you like to see them? (Later) Broadcast safely over. I may get a contract for more performances. [29 August 1939, Montreal]

The time has come the Walrus said to bid you adieu: it seems strange to have you going to England, with me remaining on this side. I sent off two small packages of books to your ship, probably there will be a library, but it might save you trouble to have oddments handy.

I am weary with domestic troubles, they take up much time and energy, and such endless pathetic tales of jobless females, many too ill to work properly.

It will seem very funny not having quick letters from you next year, I shall be fearfully eager to know how everything goes, so do write me every detail.

And, to continue on that subject, remember that they really want you there, and there is obviously an opportunity with the new interest in that Experimental Institute [Nuffield Institute for Brain Surgery at Oxford]. Let the success of Ohio do something towards dislodging your "hampering inferiority complex."

I must stop, I'm following a patient, aphasic, one of the Chief's [Wilder Penfield] while he is away, and have two important epileptic records to get this p.m. The question of whether or not sedatives really alter the Rorschach. These people have been kept off sedation for some days, so now's my chance.

All good luck and my ever-present thoughts go with you. [2 August 1939, Montreal]

When Koffka sailed for England a week or so later he reported: "I had a telegram from the members of my Columbus seminar. Also a book and a long and touching letter from Holmes, my assistant in Columbus. I'll try to send him a nice letter in return. So far the trip has been a grand vacation, the kind of rest I needed."

Club Affiliation and Political Orientation

Rather to his own surprise Koffka was an enthusiastic member of a discussion group at Smith, a club with some twenty members of the faculty. His talks, when he was the presenter, may have suffered from his "too deep" approach. But as a discussant with a cosmopolitan view, a wide background in French and German literature, and the capacity to summarize, he was invaluable. He also played the role of peacemaker on various occasions during turbulent discussions. His letters report many of these evenings in detail.

Orton [Smith economics professor William Aylott Orton] spoke about the historical causes of Hitlerism, and gave a very intelligent paper. Briefly his point was that in the Weimar Republic what he called the "tribal culture" and political organization had never been brought together. And that Hitler was the revolt of tribal culture against an alien political system. The discussion was conducted in such a way that each member was to have his say in the order of the seating places. On such an occasion, Borgese [Smith Italian literature professor Giuseppe Borgese], is at his worst. He began very reasonably, agreed with many of Orton's points, modifying them in some parts, and then instead of stopping and giving the floor to his neighbor, he launched into one of his violent fiery, and completely repetitious harangues on Italy and Mussolini. The worst of it is that he has absolutely no feeling for the impression he creates. The social atmosphere simply does not exist for him. Again and again Club members tried to utilize the momentary pauses in his eruptions to say, "Now let us hear from Kimball [history and government professor Everett Kimball]."

The Chairman formally explained that we might have a second round, but that time was progressing and the first round should therefore proceed. All in vain! He does not hear it. And when finally a sort of revolution is impending, and the Chair seems to be willing to take strong measures, he is astonished because it is now Kimball's turn.

After Kimball, I spoke, and succeeded on the spur of the moment in reconciling two ideas which, both implicit in what Orton had said, appear at first sight quite contradictory. Orton had begun with a quotation from German writers, according to which the Germans are the people with the deepest and most earnest thought. Now comes Hitler who, although in a way, following in the footsteps of these authors, decries reason and appeals to "the bold." As I said, I succeeded in showing the solution to this apparent contradiction. . . . Then came a new climax! Oliver Larkin [art professor] angry about Borgese's behavior began by saying that he found it difficult to make any contribution because his view of history was so entirely different from that of most of the Club members. He then continued: "Thus I would consider Mr. Borgese's view that great personalities are the dominating factors fantastic nonsense!" Borgese winced, but apart from a jocular remark said nothing. At any rate, Larkin continued, when all of a sudden Aetna erupted. Like a roaring lion Borgese attacked Larkin, grew more and more excited. Helgesson [psychiatrist] poured him a drink of whiskey, Borgese took it, lifted it to his lips, but before drinking thrust it back on to the table, and with a crash, completely unconscious of anything but his hurt vanity. It was in a way pitiful, in another way excruciatingly funny. . . . I had my say, suggesting to Larkin that at a later meeting he speak about the problem of tolerance (your problem) which arose out of things he had said. Then I left . . . as to what happened afterwards I have only to report that "everything concluded in perfect amity. Larkin and Borgese embracing each other."

Borgese assured me at the Sunday Club that he had not really been angry, to which I could not help remarking "but you gave to all of us the impression that you were."

I think that "sachlich" [objectively] that Borgese had a good point, but he spoiled it completely by his egotism which is such that at these moments breaks all bounds. I like him and therefore I do not really mind, but many of the others, I am sure, do mind, and that is a pity. [29 October 1934]

. . . Club on Saturday was very interesting with Beard's [historian Charles A. Beard] highly suggestive paper, the topic of which is much too complicated to be explained in this letter. As so often, I helped him in the discussion, a service much appreciated by him and his wife [historian Mary R. Beard]. In the discussion Borgese claimed that a quotation from Aristotle's poetics could not be as read by Beard. You know how emphatic Borgese can be. IMPOSSIBLE he shouted! Beard remained very composed and polite insisting only that he would not have put a passage in quotes into his paper if it had not come from the original. Last night Borgese showed me a letter which he had already written to Beard, for Beard, had, of course, been right. [16 March 1936]

The Club, joined by Neilson [Smith president William Allan Neilson *] after dinner, was in a curious temper. Borgese's topic was the policy of the Roman Catholic Church. From the very beginning, he was interrupted . . . by irrelevant questions asked in a distinctly aggressive manner. The host and chairman did not succeed in getting order in the discussion so that Borgese could not develop his ideas. I have never seen the Club behave in this way [Several people were] furious at the very real discourtesies shown to the guests and rumor has it that [they] intend to resign from the Club. Of course Borgese stood his ground. But naturally he became excited too. Neilson who was thoroughly disgusted, left at midnight, I left half an hour later. But Borgese told me yesterday that the worst happened after I had left, namely [another] violent quarrel. . . .

Of course, Borgese has his peculiarities, he is easily offended and very self centered. But his "niveau" [level of intellect] is so superior, the power of his personality so great, his moral fervor so serious, that it reveals a sore lack of finer feelings on the part of his adversaries. Borgese's interpretation is—and this will interest you, since it has a direct bearing on a question in your letter—that Pacellie [Pius XII] is the Rome-Berlin Axis Pope par excellence and that the Roman Catholic Church is at this moment a grave danger, also in this country.

Borgese will be here for half an hour. He leaves tomorrow.
[6 March 1939]

At the time of his correspondence with English astronomer Sir Arthur Eddington,* Koffka shared his ideas with his friends at the club (see Appendix E).

I spoke for an hour and a half at the Club on Saturday, of course with interruptions for explaining many points more fully. But even so I presented not much more than half of my material. I gave a very brief and easy introduction in which I indicated what Eddington wanted to do. And gave a general outline of his theory. That, I believe, everybody understood. The rest they found difficult, not surprising, because it is difficult. In the discussion Borgese delivered one of his long speeches, far too long for what he was actually saying, but about the lack of philosophical background in Eddington and his colleagues, and how true philosophers who had known the metaphysical truths long ago, need not be impressed by the fact that physics now, has also given up determinism. Knowing my Eddington well, I could answer by reading quotations from Eddington, the first was so absolutely striking that Neilson, jokingly insisted, that there must have been collusion with Borgese producing his arguments only for me to refute them.
[3 February 1936]

Occasionally there were guests at Koffka's club. Here he reported on a visit from the son of the German philosopher Edmund Husserl:

Rather a full week. At Club there developed a very interesting and equally heated discussion on the social implications of Christianity, started by Kraushaar [philosophy professor

Otto F. Kraushaar] and carried on with great fervor by
Borgese. . . . The Neilsons had the son of Husserl as a guest.
He is a German professor, philosophy of law, and because of his
Jewish origin has lost his position. I called on him in the morning and took him for a drive. A curious but rather nice person,
strangely inhibited. . . . Afterwards Club with Borgese speaking about Bergson [French philosopher Henri Bergson] chiefly
about his last book. A marvelous presentation. He shares with
Bergson the plasticity of mind, things come out in full rounded
contours, but scientifically there is not much to say in their
favor. The discussion was long and heated. I had to assert my
authority rather forcibly to get the discussion back from a
futile discussion of Greek philosophy and succeeded in making Husserl speak about the relation of intuition and Wessen-
schau [the seeing of an essence], which however, was not very
helpful. It was clear that everybody disagreed thoroughly with
everybody else! [20 April 1936]

Koffka also reported with sensitivity other group meetings in
which he was an observer.

About my last two days. I arrived in New York and was met
by Dr. Bohn [a personal friend], and taken to the apartment of
friends of his where he had been for a small dinner party before coming to the station. A number of socialists, key people,
interesting and rather charming. We stayed till about half past
eleven, and then went to my host's small apartment on West
12th Street. There we began to talk and did not stop till 2:30
a.m.! I like my host very much indeed, active in the socialist
party, but sound and sane, and not carried away by wild hopes
as the communists are. We talked on almost every subject under the sun. Yesterday he had asked two younger philosophers
for breakfast at 11 o'clock, I had a very good discussion with
them.

Then we went to Harlem where Dr. Bohn had to speak to a
small colored group. . . . This group assembled for a kind of
unitarian service, hymns are sung, bible passages are read,

and then the lecture given. A long narrow room on the ground
floor, the president, a smallish man, from the West Indies. Over
50, a rather broad face, very kind and dignified. He sits down
at the piano, announces the hymns, and plays, as well as he
can, the audience sings. Not any better I would say than an
ordinary white audience. Then some reading and Bohn's lecture. How capitalists got the power in the country, his moral
being: don't say it's no use to get hold of the Government. The
U.S. is ruled, not by the Government, but by the big capitalists,
because these great capitalists, have the power they wield over
us because they had first got hold of the Government. Now,
what they could do, you, the working people can do. Of course
he did not mean by force, but by intelligent organization and
cooperation. His talk was chiefly historical, about the Morgans,
Rockefellers, Carnegies, very good for that kind of audience.
Small middle class negroes, not a bit cheap. After the lecture,
collection, solo sung, accompanied by the president again, who
played it about half as fast as it ought to have been played!
Thereby upsetting the singer completely, who usually arrived
at the end of the line a bar or two before him! Then a long
discussion, which lasted till 11 p.m. [5 December 1932]

Koffka was not a very active member of the American Psychological Association, although he occasionally spoke at APA meetings. But he greatly enjoyed belonging to the Experimentalists, a
select group of experimental psychologists. Here he described the
Experimentalists meeting at Vassar and the APA meeting in New
York at which he spoke, both in 1931.

Driving up in the blinding rain . . . they have given me the
best room in the house, the only room with completely private
bath. The first meetings were not too exciting, the best report
so far Dashiel's [probably Columbia University visiting professor John F. Dashiell]. . . . Herewith a brief report on the
meeting, brief because nothing much has happened. We were
fifteen people in all, [Harry P.] Weld* and [Karl M.] Dallenbach* from Cornell, Bentley [Madison Bentley,* also from

Cornell], [Raymond] Dodge,* [Edward S.] Robinson* and
[Walter R.] Miles* from Yale, Dashiel, [Robert S.] Woodworth,*
Peterson [unidentified] and [Albert T.] Poffenberger* [all from
Columbia], [Herbert] Langfeld* [from Princeton]. Very little of
interest was reported. Discussion, as always in this group, is in
the best of spirit. It was quite nice, by 4 p.m. everybody went
away. I was too tired to face the long drive, so I stayed on and
had dinner with Miss Washburn [Vassar psychology professor
Margaret F. Washburn*]. Quite a friendly chat. I think she enjoyed the meeting, whose chairman she was. . . . I told Poffenberger, after my report that you relied more on his book than
on any other in your course on Applied, and that you had found
valuable confirmation for our results in his book. My report at
Vassar, I suppose you want to know about it. Well, it is hard to
say what they thought. Dodge said that the chromatization
should be considered, but that it by no means explained all our
results. [4 April 1931, Poughkeepsie, N.Y.]

Whether my paper [at the APA] was at all successful I cannot say. I am sure that objectively it was a good deal better
than Thorndike's [Columbia psychology professor Edward L.
Thorndike*] who is not much good at this sort of thing. General
theory is not his forte, he feels it himself, even his delivery is
rather poor. Of the morning papers I heard nothing as I took
part in a round table on theoretical psychology. It started much
too late to make any headway. Lunch with Hull [Yale psychologist Clark Hull*] and Dallenbach and Weaver [unidentified],
with whom I talked most of the time. At the banquet I had
a place of honor, and a really interesting time with Mrs.
[Howard C.] Warren. Warren's [Princeton psychology professor
Howard C. Warren] presidential address, was nice but rather
naïve. The film afterwards, made at Brown, prenatal behavior
of kittens, showed a perfection of technique, operating on pregnant cats, extracting one of the foetuses, severing the umbilical
cord. But I am not convinced that the results warrant such an
interference with life. A point of view which hardly one of my
colleagues here would understand. [21 April 1931]

It is hard to put a scientific label on Koffka's political affilia-
tions. From the letters he appeared, in many areas, as a liberal in
the widest sense of the word. Here follow a few sample reactions to
issues of various kinds. Speaking of the Spanish Revolution (1936–
39), when the Franco regime, the Insurgents, fought against the
popular front, the Loyalists, he wrote:

> Only a truly objective statement will convince people of the
> merits of either cause. To be objective one has to examine the
> history of this and the previous governments, then it is cer-
> tainly much more difficult to take sides; nonetheless I continue
> to be anti-rebel. They seem to me more guilty of the present
> hopeless issue than the others. In Spain, as in most other coun-
> tries, it is the fight of two orders, the defenders and the bene-
> ficiaries of the old consider any change an immoral action. For
> example, the enemies of Roosevelt here. And the champions of
> the new order can see no good whatsoever in the old, so each
> party must call forth the worst sides of the other, smug con-
> tentment and arrogance versus fanatical hatred. [8 October
> 1936]

In the same year, Johns Hopkins philosophy professor Arthur
Lovejoy* was a guest at Smith. Koffka reported:

> Lovejoy, Neilson and I had a long talk on politics, during the
> course of which I related your Spanish experiences.† Lovejoy
> seems to me by far the best American philosopher. His book
> *The Revolt Against Dualism* is excellent. It shows the fallacies
> and absurdities of this revolt, criticizing the American Neo-
> Realists [Alfred North] Whitehead and Bertrand Russell. But
> philosophy is a curious occupation. If those people had not ad-

† The Spanish experiences to which Koffka refers included Harrower's being
in Vigo on the west coast of Spain in 1936 when the Insurgents took over the city.
She witnessed fierce fighting, and the windows of the room in which she had
taken shelter were shattered by gunfire. She and her family were finally res-
cued by the British Navy, which sent warships into the area to pick up British
citizens.

vanced such absurd theories Lovejoy's good book would never have been written. Dean Nicolson [Smith dean and literature professor Marjorie H. Nicolson*] studied under him at Hopkins and thinks he has the best mind she has ever come across. [27 October 1936]

On Franklin Roosevelt's reelection over Alf Landon in 1936:

[MH] I listened with deep thankfulness, even if not with excitement, to the election results. To me it symbolizes something very important. A genuine desire to help the average man, courage, initiative has been recognized as such, and the various scares of communism and insecurity and whatnot have just not been paid attention to. The extremely wealthy people are a minority and it's a mercy that their panic to save their own skins was recognized as such. I feel that Roosevelt himself must be tremendously happy, for I feel it is not enemies that he minds having, but if the crowd that he had worked for had been blind to what he had done or swung into ingratitude through ignorance, it would have been terribly bitter for anyone to bear. [4 November 1936, New Brunswick, N.J.]

[KK] What you said about Roosevelt expressed the meaning of the election beautifully. It occurred to me today that we are less apt to ask the question: "Is F. D. R. a great man then is Hitler, or Mussolini, or Napoleon?" Not, I am sure for any intrinsic reasons, but rather for the extrinsic ones which these so-called great men create for their own glory. [5 November 1936]

When professional organizations took a stand on moral or political issues, demanding a vote from the membership, Koffka was troubled:

I should like to know what you wrote in reply to the APA circular. I find it very difficult to make up my mind. For I feel that qua psychologists we are hardly entitled to say anything.

If a physicist speaks out, i.e. he does it not as a physicist but as an ordinary citizen who has proved his worth in the fields of physics. I doubt whether the psychologists can do more without exposing themselves to the reproach that they were pretending to know professionally what in reality they know as little as anyone else. Of course it is bunk to speak of war as inherent in human nature, if one means by that an instinct for war. But if a psychologist tried to refute that by scientific psychology then an opponent might easily play out one scientific psychologist against another, then he might refer to [William] McDougall's* instinct of aggression. That as individuals and as citizens we have a great responsibility, greater than that of the average man because of our privileged and responsible positions, I grant freely. But I see some danger in organizing a struggling science for practical purposes of terrific importance. Here is my main difficulty for this raises the problem of the relation between science and the State. I still think it is the best solution that the State lets science alone, or supports it in its autonomous work, and that science becomes subservient to nobody. The examples of Italy and Germany and Russia are rather alarming. We can do most for society, I believe, by teaching disinterested work governed only by the search for truth. If you have a carbon of your letter please let me see it. I might possibly send an answer myself, which so far I have not done. [24 March 1936]

British politics interested Koffka particularly, and in 1936 he followed in detail the drama of Edward VIII's brief reign and his abdication to marry Mrs. Wallis W. Simpson.

Yesterday was a very rich day. The King's speech. Tremendously moving, particularly the last part when he spoke about himself. One was compelled to understand how he felt the crown to be a tremendous responsibility, he seemed himself still awed by the knowledge of being a King and afraid that the crown would cut him off from his fellow-beings. [2 March 1936]

Have you heard the news about the King? Apparently it was announced on the radio that the king had declared his intention of marrying Mrs. Simpson. I can hardly believe it, since she is not yet divorced. I am terribly sorry for him. A night club acquaintance seems hardly the right person for the British throne. [27 October 1936]

The King's affair is terribly exciting but now I am beginning to be shocked by the people who are championing his cause, Beaverbrook [influential publisher William Aitken, Lord Beaverbrook] and apparently the Black Shirts [a fascist organization]. I am sure that [British prime minister] Baldwin mismanaged the business very badly, but I'm no longer sure of what the political result would be if the cabinet were defeated. [7 December 1936]

Yesterday I had one of the greatest experiences of my whole life: "Prince Edward's" farewell speech. I hope you heard it. Absolutely great in its simplicity and sincerity. I was shaken by emotion. He is a good man, and England has lost a great King with enormous potential. Please let me know how your family feels about it. [12 December 1936]

To this last request Harrower replied: "My mother's letter is still too upset to be coherent. My father has called her 'a King's man' and accused her of failing to see the real issues involved. How I can hear it all going on" [27 December 1936, New Brunswick, N.J.].

Koffka was rarely emotionally involved in matters of judgment. The final quotation in this section shows an interesting admission of an unusual experience of confusion.

Intellectually I am in a great turmoil. I know less and less what kind of political development of the world I shall hope for. The book *Gone with the Wind* [Margaret Mitchell, 1936] has given me much food for thought. Not that I defend slavery as an institution for it lent itself to too horrible abuses. But an aristocratic society of individuals that are modest and have a high code is so much nicer than a democratic society of boastful and self-assertive people. What matters seems to me the human relationship between man and man. I am now quite convinced that often it was a finer relationship between a planter and his slave than between an employer and his workmen or even between the trade union secretary and the members. That this kind of thinking does not take me nearer fascism I need not say. For in fascism you have an exaltation of selfish values, even if the self is not the individual but the State; and the really fine things have no currency in fascism.

Another idea which developed while I read Brown's [psychologist J. F. Brown] book was that men are not born equal and that no amount of difference in environmental conditions will account for the differences between persons. Compared with Beethoven I grew up under most favorable conditions! [22 January 1937]

Reaching Out to Other Thinkers

Although it was never actually stated in the letters, Koffka felt himself isolated from the mainstream of creative thinking in psychology while at Smith. This feeling was one reason why he was so anxious to find another position and was so disappointed when each attempt fell through.

This isolation rekindled his particular interest in discovering or getting in contact with Gestalt-oriented thinkers in other fields. The Gestalt concept, for instance, was near enough to South African General Jan Christiaan Smuts's* Holism to lead to a correspondence:

Dear General Smuts: Twelve years ago I read your great book on Holism, a book that propounds a philosophy similar in its general spirit and in many detailed applications to the ideas which had guided a number of psychologists in their work. I am referring to the Gestalt Psychologists whose principles you

may have come across since you wrote your book, perhaps in
W. Köhler's *Gestalt Psychology*.

Today I am taking the liberty of asking my London publishers to send you two books, one a long-winded, but I hope
systematic exposition of psychology from the point of view of
Gestalt theory by myself, the other a brief and much more
readable introduction to experimental psychology, just come
from the press, by Dr. Mary R. Harrower, a former student and
collaborator of mine. Miss Harrower, who joins her compli-
ments to mine, was incidentally born in Johannesburg.

These books may interest you in that they show how holistic
principles are required in psychology and how they influence
the active experimental work of the psychologist who with
their help may even some day hope to approach the problem of
personality.

With expressions of my sincere admiration. [18 October 1937]

Smuts replied promptly [22 November 1937]:

Dear Professor Koffka: I am sincerely obliged to you for
kindly sending me your *Gestalt Psychology* (1935) as well as Dr.
Harrower's *Psychologist at Work* (1937). Both are very welcome
additions to my library and will receive careful attention.

I am also pleased to hear that you have been interested in
the wider principles of Holism and have had the opportunity to
read my book on the subject. Holism is proving more and more
the next great phase in science, in distinction from the predominantly analytical procedure of science in the past.

Years ago I read your *Growth of the Mind* (1924) with deep
interest and much instruction. Long since I have followed, as
far as my circumstances allow, the great developments which
have taken place in Gestalt psychology. In some mysterious
way structure and pattern are at the very root of the universe
and of mind, and Plato had a distinct vision of this when he
developed his ideal Forms as basic to all true knowledge.

With grateful thanks for your kind thought in sending me
these books.

Koffka had had over the years more than a casual relationship with Erwin Schroedinger,* one of the great physicists of modern times, and valued discussions with him highly. "In the evening I went for supper to the Schrödingers, most cordial reception. Excellent supper (they have a Viennese cook), and a long talk. I had quite a long discussion with him on the question of physics and philosophy of science. I must count myself very fortunate since he usually avoids such discussions even with his colleagues" [8 July 1930, Berlin].

Koffka had always valued highly his discussions with Albert Einstein in Germany, before either of them came to the United States. He was therefore delighted to link up with him again when Einstein reached Princeton.

This morning I had an extremely nice letter from Mrs. Einstein. My letter forwarded to him to Port Chester had been lost completely among piles of others owing to the fact that for the time being he is without a secretary and is very untidy. So they both apologize for the long delay and ask me to their house whenever I get near Princeton. [15 October 1936]

I told you that I had heard from Mrs. Einstein. Since then I had a letter from Wertheimer in which he quotes from a letter Mrs. Einstein wrote to him asking him to forward her letter to me. In that letter she says also how very sorry they both are that they had missed me. In German from Mrs. Einstein: "Dr. Koffka war meinen Mann immer ganz besonders sympathisch." ["My husband always felt unusually sympathetic to Dr. Koffka."] I was rather pleased because I did not expect him to remember me that well as I had not seen him since 1916 and 17. [20 October 1936]

Koffka's correspondence with Sir Arthur Eddington,* English astronomer and physicist, turned into a major undertaking and began in a letter to Harrower.

The book reviews which you sent interested me immensely, particularly that on Eddington. Why is it—and this idea has

surely occurred to you also—that he assumes the essence or
the workings of the mind to be totally different from those of
nature. How much more satisfactory would the solution of the
great mystery of the world be if this assumption were wrong.
Why does he not even envisage the possibility? If he did he
would try to find facts to justify decisions pro or contra and
such facts may be found. I wish I could talk to him once and
that I were inspired on such an occasion. [19 March 1935]

A face-to-face discussion was out of the question at that time,
but Harrower persuaded Koffka to write instead. His forty-page
typewritten letter (see Appendix E) was taken very seriously by
Eddington, who replied with equal thoughtfulness. Koffka was
delighted:

I am writing again today because I just received a long letter
from Eddington, 4 sheets in fairly small handwriting. He explains several points, accepts many of my statements, but
makes it clear that his system is much more dualistic than
mine. At the same time he begins with these words: "It is not
often that I receive (amid a rather unmanageably large correspondence) so profound and clear-sighted a letter as yours. I
cannot reply adequately." And he ends on an even nicer note: "I
have read your letter with great interest. On pp. 9 through 12
there are some points I think I might argue against; but as a
whole even where it criticizes my own view, I recognize that
your ideas are profound and am quite prepared to believe you
may be right."
So I am so awfully glad I wrote and very grateful to you for
having encouraged me to do so. At the end, in a postscript, he
has a quip at Economics. "Unfortunately science is too wide a
term to mean anything definite and includes not only respect-
able sciences, but—well, the British Association has sections
for Economic Sciences and Educational Sciences!" [3 December
1935]

I discovered another nice feature about Eddington's letter. It
bears the date on the top November 3rd but the postmark is

November 21st. He must have begun writing almost immediately after receiving my letter and must have returned to it
again and again. [4 December 1935]

A year or so later, when Eddington was planning to visit the
United States, Koffka reported: "A letter from Eddington. He does
not want to give any lectures during his stay over here but wants
to meet me" [6 March 1937].

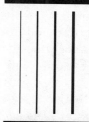

koffka as mentor

The Early Letters, 1928–30

The concept of mentor is a popular one now; graduate students badger the old-timers about their experiences with their mentors. I would sooner describe Koffka in a more old-fashioned way as guide, philosopher, and friend. But regardless of the terminology it is clear that during the first three or four years of the correspondence (1928–32), Koffka was aware of his seniority, and his letters reflected his desire to further the growth and development of his pupil.

In 1933, the relationship changed, subtly at first, but then quite clearly, for the discussions became a dialogue between colleagues. This chapter and chapter 5 reflect first the early mentorship and then the shift to an intellectual partnership.

Before any relationship existed, however, certain features of personality and background allowed—even encouraged—a systematic correspondence to develop. It seems unlikely that anything of this sort could occur today since letter writers are a vanishing breed, so one might ask what produces letter writers?

Koffka never spoke of an early interest in letters or the need to communicate by mail in his youth. But it was clear by his general correspondence, which as the laboratory's secretary I typed and edited, that he found letters an easy mode of expression. Throughout his adult life, he wrote long personal letters to his mother and a close friend in Germany every week. His earliest break from home as a student was to visit Edinburgh, where he developed a particular affinity for things British, a fact which unquestionably influenced his sympathetic understanding of my background. As the years passed, his correspondence with my mother became sizable. It could be said of Koffka that he found it easier to communicate by the written than by the spoken word.

In my case the antecedents are clearer. In true British style I was banished to a boarding school at the age of ten until the age of eighteen. Since only two months of the year were actually spent with one's parents, letters from home were the major source of contact. My mother, a born letter writer, wrote to me daily for those eight years. I replied with increasing frequency, from the Sunday letter of the small child to spontaneous accounts of school activities as they occurred. But from these hundreds of written communications was built up, I think, the feeling that through the written word one achieves the necessary security, and perhaps the more ultimate reality, in a relationship than is achieved through day-to-day contact.

In addition to the frequent exchange of letters with my family, letter writing in England in the early 1900s was the accepted means of communication. The telephone was for emergencies; we children would never use it. Letters would be written, mailed, and delivered the same day to friends a few streets away in our small village. As children, we frequently included verses or drawings in our letters.

The kind of correspondence between my parents and their friends was probably also important. With two college presidents and a renowned professor of Greek as part of the larger family, there existed no barrier to spontaneous exchange with what could have been considered venerable figures. It did not seem in any way unusual, therefore, for me, the twenty-year-old student, to reply to the Herr Professor's letters with poems or enclosures, as, for instance, a mock Christmas card:

> When genius smiles on little girls
> And condescends to pat their curls

The world demands—the world is right
That these in turn should shed some light
(Of course not much, and not so bright)
Upon mankind at large:
So I, in nineteen twenty-nine
Hope that my feeble ray will shine
Since courteous Kurt does me applaud
(At times) May I rise o'er the horde
And grasping gifts the gods have poured
Profit—like Mrs. Humphrey Ward.
[25 December 1928, Northampton]

A systematic correspondence began during the summer of 1930. After two years of working on problems of perception in Koffka's Northampton laboratory, Harrower was appointed on Koffka's recommendation for a year as instructor in psychology at

Matthew Arnold (1822–88), British poet and scholar, smiles down at his young protégé Mrs. Humphrey Ward (1851–1920), who later became a successful novelist.

Wells College in Aurora on Cayuga, New York, substituting for
Professor Ivy Campbell. Head of the psychology department at
Wells, Campbell planned to take a sabbatical year in 1930–31 and
had asked Koffka to suggest a psychologist with Gestalt orientation and training.

In the letters, Harrower expressed concern at the thought of
leaving the Northampton laboratory and embarking on her new
assignment. Koffka's letters were full of encouragement for the
new undertaking, in addition to his own news. He wrote first from
Berlin, where he spent part of each summer until 1937, to Harrower spending the summer at her old home in Cheam, England.
Later, he wrote from Northampton to Harrower at Wells.

> I have been about a good deal. I spent a few hours with R. M.
> [Robert Morris] Ogden [education professor and dean of the Col-
> lege of Arts and Sciences at Cornell] who had been in a place
> near Berlin. Afterwards I had lunch with Dr. Berliner, the edi-
> tor of the *Naturwissenschaften* [*Natural Sciences*] at his Club,
> Die Deutsche Gesellschaft [The German Society]. It was a
> small party of five people, the other three fitting in very nicely,
> one was a Ministerialrat in the Prussian Kultur-Ministerium
> the man who is responsible for the Technische Hochschulen
> [Technical High School]. We talked a lot about America. It was
> very entertaining. I have always been particularly fond of
> Berliner. In all likelihood he will visit me in Northampton
> some time.
>
> . . . Letters from [Northampton lab psychologist] Eugenia
> Hanfmann, who has now got her non-quota visa. That's all the
> news, except that I am dreadfully lazy, the very opposite of you.
> But you seem to progress beautifully. If you arrive in Wells
> with a bag full of lectures you will have a much better time
> than you expect. You will be able to discover friends among
> students and faculty. You always have accomplished to meet
> the right kind of people.
>
> The impending departure [from Germany back to the States]
> sometimes puts me in a queer state of mind. Again a chapter in
> the history of several lives is written. And, fortunately, nobody

knows what the next chapters will be like. To you the impending farewell to Cheam must be similar. I know how you dread
it. And therefore I hope that the time you are spending there
now is so perfect that its afterglow will help to erase the pain of
parting. Your return to America, how different will it be from
your flight to America two years ago. This time you go from
Cheam, a regained old home, to the States where you have a
new home, then you had cut yourself off from that old home,
and went homeless to an unknown and utterly strange country.
[24 August 1930, Berlin]

I have not had a minute to spare, although I really wanted to
write at once. I wanted to be near you, make you feel that you
must open up in letters as much as you have opened up in talk
and deed. I know you well enough to understand your gloom-
iest mood, to know its significance, its place in your total personality. . . . Please do not consider this coming year as a
separation. Though we shall be living in different places, we
shall share our lives. I do not want to give up that complete
exchange of views and events of our last two years. And you
must not either. It is one of my great aims to keep the flame of
your youthful enthusiasm burning brightly like a beacon.
    If it begins to smoulder, you must tell me about it so that I
can rekindle it.
    I am glad your meeting with [Charles] Myers * [head of the
Institute for Industrial Psychology in London] was so successful. I have a great liking and a great admiration for the man. If
you see him again, please give him my very kind regards. . . .
You must tell me all about the failure of the sophisticated
party. But I am convinced that your conclusion is quite wrong.
You really have no reason to feel inferior to anybody!
    . . . I went to the tennis courts to see the English German
Club match. It was heavenly. For five hours I sat in the radiant
sun and saw some excellent games. . . . Andrews beat the first
ranking German player, Presser. Then the most beautiful
game; Bunny Austin against Dr. Lanfsmann a former Giessen
student. Bunny won eventually in three sets. But the firmness

and beauty of the play was thrilling. My mother and I saw a
new and very interesting film: *Dreyfuss*. A reconstruction of
the famous Dreyfuss case which happened before you, my
child, were born! Quite impressive and the main parts well
played. [31 August 1930, Berlin]

Such a good long letter today. . . . You are wonderful, the two
year books which I asked about were exactly where you said
they would be. Many thanks. Also the other question is satis-
factorily answered as the protocols have shown.

I am so glad about your classes and I admire your energy in
obtaining a suitable classroom. [Harrower was at Wells College.] My brave missionary! Your uncle is so proud of you.
Don't worry about the future of your lectures, you'll pull
through splendidly. I have not the slightest doubt about that.

I was much pleased at what you said about your experiences
in the Cornell lab. Your making a good impression may help
me in the long run. . . . One passage in your letter is a matter
of grave concern to me. Your dread of driving on those bad
roads. Don't take any risks. You are under no obligation to kill
yourself! [30 September 1930]

How splendid! I am more than delighted by the idea of your
reporting to the meeting of the N.Y. State Psychologists. I suggest as a title: "Some Experiments on Color and Organization."
That will give you full freedom to select whatever you want. I
feel your excitement. Every line of your short note exudes it.
And you have almost infected me with it too!

. . . A big hug for the enclosure.† You are trying to express

† Life, you will lose a lover when I die!
  For whom have you encouraged more; have I
  Not always claimed
  A thousand burning favors from you,
  Proud, untamed and exquisite enchantress?

  You say I should not love you, in my face
  You have flung hardships, shown me to my place

the one thing again and again. You have phrased it in several of your letters to me, now you bring it out in a new tune which connects it with other tunes. It is a great truth, because it is a living truth with you. [8 October 1930]

All good luck for the meetings in Buffalo [New York State Psychological Association]. I shall think of you all Friday and Saturday, not knowing at what time your are scheduled to appear. And I shall wait with great tension for your report. I am so glad you found that McLeod man.

Your problem of thought organization is as interesting as it is important. There is no better field for research than this. And if you can discover a good method, then, you will have done more than most psychologists! Nothing would please me more for a dissertation. Even before your letter came I had written to [Edwin] Boring about the reader.

> For my bold daring;
> Yet as you spurn me, with the other hand
> You cast the colored splendors of the land
> For my own keeping; sun and wind and youth
> You give me in each kiss. Ah! Life, in truth
> You will have lost a lover when I die. . . .
> But while I live, leave me this ecstasy. [Harrower 1946]

†   To a Eucalyptus Tree
> O flexible enchanted!
> To whom the earth has granted
> The joy of subtle charm and graciousness,
> Kissing the sun with eager face,
> And with your swift disarming grace,
> Casting your garment round the place. . . .
> O flexible enchanted!
> Now you are hushed and to the mist
> Are turning leaves that never kissed
> In jubilance the sun,
> You let a silver shiver run
> Throughout your frame, and like a nun
> Pray that the miracle be done. . . .
> O flexible enchanted.

[Published by Harrower (1946), without the word to which Koffka had objected.]

Harrower in 1929.

About the poem. . . . I do not quite like the word "enchant-ress," it is to me a little hackneyed poetically. A stronger word with some concrete and individual connotation would be better. You see, I love the spirit of this poem so much that I want its form to be as perfect as possible.† [28 October 1930]

I was so uneasy this morning when no letter came from you that I had to wire . . . then I found your letter and the pro-gramme of the meeting. What a relief! And a hundred million congratulations. Splendid! I am delighted. Could shout for joy,

[you] "giving the best paper" and "Becoming segregated." What a step forward. And how your chances for a career must become improved. You will now be one of the young psychologists that will be watched. And to have spoken in the discussion, not once but five times! Perhaps the incoherence of this scribble will give you an idea of how pleased I am.

. . . A party at Leland Hall's [professor of music, Smith College], with plenty of music. He is so delightful. However, at the end I was saturated and could no longer listen, so I began to think through a problem in color, or rather brightness vision, and found an important connection. . . . I want to know heaps more of your days. [3 November 1930]

I write a line because I want to communicate with you. I got your Buffalo meeting paper yesterday, but otherwise no news from you for ages.

. . . I had a letter from Dean Weld [Harry P. Weld,* Cornell psychologist]. He spoke of the excellence of your report at the meeting in Buffalo!

. . . Later: Another piece of congratulations, your Buffalo paper was excellent. At last I have read it, and was delighted. Clear, simple, dramatic, impressive and convincing, you are the brickest brick! . . . Feel my implicit trust in you, my delight in your being and doings. Please be happy again. Just think of the great success you have made already. Just think how much you could have done with your young life. Be a little proud of yourself. See yourself as with your uncle's eyes! [11 November 1930]

Your two letters were such a joy. And good news too. Splendid this change of your schedule for the next term.

Why do you think I would be cross about your remarks on Chapter 1 of Color and Organization [Koffka and Harrower 1931]? In writing such a thing one is so engrossed with the subject, everything, even the minutest detail, becomes so alive, that one easily makes the mistake you criticize, namely to obscure the main argument. There is only one circumstance which you may have overlooked, and which may partially remove some of your justified criticism, viz that those passages about experimental and methodological detail would of course be set up in small print. But please, make all the corrections you like. I shall be immensely grateful.

Now to your special honors work. You want ideas, I wish to God I had any. The nicest thing, as we both know, would be to find something about the process of organization itself! How does the field reorganize itself and when? A vague idea about a possible mode of procedure is this: Present jokes, some of them in proper form, some so changed that although all the facts are contained in the narrative the "point" will be missed. Then after an interval ask for recall. The critical joke will probably not be recalled at all, or in the wrongly organized form. In either case proceed by telling new jokes, one of which has the same logical structure as the critical one—though entirely different material! I expect that in some cases this new joke will reorganize the old one, and may even lead to its recall in the cases in which it was originally not reproduced. What do you think of this idea, the special form of which has of course to be worked out? Or, conversely, try to intersperse the joke between other stories in such a way that the point will be missed, although the story has been properly told. Make again the recall test, perhaps also in such a form that the joke is to be recalled, if possible without the context that spoiled it. See whether then it is understood. Of course, since recall methods would be applied all through, you would at the same time get results about memory and organization!

I'll keep my mind on this problem and let you know any spark that may illumine my darkness. [26 November 1930]

Following a successful year of teaching at Wells College, Harrower returned for another year at Smith to work toward a Ph.D. under Koffka (1931–32). The correspondence is naturally suspended at this point.

The Early Letters, 1932–33

In May 1932, Koffka sailed for an expedition in Uzbekistan organized by Alexander Luria (chapter 6). Harrower remained in
Northampton to take the first of several written examinations for
her Ph.D. Five examiners had been chosen: Edwin G. Boring*
from Harvard; Arnold Gesell* from Yale; Koffka; George Humphrey* from Queens University, Canada; and Harold Israel* from
Smith College. Sailing on the SS *Europa*, Koffka sent the following letter to be read on the day of the examination:

This the day, the piobroch [bagpipe-like instrument] sounding full and high. Be "mutig wie ein Held zum siegen" ["proud
as a hero going to victory"]. Just go to the appointed place, get
your questions, read them carefully, and then start on the required answer. Think it over, you have plenty of time. Parade
them! Then select among the remaining questions those you
can answer best, not those you think are the most difficult.
You'll find more than enough easy ones. And follow the same
procedures on the other days. Don't worry, I don't, I know you
can, and you will, pass. A bottle of champagne will be drunk to
celebrate the event, some day we shall drink that bottle together. In Berlin, or London, or Switzerland. We can wait. You
know how to do that, impetuous though you are. Think of that
bottle while you write.
    . . . You are a good person. You deserve your degree, and your
degree will mean something. You have burning enthusiasm,
and you have imagination, and have worked hard. You have
the gift of getting away with things, and yet you have spurned
to do that. You have come to real grips with your stuff, you
found many inconsistencies and gaps in what the textbooks
said, don't be afraid to point to such faults, should occasion
arise in your exams. You're a cricketer, and now your hand
must wield the pen rather than the bat or ball. But good work
is good sport too. Tell your fingers to be careful of spelling, dimensions, etc. I forget other pitfalls! Chiefly be yourself, not
your knowledge only, but yourself is being tested.

Ni Puahta ni Pera [an Uzbek expression of good luck].
The third reader! [May 1932, SS *Europa*]

By October 1932, Harrower had begun her year as senior lecturer at Bedford College, London University. Professor Beatrice
Edgell,* with whom Harrower had taken her undergraduate work,
had issued this special invitation. Back in Northampton, Koffka
gave the first report on the results of Harrower's ten examinations:

. . . I enclose my report on your exam. And I can only add
that you have done a first-rate job. I am full of admiration for
your achievement. You are a real psychologist now, and you
know a great deal more, in several subjects than your old
teacher. I had a talk with [Harold] Israel this morning. He had
been bound to secrecy and therefore did not say much, but my
impression is that he passed you with commendation. He called
your treatment of the first question in Part II "brilliant" and
that quite spontaneously. When I mentioned your plan of com-
pleting your diploma, he said at once that it would do away
with your minors, I said I fully agreed, and would be very
thankful if he would bring this matter up for discussion before
the committee, when the details of your procedure had been
settled.

. . . You must treat my information as strictly confidential, as
a matter of fact I violate the rules laid down by the Dean although, fortunately she has never said anything to me. Thus
although you don't know the outcome with absolute certainty,
you need not worry a moment longer. I cannot see how anyone
can fail you on your showing. I am now very curious to hear
what you have done about your diploma.

. . . Two letters of yours arrived last Friday (letters of Sept.
20th and 23rd). Such a joy to see your handwriting and to hear
of your doings. A somewhat supercilious crowd of your old
friends! Some people show their jealousy by callousness. Never
mind what they are saying and don't generalize from one experience that English people don't like you! Professor Edgell is
very English and she likes you immensely. Don't let unpleasant experiences bias you against your year in London. I am

sure you will find that you get on beautifully with ever so many people who have no axe to grind. You stick to it, and be what you are. Your personality, your enthusiasm will oust and worst their blasé skepticism. You have something to say, so say it! The more you are yourself the more will your influence be for good.

. . . My classes have started. How well, I do not know. The girls seem quite nice. How much they get out of it, I have no conception as yet. I have finished three-fourths of Tolman [University of California psychologist Edward Tolman*], find the theoretical discussion very disappointing [Tolman, 1932]. He is a charming fellow, that comes out in the book again and again. But he is not big enough for the great task he has set himself. And therefore I cannot find that his new terms and concepts advance our theoretical knowledge in the slightest.

Your translations are good.† I am terribly proud of you. The first closer to Goethe's rhythm than the second. [3 October 1932]

Your despondencies are partly due to what Stapleton [Smith graduate student Lawrence Stapleton] rightly called "your exasperating modesty," of course you are doing a great deal of

---

† Goethe's original verse and Harrower's translations:

> Wer nie sein Brot mit Tränen ass
> Wer nie die Kummervollen Nachte
> Auf seinen Bette weinend sass
> Der kennt euch nicht, ihr Himmilischen Machte

> Who has not ate his bread with tears
> Who has not sat through the long night
> Tormented by his woes and fears,
> He knows you not, heavens' powers of might.

or

> Who ne'er in sorrow ate his bread
> Who ne'er whole nights from dawn till even
> Sat weeping sore upon his bed
> He knows you not ye powers of Heaven.

good at Bedford, of course Edgell needs you, of course your presence and influence make themselves felt. I know that, and you ought to know it too. Edge would never have asked you to give the main paper at the British Psychological Association if she did not have a very high opinion of you. And I am absolutely convinced that you will justify it. I have no uneasiness whatsoever about your lecture.

But I am quite upset that you have decided not to apply for the Readership [a permanent position higher on the academic ladder than senior lecturer] on the basis of the chance of getting the position at Bennington College, apparently because you understood me to want you to do that. But I cannot possibly want such a thing. I cannot possibly bear the responsibility of your abandoning a post which does not only mean a brilliant career but also a task of great sachlich importance. . . . If you got the Readership you would be a woman of some importance now, but in a few years a woman of great importance. You would be one of the leading psychologists in Britain. Now it is very hard to say, except you yourself, how much that means to you. I know that there are things that mean infinitely more to you. The question is, would you at Bennington get as much of these more invaluable things as to compensate for the loss of valuable ones. It is devilish decision. [1 December 1932]

Koffka continues in his next letter to urge Harrower to apply for the readership, particularly since she has been sponsored by Professor William Wilson,* a well-known physicist.

I must write to you on the last day of the year . . . you ought to get the Readership. I wish you would talk the matter over again with Wilson provided there is still the time since he was the first to ask you to apply for it. He ought to be told the whole situation, why you think it is conceited to apply is beyond me! So you are "not a scholar" well, of course if a scholar is a person proud of all things he has learned and at the same time contemptuous of them, a clever player of the game he likes to call science, then indeed you are not. But if a scholar is a person who sees important problems and invents methods for their solutions, who can arouse interest in things scientific, enthusiasm for things purely theoretical, then you are a true scholar if ever I knew one. Damn your modesty! [31 December 1932]

The delay of transatlantic correspondence, with Harrower in London in 1932–33, was in marked contrast to the next-day delivery which the correspondents had been accustomed to. A give-and-take discussion which could have been completed in a week in the United States required almost two months to bring to a conclusion. Koffka in particular fretted when his questions were not answered. He kept a systematic list of all the items mentioned in a letter and made note of the ship the letter would travel on and the date when the letter dealing with his questions could be expected. It is true that at this time every page which he had written for *The Principles of Gestalt Psychology* was sent to Harrower for revision, but Koffka's need for quick replies extended beyond this editorial assignment.

This morning your cable, thank you for your encouragement, it made me glad because it was a sign from you. By now you will have seen that your letters did arrive. It is only the damn long interval caused by the infrequent transatlantic mail which I curse.

Saturday night club [Smith College discussion group] was nice. Men are at the present time and in these surroundings more club-able than women, on the average at least. It is easier to have a group spirit in a properly selected men's group than in a mixed one.

I am sorry if you are discouraged. Please . . . compare your standing in science, your grasp and knowledge, your methods of working at the time you came to Smith, with what they are now. Just as in climbing a mountain one should look down to see how far below one has left the valley, and not up to be discouraged by the remoteness of the summit, so you should look backwards.

Harrower in her next letter replies to a question of Koffka's about what Lawrence Stapleton had said about her poems, and Koffka later reacts to her answer.

[MH] O.K. The poems: Stapleton [spending a year in London] said: 1. They were evidence of possible, really valuable work in the future. 2. They were unlike all modern poetry in that they had no conscious technique. But whereas all modern poetry suffered from anemia of the heart, they were full of very genuine feeling. 3. I ought to give up some time to reading poetry, and do something good as a result. 4. That it was interesting how many avenues of thought I had opened up from one and the same central position. . . . I was surprised at the kindness of her criticism. For, as people, you and I are much criticized by her. Actually she discussed you, not me, but I felt how everything she said applied equally to me. The strange thing was that one could not be in the least upset by it, it was all so unprejudiced, and absolutely inevitable that she should find these aspects of behavior worthy of criticism. I have a tremendous admiration for her, but ultimately, I would rather face life as I do, and be wrong, than change and be right. I wonder if you understand. . . . I'll let this go. I have to make up my mind whether to play hockey on Hampstead Heath with the physicists or go to sleep . . . since I only just got up, I suppose I ought to play hockey! [12 November 1932, London]

[MH] My only points of interest this week are Lawrence Stapleton, and my dancing. The first being the only form of real intellectual enjoyment. The second an amazingly tonic physically and restores my sense of proportion. Lawrence amazes me by her grasp of problems and by her range of, and clarity of expression. But what I like most about her, and I am afraid will always determine whether I like a person: She has a directness and sincerity which makes for a complete confidence in her. She is the first person of my own age, actually five years younger, in whom I find a real common ground of the things which matter to me. You are probably bored with my singing her praises but you will be glad to know that I like her. [21 November 1932, London]

After three weeks or so, Koffka was able to react to the answer to his question:

[KK] Stapleton: what she said about your poems is distinctly good. I fully agree with points 2 and 4. . . . No doubt reading good poetry will do you no harm, but reading it en masse, so to speak, especially for using your reading for future production, seems to me to be quite alien to your kind of art. Does Stapleton not say herself that your poems are quite unlike all modern poetry, by having no conscious technique. And that is one of your charms, your expression is direct, not dictated by literature, and it should remain such direct expression.

What she thinks of me and finds worth criticising I do not know. I will try to guess at it: She thinks I am a person of absolute standards, not knowing the relativity of all. She thinks I am a dogmatist, a believer in something whereas skepticism is the only believable attitude. If so, she does not know what you know, that relativity is only one turn of the Spiral, the turn away from primitive absolutism. The turn towards a new kind of absoluteness. She is on that second turn of the Spiral, I do not believe she has a great chance of ever reaching the third. But really creative people never stop at number 2. And in that, I think, I am one of the really creative people, and after all, it is they who count, and not the mere critics, however keen and well-trained their intelligence. She will probably one day be a really first-rate critic, that is much, but she will not in my judgment be a real creator. [25 November 1932]

[MH] You are both right and wrong in what you say about Stapleton. She is far more than a critic because though professionally a philosophical skeptic, she has such tremendous beliefs. A real faith in something, but she has all the qualities of a person who will create and contribute something big in the

world, I think. She said the other day that in reading Stebbing's [London University philosophy professor Susan Stebbing*] paper for the Aristotelian Society, (advance copy) she
felt that the criticism that she (Lawrence) was making, is what
you would have made, only you would use different language.
Further, tho this is difficult to state correctly, she felt that the
difference between her thought and yours was that there were
more things which could be intellectually expressed, or adequately represented, for you, than for her. Her beliefs are somewhat divorced from all intellectual renderings, she thinks we
can never be completely objective in thought, and no theory of
philosophical systems can give us the kind of picture of the
world that we think it does. She believes in very little intellectually, because her other beliefs which cannot be intellectually
rendered are so strong. Gosh! how differently and clearly and
precisely she would have put it all. [14 December 1932, London]

[KK] Stapleton: I am very glad of what you said. If she has
real strong beliefs it is all right, then it should not be so difficult to convert her away from her intellectual skepticism.
Could you not say: "Our intellect, like our whole mental life is
part of reality. It is a string of events, of happenings, in this
world, since that is so we have to face the alternative, either
the world is all heterogeneous, all its events totally different
from each other, or the heterogeneity is not complete. Only in
the first case would knowledge of the world of any kind or degree be impossible. But not in the second. The first case seems
utterly unlikely and in contradistinction to the progress of science. Therefore we may all pin our faith on the second, and
build our philosophy accordingly. Quite probably you know that
I made a great point of that, our intellectual life, if divorced
from the rest of our mental life would give a very incomplete
and in many respects a much distorted picture. If that is so,
don't despair, but try to include more into our great picture
than just the skeleton of our intellects, particularly if they are
skeletons of formal logicians." What will Stapleton's argument
to this be? [27 December 1932]

Shortly after this discussion Koffka added the following note: "I had a long and good talk with [American anthropologist] Margaret Mead about relativism of values. She is a thorough relativist in her anthropology, but to my surprise and delight not at all as a human being. So I pointed out the discrepancy to her, and was supported by [Harvard psychologist] Harry Murray*" [3 January 1933].

koffka as colleague

The Later Letters, 1933—41

Clearly no single letter, no one month's correspondence, actually marks the shift on Koffka's part from mentor to colleague. Rather the different roles being played out through the letters can be seen in general trends, for instance, the greater freedom on Harrower's part to write securely of her work and ideas and to accept the new status that the position as senior lecturer in psychology at London University had introduced.

It was also borne in on Koffka that he depended completely on Harrower for editing *The Principles of Gestalt Psychology*. Although he spoke English flawlessly in conversation and had a knowledge of English grammar that put "natives" to shame, his German sentence structure, his tendency to be too abstract for most readers and to overload paragraphs with additional clauses, required severe editing and often rewriting.

Fighting her way through the original draft of *The Principles*, Harrower reached the stage where, if she could not understand a paragraph, she was able to blame the paragraph and not her own lack of erudition. Koffka could not have been more aware and appreciative of this work as it was done and let it be known as early as 1933 that he intended to include this recognition in his book. "But of all I have received the most active help from my former student, Dr. M. R. Harrower. To her not only the author, but also the reader, is greatly indebted. In scanning every line of the type-script and the proofs with the greatest care she thought con-stantly both of the content and of the reader. In many hours of discussion she made me reformulate a number of passages so that they carried meaning not only to myself but also to those who might take the trouble of studying the book. It is also due to her skill that the English of the text is as correct as it is."

It was at this stage that Koffka suggests Harrower write a text-book jointly with him, a project which did not materialize; but he then urged her to write her own Gestalt-oriented book. It was with more than interest in the work of the student that he as-sessed and praised the finished product, *The Psychologist at Work* (Harrower, 1937).

The interchange of letters in 1933 and after might be subsumed under the heading of work-oriented interests. The letters dealt with experimental studies contemplated, accounts of unusual ex-changes with colleagues from other disciplines, tests and test pro-cedures, the recording of the inevitable struggles to produce, on schedule, a paper or a lecture. There were examples of Koffka's insightful concern that psychological concepts may be too easily accepted as explanations, a problem never far from his mind.

And in the background is reflected Harrower's ability to ex-press, with determination, her need to leave experimental psy-chology and move into the unknown territory of the hospital en-vironment. She had become dissatisfied with the study of vision in the abstract and needed to relate her studies to a *person's* vision.

Early in 1933 Harrower told Koffka of her idea to set up an ex-perimental situation to test some of Piaget's* underlying as-sumptions.

The vacation is nearly over. . . . My goodness how I have en-joyed it! I have really done nothing, but the leisure, and the time to enjoy this room, and to get out when I want to, and to read a little without the pressure of actually preparing lectures has been wonderful. What I have been reading, and enjoying as I have not enjoyed a book for years is the new *Piaget* (1932). He is dealing with the origin of such ideas as justice and morality, and contrasting all the way through to heteronomy and an autonomy . . . the arbitrary conformity to something external as opposed to the "sachlich" compulsion of something that is part of oneself. I have seldom found so much of what I am interested in in one book! In addition to this I think I can make something out of my interest, and am going to suggest to Ginsberg [British social psychologist Morris Ginsburg *] that I do this for the thesis that Becher [Smith sociology professor Howard Becher] is going to have to read. Namely, since the stages preceding the autonomy are the outcome of what Piaget calls the constraint of the adult, and since his children are all taken from ordinary and non-progressive homes, it seems that there surely must be a difference in children who live in an atmosphere where cooperation rather than constraint is the order of the day. They should grow out of this first stage much more quickly, or so one would think, so I want to repeat Piaget's questions at some progressive school and see what happens.

As I was reading I jotted down several points which seemed to be questions that might be experimentally settled. I will give them shortly.

1. Instead of telling stories (embodying certain moral situations) and asking for the child's comment, let them act the situation as a little play: this is to obviate the merely verbal situation which P has found to differ in many cases from what the child would have said when the story happens to coincide with something he has actually experienced.

2. In an atmosphere where adult constraint is minimized, and where the attitude towards morality is very different from the start from that in the majority of homes, will (a) ideas as expiatory punishment appear at all? (b) will there be stages but will the age levels of these three shifts from heteronomy to autonomy be different? (c) will cooperation with other children appear earlier, with the consequent shift in the idea of justice which P finds bound up with it?

3. P found that suggestions had no effect when for example the child is experiencing a sort of moral realism and looked on

the rule as an entity outside him: suggestions as to its relativity were useless, I wonder if, provided one that did not find this stage (moral realism) in the "progressive child" whether he would be equally resistant to a counter suggestion, namely a suggestion of the absoluteness of the rule. [6 January 1933, London]

A few days later Harrower continued but was now concerned with the lack of her inner need to work, despite success in teaching:

Your letter arrived this morning, a send-off for the new term. . . . I had lunch alone with Edge [Bedford college psychology professor Beatrice Edgell*], the nicest time I have had with her. She showed me a letter which will please you, from the Registrar saying that a student who had to give up all her work because of ill health, had asked particularly if she might continue with my psychology.
 . . . My reprints have come! I am really going to work. I must write to you less, I must somehow get an interest in, rather than an external compulsion towards, working. It is simply my only chance of existing, and I know it. Until I have an inside desire to work, I'll never stand the strain. . . . Until I have some real purpose to go for, some work to make my own, it can justly be said that I am drifting and wasting my life. You— seeing things from the outside—little know how things are, I would sacrifice every atom of popularity and being a wonderful lecturer for one genuine shred of interest in what I have to do. Don't tell me I have it! I know only too well how I have to drag myself to do this work. And tho I need say nothing about it, to please you, or because you can't bear it, there is no way, in fact, I cannot, deceive myself.
 . . . [Morris] Ginsburg thought the Piaget scheme too much work, he also said he could not see why I did not stay at Bedford, "I can't understand you, but then I don't see why I should I don't know you."
 . . . We have decided on the possible "Contribution of Gestalt Theory to Social Psychology" as a thesis topic. He wants me to

attend another seminar. . . . I am terribly down, a sort of blank wall feeling. Heading for a job I don't care about either way. It's a mess, to say the least. But I am going to have one desperate effort to put myself into all this, and try to find out where I want to go and change my attitude of "how much can I do without reading" to "how much can I read"! I am pretty near sinking in many ways these weeks, but I'll come out somehow. [9 January 1933, London]

Harrower has been invited to speak to the London University Philosophical Society. On receiving the paper she presented, Koffka wrote:

Your Philosophical Society paper: of course I read it in the afternoon of the day on which I sent my last letter. Busy as I was I could not withstand the temptation. I must say you have done a good job getting that mass of material in without over-cramming and keeping it full of interest for a group not especially interested in psychology. How much energy and enthusiasm you have thrown into that paper. I was deeply touched because in a way it is not the kind of work to which your real love belongs. But nobody could guess that from the paper. I hope they startle with surprise and thrill. It is so dramatic as you present it. I wish somebody would ask you to publish it.

If they do, you should have to do two things: Give references to Liebmann and Gelb* and minimize your claim that at the coincidence points, the figures disappear completely. [The coincidence point is that moment of equal brightness, when a colored figure on a differently colored ground disappears—or nearly so.] So you'd better modify your text a little, lest the critics pounce upon that one question. [17 February 1933]

I read your report of the figure-ground experiments [Harrower 1936] yesterday. As a matter of fact I referred to it in class because it fitted in so beautifully and I have reread it just now making a few penciled notes which you will understand.

This is a fine piece of work and I'm delighted with the results. I should like a few things fully cleared up. But your results are splendid. I shall list them briefly in the synopsis of my fifth chapter. One, orientation; two, relative size; three, enclosing and enclosed area; four, density of energy articulation; five, simplicity of resulting organization (good shape, good continuation); six, effect of one organization upon another; seven, attitude.

So you see how valuable your results are to me. I suggest that I incorporate these in my text this summer when we are together. By that time your results will be more complete than they are now. But many many thanks for writing this clear and concise report for me.

I worked well yesterday, giving a brief theory of constancy of shape based on the two principles of a normal level and the invariance of relative properties. Exactly the same kind of arguments which I used in my color constancy article [Koffka 1932]. Seminar in the evening. I find Boring's book [*The Physical Dimensions of Consciousness*, 1933] most unsatisfactory! [3 March 1933]

I have discussed a result in [B.] Zeigarnik [psychologist in Berlin] in my book which fits beautifully with your dissertation. In a state of fatigue the completed tasks are better remembered than the non-completed ones. She explains it by the fact that they have become completely structured and thereby stable. While the incomplete ones lack that stability. So this is another case of your general law. Anything that favors structure, favors recall. Good for you, this was entirely your idea!

Have you got a lab course which you could do the following Zeigarnik experiment? You remember that recall twenty-four hours after the performance of the tasks yields but a very small superiority of the incompleted task. The explanation, supported by special experiments, is that other events interfere with the insulation of the sub-systems. But one could test this, in the manner of the Jenkins-Dallenbach experiment on retroactive inhibition: choose a twelve hour interval, one filled with

In 1937 Harrower visited Koffka and his relatives on a farm in Bavaria. Earlier that year Harrower's first book, The Psychologist at Work, *had been published, Koffka having written the preface.*

sleep, the other with work, i.e. have one group do the tasks at night just before going to bed and recall in the morning shortly after getting up and reverse the procedure with the other group. I'm afraid you won't be able to do it. It requires too much time from you and the subjects, but we will keep it in mind. [18 March 1933]

Koffka had suggested that Harrower, then at Douglass College in New Jersey, write an account of experimental psychology from the Gestalt point of view. He was delighted that his suggestion was taken seriously, and from time to time in 1935 and 1936 he expressed enthusiasm about the book's progress.

I must write again. Your New York letter thrilled me too much. You can't know how pleased I am that you want to write that book. Of course I meant the suggestion seriously, and of course you may, nay, you should, take all the steps you consider necessary at once. So do write to Harcourt Brace [the publishers of *The Principles of Gestalt Psychology*] and tell them that I not only approve but I suggested the plan and that—if you like—I shall read and sanction every line of it. I am absolutely delighted.

This also puts for me an entirely new complexion on your wish never to teach again, if it means employing your spare time in research and writing it is entirely different from what I thought it meant. I know, and I knew when I wrote that letter of mine, that I was making myself unpopular by my admonition. But I always consider friendship to include the obligation of perfect truthfulness. I was afraid that your decision was made too hastily and therefore I sent my warning, but you are the ultimate judge of what is good for you. All I want is that you consider every angle before you make a final decision. Since you have done this, there is no more to say. However, I believe that you need not decide now. The question of your position next year will, I suppose, not be ready for some months so you need say nothing about it. [29 September 1934]

I am so happy about the book. If after some thinking I have any suggestion it is: You should use your after-image experiments with the irregular circle to impress the reader all the more, that no mere color theory, will ever explain color vision. You might, for example, mention that contrast disappears if the infield is spatially removed from the surrounding field [see Harrower 1937, chap. 3]. . . .

I have thought a great deal about your first chapter, and I have now discovered what is perhaps its outstanding merit: the way in which you keep the reader in suspense by your vivid exposition of the mechanistic and vitalistic solution which are at first offered as the only alternatives. I believe that you force the reader to conclude for himself that there must be something basically wrong in the fundamental assumptions which are responsible for this alternative. The reader must feel truly relieved when you present your final solution, and this feeling of relief should do much to keep this issue and the new principles before his mental visions in all that is to follow. At the same time you never allow your reader to forget that what you are discussing is relevant to *psychology* and is not mere philosophical speculation. Honestly, and without exaggeration, it's an excellent piece of work. I was tremendously thrilled by it and the method of delivery could not have been nicer. [17 February 1936]

No news. My main point is naturally that I am reading your book. When it came I was still busy with my congress paper [unpublished paper prepared for the International Congress in 1937], but that went off on Wednesday. Since then I have devoted every spare moment to the book and have actually read two-thirds, i.e. five chapters. It makes very good reading and I am enjoying it thoroughly. I shall finish it on Monday or Tuesday and then return it and explain the kind of work I have done. For you there will be very little to do; I should say that one Sunday would be ample to deal with my suggestions.

This is not a final judgment, of course; that will be given when I have read the whole. But I am sure you are curious to

know how I liked it, and therefore I must tell you "VERY
MUCH." [7 April 1937]

I just finished the book. There was so little to do in the last
chapters that I got on more quickly than I expected. My general judgment is that the book is extremely readable and that
it ought to have an appeal to the public to which it is primarily
addressed. I think it will be a very useful and appreciated book
for students who without majoring in Psychology have had
some courses in it. It will crystalize for them what they are to
remember. You have succeeded in making your subject easy
without making it trivial. The balance between fact and theory
will be just right for the lay reader, and I hope that our subject
as represented by you is attractive enough to the general public to make them buy it in large numbers. I have the feeling
that the class of people who want that kind of book is larger in
England than it is here. I'll send it back by Express as soon as
possible. [12 April 1937]

By 1936, Harrower had decided that the clinical field, not yet
considered the province of psychology proper, had captured her
complete interest and enthusiasm. The topics discussed in the letters shifted in this direction.

[KK] Thank you for your long letter which came this morning. I am simply delighted at your vigorous and determined
interest, and I only regret that I cannot do more to foster it. I
looked through two of my off-print cases Abnormal Psychology
and Psychopathology but I chose only two papers which might
be of help to you. Both methodological criticism of psychoanalysis. One by J. F. Brown, the other by C. M. White. I have
scores of reprints by [American psychologist] Trigant Burrow
but my general impression is that the author is vague and
somewhat mystical.
What factors are responsible for Ego organization? What
kind of properties must processes have in order to operate in
the Ego? From this point of view the normal and pathological

case is equally in need of explanation. The second possibility seems to me to offer the advantage that it sets the problem in broader terms. We do not necessarily have to search for Intra Ego forces, but may envisage the whole structure of the person's mind, including both Ego and Environment processes, and looking for special characteristics in either field. It is perfectly possible that in this search we might find something corresponding to a censor, but if we did, then such a result would be more firmly established, since it was arrived at by a more inclusive survey. Do you understand what I mean? The whole subject is fascinating, and I am very glad that you are collecting facts for future work. [25 May 1936]

If I think about problems of psychopathology what stands out in my mind is the problem of reality. What is it that makes normal people aware of the "subjectivity" of their thoughts and impulses and lends the character of forceful objectivity to these processes in diseased minds?

Ever since I heard Mary [a young woman known to both writers] talk of her "voices" this thought has been uppermost in my mind. It has a very wide range, since probably all schizophrenia and perhaps many other deviations from normality involve a changed picture of reality. It is certainly not purely, probably not even predominantly, an intellectual problem. I am sure it will protrude itself into the work you are proposing to do. What is the reality of a person before a critical operation. What afterwards? How is what Head [British neurologist Sir Henry Head*] calls *Vigilance* connected with it? How degree of integration? What parts do success, failure, frustrations, play in forming reality? I believe one could formulate quite an interesting and promising program of research. If you are at all interested you might provide yourself for the summer with some literature on hallucinations, psychoanalytic and otherwise. There are also those intermediate states between relief and rejection, which you described to me as your own experience when Taylor [Smith psychology professor William S. Taylor] hypnotized you. They might give some clues, and then of course there are the dreams with their reality. The problem is immense but I believe intensely interesting and important. Then the study of the influence of drugs comes in, through what agency do drugs change our picture of reality? There are endless avenues of research which might well be systematized in a good program. Are you at all interested in this? If so, you may give me your reaction when we meet. How I would love to work with you again. A subject like this would probably fit the interests of both of us. [21 May 1936]

While Koffka approved the general idea of Harrower's working in the field of what was then termed abnormal psychology—now clinical psychology—he was skeptical of psychoanalysis.

It was nice at [Max] Wertheimer's.* Several people in the afternoon and from midday dinner on his former Frankfort assistant Levy (M.D.) [unidentified] who has done interesting work on hysterical patients. I was consulted about the best form of publishing this work and made a suggestion which to both of them seemed to solve the problem on which they had been stuck for months.

I also reported on [psychologist and psychoanalyst] Erik Homburger Erikson's* paper. You would have liked my defense of him and his theory against Wertheimer's first emotional reactions.

Here are some interesting facts about psychoanalysis: The large and leading Psychoanalytic Institute of Berlin has just published a statistic of its cases, cured, bettered, et cetera. Then somebody in this country conceived the idea of comparing these statistics with those of institutions which do not use psychoanalysis, like the State Hospitals over here which are precluded from using this method by the number of their patients. To the greatest surprise of everyone concerned, this statistic was identical with the one from the Berlin Institute. Considering that the Berlin place selects its patients, rejecting those it does not want to treat, whereas the State Hospitals have to accept anybody, the comparison of these two statistics, as far as it goes, indicates that psychoanalytic treatment is even inferior from the point of view of therapeutic results to the routine treatment of an ordinary hospital. A committee of psycho-analysts has been appointed to investigate this further.

I should have liked to have Dr. Levy come to my seminar at the time when Homburger Erikson comes, but he cannot get away from his job. [6 January 1936]

Koffka was also skeptical about the value of a "normal" person seeing a psychiatrist—a disturbing thought to him.

I know what excellent, productive and humanitarian work was done by Gelb [Russian-born psychologist A. M. M. Gelb*] and [Kurt] Goldstein,* but I still have to be convinced that psychoanalysts or clinical psychologists have done anything of like value. I admit that this is a personal bias, but you want my opinion and I am as deeply concerned in this decision as you are.

Now you want to consult Goldstein yourself; why then don't you try to see him before you decide? He will be able to gauge your possible contributions better than anyone else; he will therefore be able to advise you how to acquire the necessary techniques. If you want, you may of course tell him, when you write for an appointment, that I advised you to consult him.

And now at last I come to that point in your letter that made me alarmed: Your wish to see a psychiatrist. Now, ultimately of course you are the final judge. It is your own mental equi-librium that is threatened, and so you must decide what to do in order to regain it. However, before you decide to put your "case" in the hands of Fremont-Smith [neuropathologist Frank Fremont-Smith*], I want you to wait till you have recovered your health. I only learned yesterday from Nathan [Koffka's physician] the nature of your disease; you either had forgotten the name, or I did not catch it. But it is pernicious anemia, something that is quite serious. I was terribly alarmed ever since Nathan told me. I described to him the discrepancy be-tween your hemoglobin and blood count tests.

But he also said that today there was an absolutely certain cure, so I am not unduly afraid; but you must realize that at this moment you are really seriously ill; therefore you must not be too surprised that the strain of traveling and seeing people, discussing vital problems and being faced with a momentous decision does upset your balance. I am terribly afraid of the consequences of making oneself a mental case. I still believe that if we are sound in mind we must be able to face and solve our own problems alone or with the help of a few very close friends. To me—and I may be quite old-fashioned—it has something of a sacrilege to go to a stranger and bare to him one's whole personal life and try to get from him a solution. Were I convinced that as a rule such solutions proffered by an outsider were really helpful, I should waive my other qualms. But I have seen too many people who have tried just that mode of escape to be thoroughly convinced. [2 February 1937]

In 1938, following six months of work with Kurt Goldstein at the Montefiore Hospital in New York, Harrower was established at the Montreal Neurological Institute working with Wilder Penfield.* Goldstein and Penfield had differences of opinion on theoretical matters, and Harrower was sometimes torn between loyalties.

[KK] That you love your work at the institute is a gospel of joy; that it gives you real satisfaction and that you feel you are necessary. You will be most loyal to Goldstein if you are most loyal to the truth. He has had great ideas and I'm sure that he has guessed at some fundamental truths. He has not, however, succeeded in becoming sufficiently concrete nor has he always seen all the facts. You continue his work if you remember what he taught you in your work. How I wish we could be doing it together. [9 February 1938]

In March 1938, Harrower in Montreal was becoming involved in various McGill University activities, and Koffka responded to her ventures.

[MH] I cannot work today, it's been awful. I've been trying to write something for the Philosophical Society and cannot get started. I announced to Hebb [Donald Hebb, later president of the APA, with whom Harrower shared an office at the Montreal Neurological Institute] that I wished silence all day and have done nothing but tear up what I wrote, no progress whatsoever and hopeless inaction. I can't get started. Since I feel the same way about my New York paper and my talk to the fellows, I simply don't know what will happen to me. Women are no use, they are lousy with unsatisfied instincts, they can't concentrate, at least this one can't. . . .

I'm afraid I have shot my bolt, academically and scientifically, I no longer feel I'm really any use. It's a pity this whole idea of women's independence ever got started!

When shall I see you again? I'm not even a good partner. I'm lousy. Neither one thing nor the other, I'm a lousy bargain. I am a mail bird, I only live for mail, I ought to be in jail.
[1 March 1938, Montreal]

Today I was able to write my paper; it doesn't amount to much but it is written. I am flabbergasted at the similarity between Whitehead [English philosopher Alfred North Whitehead] and Gestalt Theory, so I have combined some of that with my other topic.

It is not to the philosophy seminar that I am to speak but to the much bigger Philosophical Society of the university. I spoke to the seminar yesterday, always in favor of or amplifying the point of view of the philosophers because the scientists can't see the philosopher's points whereas the philosophers *do* see the scientist's. Otherwise stated psychologists are closer to philosophers on many issues.

The scientists can't see that the "red" of redness is something other than the chain of events, physical and physiological that leads to it . . . . How I wish you were there to tackle it. The perspiration pours down my arms, I get so excited! I see things so terribly clearly, and I see what the other fellow doesn't see, but I can't explain, it's like tetanus.

Probably [if I gave] a few joint seminars with you I could.
But the weight of the responsibility alone is too much for me.
[2 March 1938, Montreal]

[KK] I was much interested in what you said about the
philosopher-scientific situation. I always felt that in some way,
though not in all, Whitehead was very close to Gestalt Theory,
but I heard several times that he himself denied any affinity.
One of the chief differences lies in his epistemology, his opposition to my kind of dualism. This is made very clear in Lovejoy's*
excellent book *The Fight Against Dualism* [*Revolt Against Dualism*, 1930], or something like it. It would be lovely if we could
sit together in these seminars, I could help by supplying a word
here or there to express your lucid vision.

I have to speak to our philosophy club, just a student organization, nothing like your Philosophical Society. I am going to
give them my Syracuse Lecture on the Universe of Sciences,
but I wish I were as well up on Whitehead as you are now, for
that seems to interest them most at the moment.

I am glad you included isomorphism† in your talk because
that is the point of closest contact between philosophy and psychology. I can hardly wait till your letter arrives with your report on the meeting. [3 March 1938]

[MH] You will be pleased to hear that the meeting seems to
have been very successful last night, 8:15–11:30! At 11 when
refreshments were brought in, Dean [Charles] Hendel* came
over to me and quite startled me with the vehemence with
which he spoke. He said he had been supposed to leave at 10
p.m. but just couldn't go—that "he hadn't had such an evening
for years," and that it reminded him of Princeton discussions,

† Isomorphism, meaning equality of form, is a bold hypothesis about the ultimate nature (properties and characteristics) of physical and physiological processes which can be applied to psychological processes (our experiences) as well.
It makes the assumption that the motion of the atoms and molecules of the brain
are not fundamentally different from thoughts and feelings, that the bodily processes which are coordinated with mental gestalten must have a similar structure to them.

that he and I must get together to try and plan some discussions covering both fields. He took away my book to read, saying that he had wondered whether it was you or Köhler that I had been quoting from!

The only person who was quite impossible was Dr. D [astronomical physicist Alice Douglas*] who saw no point whatsoever in my physical examples, i.e. "of course nature takes the line of least resistance but man acts according to duty." Hoskins the biologist was there and he nonplussed me completely, but he was not antagonistic, only tantalizing.

Hendel was wonderful; he helped me tremendously. Curry and McClennen [members of the philosophy department at McGill] were also nice. But I think I see things in the same way as Hendel does, or something, it is easier for him to get the point of everything I say.

You'd be surprised though how much difficulty there was in that really very simple paper.

Altogether it was quite worthwhile, for Hendel is the most influential man here, and since it was he who had asked me to speak I was glad he got what he wanted. It would be very nice to be taken into the philosophy department as a kind of appendage. I wish you could meet Hendel; he has a very incisive way of dealing with things. McClennan, though perhaps a deeper thinker, is fuzzier in his expressions. I must get on with something else. [9 March 1938, Montreal]

[KK] How absolutely wonderful! This is a grand success and may help you a lot. I cannot tell you how delighted I am. Now this will be followed up by Hendel's reading of your book and he will be even more enthusiastic after that. For all you say to the contrary, you are making a position for yourself in Montreal. I am sure that it is your clarity, your enthusiasm, and your occupation with real and essential problems that has impressed Hendel and the audience!

Your draft for your APA paper is excellent. You may have time to expand the theoretical conclusions a bit, perhaps hint-

ing at what your results may mean for the law of pragnanz.
[11 March 1938]

The tests that Harrower was using in Montreal came up for discussion, the Vygotsky test for concept formation considered in an
exchange during the fall of 1938.

[KK] Now, a question. I seem to remember that you spoke
rather critically about the Vygotsky test. I have just read the
interesting paper by Kasanin [Russian psychologist] and Hanfmann [Eugenia Hanfmann, Northampton lab psychologist] on
concept formation in schizophrenia. The results are very clear-
cut and significant. I think they show that something like the
categorical attitude is gravely impaired in schizophrenia but I
should like to know your criticism of the test. [27 September
1938]

[MH] About the Vygotsky test. First, have you tried it? Done
it? Given it? It makes a great difference!
    Second, I have written to Hanfmann and not yet had an an-
swer about one point which bothers me greatly, since I don't
know whether I have just missed the point, or whether it is a
real source of difficulty. I rather hesitate to be too critical.
    Thirdly, [Kurt] Goldstein, from his own point of view made
much the same criticism as I do, he said there is really no guarantee that it touches conceptual thinking at all, for it may all
be solved at a purely sensory level.
    I am waiting for the article you mention to come from the
Library, perhaps some things are cleared up in that.
    I will tell you my particular difficulty anyway: You have to
give a series of hints or aids, when, let us say, color grouping
has been tried and discarded, you are supposed to turn up one
and show why it cannot belong in any one group. Now, any
time that you have to do that there is an almost limitless number of things you might do, some of which would help a given
individual much more than others.

I have now read the article. Page 39 does nothing to help: "[In the Vygotsky test] The examiner turns up one of the wrongly selected blocks . . . after each new attempt another of the wrongly placed blocks is turned up . . ." but *which*, as far as I can see it may make a great difference in the subsequent train of thought.

Then again, I have repeatedly found, both with what I would call an exceptional group, the fellows, and with other people on whom we have to give some estimate of general level of thinking (not necessarily organic) that the actual nonsense syllables are never taken into account at all. No one sets about it with the idea of finding out what LAG [nonsense term in the Vygotsky] is, the four groups, or the four corners are filled, but with very little thought of the "new concept LAG." This is what Goldstein means about the correct and quick solution being possible at a purely perceptual or impressionist level. [30 September 1938, Montreal]

[KK] Thanks tremendously for your remarks about the Vygotsky test. I took it once, [Eugenia] Hanfmann administering it, but I remember little about it. It has, very clearly, nothing to do with real concept formation, but with what Hume [Scottish philosopher David Hume] and Vygotsky thought concept formation was.

It may, however, test a very abstract and formal type of behavior, that particular kind of abstraction which I consider barren from the point of view of productivity. Your technical criticism of the method seems justified until Hanfmann has explained more about the way in which she gives her aids to the patient. Her results are nonetheless rather interesting. The differences between normal and schizophrenic subjects seem significant enough to be indicative of something. [4 October 1938]

[MH] I had a letter from Hanfmann in which she accepts my criticism of the Vygotsky and says: "You are quite right about the possibility of giving the subject different types of help. I have classified it into a few groups, I do not remember them exactly, but always note what kind of help has been offered and what kind proved effective. Of course one cannot talk with certainty how some other kind of help would have worked but, after having given the test a number of times one gets some sort of feeling as to what kind of help will work in a given case, so the examiners' choice of the kind of hint to be given is to a certain extent typical of the patient's performance. That is the best comfort I can offer you in difficulties with which I am very familiar, believe me." [8 October 1938, Montreal]

One of the chief concerns of a psychologist working at the Neurological Institute in the late 1930s was the question of the "epileptic personality." At that time Dr. Wilder Penfield was developing an operation for the removal of the focus of the epileptic excitation. Harrower was particularly concerned with contrasting the psychological picture of patients with focal seizures and patients with widespread cerebral damage.

I am beginning to get quite worked up about the epileptics I am testing. Chiefly because I am trying to get across the idea that psychological difficulties in epileptics may have nothing to do with the organic condition per se, but may result from the psychological frustrations that are imposed on them. I will send you some of the analyses I am making these days. I am finding that I really have to use different tests and do different procedures from what I intended. It's all very nebulous still, but exciting. [4 October 1938, Montreal]

[KK] Your ideas about certain of the difficulties of the epileptics seem excellent. Of course you have to go carefully. I am convinced there is some truth in what you say, simply because you, after seeing these patients, say it. But you have had to be very careful lest they discover some connections between something you call psychological and an organic condition. We must discuss this point at length. It interests me very much. Could it not even be that your work might give a somewhat changed emphasis to the whole picture of the epileptic syndrome. [10 October 1938]

When established in Oxford in 1939 working with the noted British brain surgeon Sir Hugh Cairns* and dealing with clinical problems himself, Koffka was in an excellent position to discuss such concepts as perseveration on a first-hand basis.

I have one critical comment with regard to the penultimate paragraph of the whole paper. I do not think that your explanation of the perseveration of the original perception is complete, I even doubt that it gives the chief reason. I do not deny that it may play a part. Perseveration is such a universal aspect of the behavior of brain injured people, it leads to reactions which are palpably wrong and recognized to be so by the patients, that I am unwilling to attribute a special cause to the kind of perseveration you found.

Without wanting to be final I should say something like this: The patients are much more at the mercy of field conditions than we are, and the trace of an immediately past performance is a strong field condition the influence of which they cannot escape. More popularly expressed: they cannot shift quickly and at will from one activity to another. Goldstein has formulated something quite like this, but I don't know that he has applied it in quite the way which I am suggesting.

Of course there must be a reason for the difference between normal people and the patients. The relative "staccato" of our behavior as compared to the relative "legato" of theirs seems to indicate a different trace organization. Sharper boundaries with us than with them. This is still rather speculative, but the all pervasive perseveration calls for some truly explanatory hypothesis. [12 November 1939, Oxford]

There is an ongoing issue in the letters over the years in which Koffka begs for more theoretical considerations by Harrower in her papers. On the other hand, Harrower continues to insist that her talents do not lie in this direction. A discussion takes place in 1940.

[MH] Since the fact that when my views do not coincide with yours is always, and apparently will always be, a source of dissatisfaction to *me*, you may start from the premise that I honestly wish I felt as you do. That is, I wish I saw myself as able and desirous to do the kind of work you consider most valuable.

But while you can, and at times have, made me feel I "ought" to fight against the grain and do the kind of things you consider "psychology," unfortunately nothing you can say makes me feel as happy in that kind of work, or as honestly satisfied that I am doing the kind of thing I am equipped for.

You allow that (as a side line) I am able to public speak in a way that you would not be interested in, and therefore "could not." Why do you still feel that I can (when not under pressure and frankly trying to please you) do the kind of things which are inherent in your approach, your capacities and your interests. I am not able to make the kind of contribution which you expect made: You always have the same kind of feelings about my things, they fall short from your point of view. Admitted they do: but you can't produce what does not grow in a soil.

The figure-ground paper [Harrower 1939], the short Carmichael paper [Leonard Carmichael *] which was in the National Society for the Study of Education yearbook committee [Harrower 1940a], even those longer things into which an enormous amount of work has gone, all "do not satisfy you" in just the same way. Yet they are satisfactory within their own more limited sphere.

I pick up this outpouring after several days! Having rather lost interest in it. However, two things bearing on it have happened. A letter from [Harvard neuropsychiatrist] Stanley Cobb in which he says that he likes the papers [Harrower-Erickson 1940a, 1940b] so much that will I present a 20-minute paper on them in Cincinnati in May to the American Psychiatric Association! They have been accepted for the Archives definitely now [*Archives of Neurology and Psychiatry*, a prestigious medical journal]. He also wrote to the Chief [Wilder Penfield] telling how important he thought they were. This coming from him is an enormous help. He says in my letter "Your results are exactly what I would have expected in epilepsy and I think that they are of great importance." The other thing is that the [McGill] philosophers, [Charles] Hendel, Curry and Fulton are going to study the Rorschach as an epistemological problem. This arose from my having made a helpful diagnosis on the state of mind of Hendel's son so that the others got interested and took the test. So you see even if I am no good myself I can stimulate other people to do some thinking in your sense of the word.

I really have a lot to do so must tear myself away from this epistle. We hear a lot about Cairns' unit to France over here, but you don't mention it. By the way, have you met Dorothy Russell [English M.D.] yet, perhaps I have told you this that Cone [the Neurological Institute's chief neurosurgeon William Cone] said Cairns had asked that she go as pathologist. If she does it will be setting a precedent. [10 January 1940, Montreal]

[KK] About the major issue that you raise, I will only say this: I am delighted with your figure-ground paper [Harrower 1939], and I am finding your patterns and observations of the greatest use in my own work; I had only a slight criticism with regard to what seemed to me too broad an application of certain of Goldstein's principles in your explanation. And whatever I may have said about your other papers was not said to spoil your fun or change your personality, but because I feel that I owe it to you as a colleague to let you know my point of view. I cannot be satisfied, nor do I think that science can be satisfied, with the purely empirical and factual correlations established in your papers. They are of great value as starting points; they pose problems, but they are as yet not even the beginnings of answers or solutions. No doubt, I should not be interested in the Rorschach method at all, had not its uncanny value been proved by work like yours.† But my interest demands more than a mere continuation of work carried out on these same lines. Whether you want to do that other kind of

---

† Koffka and Harrower exchanged a series of letters in September 1940 on the Rorschach inkblot test and its validity (Harrower 1971b). The Rorschach is one of the best known of the projective tests, which allow an individual to project outside of himself the pattern of his inner stresses and strains. The test was published by Swiss psychiatrist Hermann Rorschach in 1921.

work yourself, or leave it to other people, that is entirely a personal question which has nothing to do with science. Your decision is yours, and you have to make it. For all you say to the contrary, however, I am still convinced that little as you like the other kind of work, you are eminently fitted to do it.

Don't mind me! Just pursue your own path. It will lead you well. [28 January 1940, Oxford]

I was much impressed with your letter about the anovia fatigue test, so much that I shared it with Symonds [Sir Charles Symonds,* a London neurologist] whom I happened to see on that day. He tells me that Bartlett [British psychologist Sir Frederic Bartlett*] was the proper authority and so, although I was very busy, I sent your letter with a note to him. I enclose his reply.

I like Stanley Cobb's letter and his corrections. I quite agree with him: "organic personality" is a horror! I had no time to read your new article [Harrower-Erickson 1940a], until this afternoon, when I studied it while having my tea. Very interesting indeed. Nevertheless I have two remarks of a critical nature. 1. The Stanford Binet [intelligence test] score might be quite sufficient and indicative in your first case. But in your third it seems to obscure the picture rather than clear it up. I want to know which tests she passed, which she failed, and why. Whether, even though the numerical score was the same after the operation, the quality of her work had changed. The Rorschach test shows that she has intellectual capacities above the average but that some serious blocks prevented her from reaping the benefits of her endowment.

Now nothing of this appears in the Stanford-Binet score, and therefore I cannot in this case, see a "consistent pattern of behavior" as you summarize it at the end of the article. Had the tests been better analyzed, your conclusion might have been found to be valid; as it is, it seems rather arbitrary with regard to your last patient.

2. The old story! I always expect, despite all your warnings, what you do not want to give. After I have read the case histo-

ries, I turn with great excitement to the conclusions: What does it all mean? And then I am disappointed, because you avoid a real theoretical discussion. You see, . . . I am interested in your work, but it does not help me as much as I feel it might. You don't mind my frankness, do you? [17 February 1940, Oxford]

When I criticize your work, it is, I feel quite sure, not your work but the kind of work I have to criticize in that way. That I am full of admiration for what you have achieved during these years, done entirely on your own initiative and responsibility, that you know.

My objection is only against confusing the clinician and the psychologist's point of view. Only when you seem to commit that do I rise in criticism. [12 November 1940]

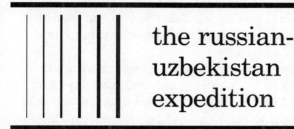

the russian-
uzbekistan
expedition

In the early summer of 1932 Koffka was invited by Alexander Luria,* the Russian psychologist, to accompany him on an expedition to Uzbekistan in Central Asia. The Uzbek Republic had just come under the Soviet influence, and the government-sponsored expedition hoped to make a psychological assessment of the natives for comparative purposes at some later date, when Soviet influence would presumably be evidenced.

Koffka was interested and made preparations to give various psychological tests to some segments of the population. In May he left for Germany where he was to wait and obtain the necessary papers for the trip.

Unfortunately Koffka became ill, with what finally was diagnosed as relapsing fever, and never able to take part in the expedition proper. However, his letters describing his experiences in Moscow and in Uzbekistan have general interest. In several excerpts, Koffka refers to Harrower's written exams for the Ph.D. from Smith. Although all the exams were passed successfully in June 1932, the committee postponed informing her that she had passed or putting the results on record until a year later, when all requirements had been met.

Since Wednesday, I have been in Berlin, seeing people and trying to get a visa. So far my efforts have been a complete failure, as a matter of fact I have become accustomed to the idea that I will not be able to go to Russia at all. I had deferred all my purchases and had begun to make other plans. Then I received a wire from Luria saying that the visa had been sent by telegraph. So I suppose I shall now get everything I need tomorrow. But it is a nuisance.

. . . Plans are now fairly definite, after five or six days in Samarkand, we take a train to Fergana about two days, and then go by cart and on foot, to a mountain village, which will be our headquarters. About 30 miles from the nearest station. These excursions across the main range of the Alai Mountains of the Alai Valley. My "house" will probably most of the time be that marvelous sleeping bag you gave me, which I unpacked on board ship and strapped to my kit bag. First, I crept into it and stretched out on the floor of my cabin, it is very comfortable indeed.

Telephone call from [Wolfgang] Köhler*: He has just returned from a tour, I shall spend tomorrow evening with him, for I cannot get away before Tuesday. I had a good time with the Schroedingers [Austrian physicist Erwin Schroedinger*], they were here last night.

It seems strange to have no news from you. Not to know about your days, whom you meet, the letters you get, the problems you discover in your reading. And all those million little things which make up our life together, with the very big things. [22 May 1932, Berlin]

My fourth day in Moscow begins. I have just had breakfast, and have another free hour, there have not been many of them! Therefore I will try and come to you and chat with you. . . . I have been given my forwarding address Fergana, Uzbekistan, post Kasten 26, Dr. Mortkovich. But it will take some time before we reach that destination. We do not even know yet when we shall get away from here, the demand for sleeper accommodations seems to exceed the supply by a wide margin. Thus we are still without tickets despite the support from various government agencies. Our plan was to leave tomorrow . . . but these are minor affairs, what you want to know is how I am faring in this new country, well, I am doing pretty well. I am lodged in a splendid room in the Grand Hotel, my windows face the Square of the Revolution, and the Red Square is just round the corner. This square at the foot of an old and magnificent wall, of the Kremlin and the Lenin Mausoleum, is truly magnificent. Otherwise Moscow is rather an ugly city. But my days have been long and full.

The two first evenings I spent in theatres, the first in the grand Opera and the second in one of the theatres of the Moscow Art Theatre. Both very excellent performances, both theatres filled to capacity. Last night was the longest performance of all, my lecture at the State Institute of Psychology. It had been scheduled for 7 p.m. but did not start till 7:30, there were over 300 people in the audience, filling the whole room and gallery. Most of them understood German, but since some did not, Professor Vygotsky [Russian psychologist, designer of concept formation test], a most charming man, acted as my interpreter.

I talked for about 5 or 10 minutes, and then he gave the most fluent translation you can imagine. He talked much more fluently than I, and it seemed to me for a much longer time. Shortly before 9, there was an interval and then I went to the Director's office, and found the table laid with sandwiches and all sorts of good cakes. A glass of tea, tasting like sugar water, and talked to innumerable people.

After quarter of an hour, we resumed the lecture, and finished at 10, but this was only the first part of the evening. More refreshments, more people. [Sergei Mikhailovich] Eisenstein, the famous film producer, a friend of Luria's had come to the first part of my lecture, and I sat with him during the interval. Now after a second report, his old but very famous film, the "General Line," was shown, extremely good. Propagandizing, a comparison of the old and new peasant. The show was over at 12:20 a.m. Then the Director of the Institute suggested that we change our plans for today, so as to give me a long morning to rest, a suggestion which I gratefully accepted.

So my next engagement is a matinee at another theatre.

Tonight we are going to have a more informal discussion of experimental problems. My topic last night, I forgot to mention, was "Die Uberwendung die Mechanismus in der Modern Psychologie" ["Overthrowing Mechanism in Modern Psychology"]. I don't know the English equivalent of Uberwendung.

Now a word about the atmosphere. It is extremely lively and optimistic. One seems to feel the joint effort of everybody proud of what has been achieved, and is being done, now, and planned for the future. Instead of unemployment, there is a scarcity of people, they have more positions in Psychology than can be filled. A great worship of Lenin, his bust or picture is in every public place. I stood under his bust during my lecture last night.

Perhaps the most interesting occasion was the great reception at 12 noon, at the Uzbekistan legislation, the Minister from Uzbekistan gave me a long lecture translated by Luria, on the conditions of his country. This was quite fascinating. He was rather a young Mongol, who had been a simple peasant in one of the least civilized and most exploited countries before the Revolution. He now spoke with poise, ease, gracefulness and humor. The stories he told were truly extraordinary. But I shall see the country with my own eyes. Afterwards there was a delicious repast, with plenty of excellent caviar, and lots to drink, all produced in Uzbekistan. The Minister from Turkestan was also present. It was really quite an occasion. An old Uzbek, in a sort of national costume invited us very cordially and ceremoniously to visit him in Tashkent, the capital of Uzbekistan, our next destination.

The Government of Uzbekistan is giving us a very fine reception there. Both the president, and a very famous prime minister, the "Lenin of the East" are to be there.

Soon Luria and Lenitcha will be here, Lenitcha is Miss Mortkovitch, the Russian physician at whose house we are going to live in the mountain village, Shaki Mordan, our future headquarters. So you see we shall be well cared for. Miss M. is one of our party.

I shall speak about your work tonight [Harrower 1932].

[Sergei] Eisenstein, who had heard a little of it was fascinated. This letter will reach you after the exam [Harrower's written exams for the Ph.D.]. Everything will have been all right. [30 May 1932, Moscow]

Here I am stretched out on your excellent and most useful sleeping bag. Well, we are now in the midst of things. The start was rather horrid. Twenty hours by train, from Samarkand to Fergana. Or rather, a station some five miles away. We left Samarkand last Thursday night, a party of nine. The night was fairly good although we had only "hard" couches, but there was a cot for every person. And here I inaugurated the sleeping bag. But the next day was truly dreadful, because of the sweltering heat, and the number of people in the carriage. The temperature in our compartment reached 100 degrees. However, even that came to an end. Late in the evening we took a cab, a dilapidated one, for Fergana, a beautiful drive towards the high mountains.

The hotel, my God! although it was not bad at all to sleep on the verandah, they had given me a room, and there I suffered from oppressive air. The next day, brought a change in our plans, Fergana was to have been the starting point for Shaki Mordan, our mountain village. But with my usual luck, I spoiled even the weather of Central Asia. A terrible thunderstorm had, on the previous day, broken over the mountains, and carried away all the bridges! It would take several days to clear the road. Therefore, we decided to make our first experiment in a somewhat more civilized district, a village, Kishlak, a native village some fifteen miles from Fergana.

When we had to leave, there was a big bus filled to capacity by our party, and luggage of same. Including provisions, things like 500 eggs. We started about 5:30 p.m., hardly had we left the town when one of the tires blew out, there were spare tubes but no spare tire. We had to wait while one of the drivers and two members of our party had walked back to fetch a new one. A matter of an hour and a half. But it was very beautiful, high mountains, over which dark clouds were brewing. Five men on camels passed us, and exchanged greetings. To cut a long story short, we did, all my expectations to the contrary, eventually arrive at our destination, but it was quite dark and no electric light.

What is it like here? I'll describe our place of abode. We have a whole house all to ourselves, and a nice house it is too. Probably it was formerly the house of a bey. But its plan is very simple, one story only, three rooms, one of which has a door to the porch. The porch is extremely pretty, high wooden columns and rafters, arching, and beautifully decorated, a deep blue color. And the furniture? Just rugs, and covers, nothing else, in true Uzbek style. One has to sit on the floor all day long and do what the Orientals do.

I am terribly happy that I have my sleeping bag. The floor is of hard dry clay. I have the bag on top of a rug, and so it is fairly comfortable, although I feel my bones in the morning, but the bag itself is a joy. Nice and warm and private.

The people here, our subjects, are absolutely charming. Suave, courteous, keen, hospitable. This whole Kishlek is collectivized and forms a Kolshos, i.e. they own and work the land together. They make a profit according to the amount and kind of work they put into it.

Their chief work is cotton growing; they are happy looking people, with always a smile in their eyes.

We are near the mountains, about two minutes from our house begins the Steppe, which stretches flat like a pancake, to the magnificent range of the Alai Mountains, which are a part of the Tian Shan. The foothills are about five miles away. The landscape is very beautiful, and because of the mud walls and the Oriental garb of the natives, the camels and the donkeys, quite un-European.

The experiments seem to be quite interesting. But of course I am lonely. I don't know the language and very few members of the expedition know mine. Besides, they are different people. Different from me, I mean, that, even without the language difficulties, I do not feel quite at home with them. I am terribly

glad I came. I have seen things I could have known nothing
about. And I am learning a great deal from my work here. But
I am sure that when the time comes I shall be ready to leave
without regret.

We shall stay in this place for about one more week, then go
back to Fergana, where I hope to find news from you at last,
and to Shaki Mordan, which I expect to be in some way the
climax of everything.

My thoughts are with you, and I miss you. There is not a
single person in our group with your gift of doing things. You
would be tremendously useful and you would enjoy it.

There is a chance of two of our young women going to Fergana this afternoon, therefore I add a few words to make this
letter ready for the post. I am much better, in fact quite all
right. I was out with my special assistant, a little Tatar
woman, who speaks excellent German and Uzbek, to make experiments. But at this time of day, morning, everybody is busy
in the fields. We went on a wild goose chase, to find the head
man of the irrigation system, walking all the way up one of the
irrigation canals, to its origin in the river. Of course the man
was not there, but we had a fine walk towards the mountains.

This is your last day in Northampton. Who will see you off?
My spirit will stand on the platform of our little station and
wave a long adieu and au revoir. And my spirit will again
hover over the pier in N.Y. when tomorrow your boat glides
into the river eastward bound. My spirit will greet you in England, and you must hunt for it in Edinburgh where it is still
walking the streets at night, looking for years that are past,
joys and follies that will be no more. I love to think of Edinburgh, but I don't really like myself as I was at that time. Too
raw a mixture. Have a marvelous time, my dear pal, try to
cheer your father, it will be easier this year, and put up with
your funny Uncle John's [John Harrower, professor of Greek at
Aberdeen University] whims and absurdities. And don't forget
your pal, who writes these lines on the porch of an Asiatic
house in Kishlak, miles and miles away from civilization.

Still the natives here are wonderful. My pet is a miller, about

45 years of age, illiterate, but intelligent. And with such kindliness in his face, such modesty. Quite medieval. [22 and 23 June 1932, Palman Bei Fergana]

We left Palman yesterday and spent the night in the Pedagogical Institute at Fergana and are to start by motor bus sometime today. I was assured by Luria that 2 p.m. would be the very latest but I have my doubts. Palman was really very beautiful and thoroughly genuine. The simple country folk in a native village. And yet I was glad to go because of the millions of flies which made life a burden. Shaki Marden our next and final station must be marvelous from all I hear. About 5,000 feet above sea level, a true resting place. Today the president of the Republic, Uzbekistan, and the president of the neighboring Republic, Kirghizstan, are going to spend a few restful weeks there. The president of the GPU [secret police] here is going with us.

It is one o'clock; we are still supposed to leave at 2. And I still have to pack and take this letter to the post office, so I'd better stop. [1 July 1932, Fergana]

I had a typewritten letter from you in Shaki Marden with the first and reassuring exam news. By the way, the strain becomes so great in my mind that I kept on dreaming about your exam. Yesterday I found your letter on June 15th and 16th and the note with the enclosures of June 21st. What a thunderbolt! And what lack either of imagination or of human understanding on the part of the committee. [Their decision to withhold their news] spoils the rest of my summer as much as it has spoiled your vacation. It is brave and probable, also perfectly legitimate, to assume that Israel [Smith professor Harold Israel,* on Harrower's exam committee] has passed you so don't worry, try to forget, it's an awful mess and I shall rejoice when it is all over.

As I have told you that several times, I understand everything you decide to do. Don't be afraid that anything you have done or want to do can in the least affect our palship. But still

I'm uneasy until I know what it is that you want to tell me [the news of Harrower's appointment to London University so that she could not return to Smith College].

And now an explanation why I have not written before and why I am writing this from Fergana and not Shaki Marden. The explanation is extremely simple, one word, malaria. We went up to Shaki Marden on Friday, Sunday I had my first attack. On the following Wednesday the second somewhat lighter. On the following Sunday my third and worst. As a consequence I insisted on being brought down to Fergana for hospital examination and treatment. We did not want to go on Monday; as a matter of fact two cars which the president of the Uzbek Republic himself had ordered for me left without us and there was no car to take us on Tuesday and so we, Luria and I, came yesterday part of the way in an Army Ford touring car. This had continual trouble and finally had to be towed into town by a factory truck, our journey lasting seven and a half hours instead of the customary three. Temperature in the truck driver's box where I was allowed to sit 104 degrees.

The city had been informed, a private room in the most modern surgical wing of the hospital was ready for me. The surgeon himself must be one of the great surgeons in the world if one goes by his own tales and has had a long experience with malaria before he took up surgery, is treating me himself. Well, of course I had no attack at the time and consequently they found no germs in my blood today, so the only proof of the diagnosis of malaria is the curve of the temperatures. However, I have been given, by our man, and most adroitly I'll admit, an injection of Biochinol, a second one is to be given to me tomorrow and if I get no attack till the day after I shall be declared cured and go back to Shaki Marden; otherwise I shall probably leave the expedition and try to get to Berlin as quickly as possible. In that case I shall send you a wire.

Otherwise you will know I'm perfectly alright and enjoying the remaining fortnight or so in the mountains of Asia.

Shaki Marden is nice at first, very impressive indeed, but it is still quite far from the really high mountains which one sees

from the way up, mountains much higher than Mount Blanc. I
am terribly glad to have seen it, even though I missed the excursion to the blue lake. Twice I was to have been the guest of
the president of the Republic, twice I was ill on the appointed
morning. Once he cancelled the whole expedition, horses, donkeys and all, but the second time, of course, he went.

In Shaki Marden, I have also for the first time in all these
weeks met an English-speaking person, an Irish woman 32
years old, black with gray hair creeping in, a nice face, the wife
of a Jewish-Russian scholar who was among the crowd that
saw us off at Moscow. We have had a few walks and talks together and to me it was a relief to be again with a person of my
kind of world.

Fate is against me. I had a rather bad attack yesterday
which made the doctor decide in favor of me going to Moscow
and Berlin. So I am supposedly leaving tomorrow night. Don't
worry, I will have a good time in Berlin and there rest more.
But please, write me at once to Berlin for God knows when I
will get your letter from the boat. Please do not worry; I will be
perfectly alright.

No, it's not malaria but a much more harmless spirochae-
tosis—so much the better! [14 July 1932, Fergana]

I've enclosed a very charming letter from Professor [Beatrice]
Edgell,* she is a brick, and tells me the conditions of your London appointment. Also, a product of my own poetic news, "Nights
in Palman." You always knew what a poet I was! In Russia,
every institution, be it a school, a university, a factory or whatnot, has its own "wall newspaper" entirely composed of contributions from the members of the institution. So our expedition
had to have one too, and I was asked to make an English contribution. I worked very hard on it, believe me. But the Rus-
sians are different from other people. Although admittedly not
one of them understood it completely since they did not know
all the words, I was never asked to read or explain it. So please
give it a kindly smile, it is quite new, only slightly exaggerated
with regard to the fact. A few words of explanation: ishak—

donkey. Chaikhand—tea house. Fiodor Nicolaievich—the nicest Russian of the group who likes to recite poetry. Kyrill Emilianovich—myself. Alexander Romanovich is Luria.

Nights in Palman

Quiet reigns and myriad stars are shining
Under Asia's lofty canopy.
Not a sound, but for a stray dog's whining
And a tired Ishak's lullaby.

Walking home from Chaikhand I follow
Sounds of beauty rare, in meaning rich
To the others, but to me quite hollow
Voice of Fiodor Nicolaievich.

Silent is my room, the flies are tired;
I can take revenge with shoe and torch.
Sleeping bag, my royal couch admired,
Give me rest! Faint laughter from the porch.

All are sleeping, man, flies, good and evil
When a mighty tom cat and a bitch
Meet past midnight screaming like the devil
Close to Kyrill Emilianovich.

Startled from my sleep and happy dream land
Silhouetted black against the sky
I behold a dozen crouching cats and
Through the door a fluorescent eye.

Plates are crashing, rending night asunder,
Screams and shrieks flow and highest pitch
Yet he sleeps through all this blasting thunder
Happy Alexander Romanovich.

I reread this letter, how hollow it sounds. How you can express within four lines in one of your poems what I cannot in two full sheets; "and my soul like a prisoned bird, flies through the vast halls of my loneliness, and against the window beats its frenzied wings, kept from the air, freedom that is you [Harrower 1933]." [29 July 1932, Fergana]

Early in August, Koffka was well enough to return to Berlin.

I have to answer three of your letters, one as welcome as the other. But let me first tell you about myself. On Saturday I had dinner with the Köhlers, I did not feel quite as well as the previous day, but it was very nice indeed. A great chance since Köhler went to Munich the next day. Sunday was rotten, a new attack, unremitting fever from morning till night. Of course I stayed in bed all day. Your letter was the ray of light. On these days I am in a state of exhaustion and depression, the best of company does not help.

Today I still had a temperature, not very much, so I got up to keep my appointment with Prof. Klaus Schilling, director of the Tropical division of the Robert Koch institute. A nice man and apparently a good one. The animal, I am indebted to for my spirochaetae, is not as I may have told you a leech, but a tick. The doctor took some blood, and after a long search discovered a spirochete which he showed me in the microscope. He ordered an injection of Salvarsan. The place here is brand new and very good, of course expensive as I wanted a room to myself. I got the injection yesterday, which sent my temperature up. . . . I have been ordered to stay in bed through tomorrow.

So much for myself, except that my boon companion in my hours of rest is my old and dear friend Dickens. I am reading after an interval of many years, *Martin Chuzzelwit*.

Now let me turn to a more pleasant subject. I mean you. Of course the lectureship is something very high in England, quite comparable to an Associate Professor in the U.S.A. And a lecturer who succeeds, and one who makes innovations, and such good and necessary ones! I admire your pluck, and [Beatrice] Edgell's good sense. I am deeply touched by her concern about me. Please give her my very kind regards.

Perhaps I can get Köhler to write a letter to the Committee

Koffka in 1932 after recovering from an illness contracted in Uzbekistan.

about your dissertation, just to show what others think of it.
[2 August 1932, Berlin]

By the end of August Koffka was finally pronounced cured: "My
mice have remained in good health and my blood is now free from
spirochaetae, I am picking up nicely and gaining pounds."
Sometime later Koffka attempted a more formal presentation of
his experiences. While this version does not have the freshness of
the immediate recording, it contains some features of interest.

I remembered suddenly that in March you encouraged me to
write something about my Asiatic experiences, as a possible
source of income. I had started at that time, but under the pressure of the book, the work has been discontinued. Since I am
relatively free at the present time I took it up again, and have
been writing a bit more. Of course it is still only the beginning,
as it stands it is no good, I am sending it to you for your judgment if you think it worthwhile to go on.
. . . I wrote a little more of that travel description but I am
utterly dissatisfied with it. I don't know why, but I feel as
though I cannot do this sort of thing. I cannot describe a scene
or landscape or a city so as to convey a living picture to the
reader. I shan't continue till I hear from you. I do not ask for
encouragement, I know too well that my own judgment is correct. [20 September 1934]

Slightly edited, the finished version is given here:

A sunny afternoon on the first of June in Moscow. I am at the
Kasan station, to leave with three Russian colleagues for our
expedition to Central Asia. The train is filled a full hour before
the time of departure. It consists of a number of "hard car-
riages," one sleeper, and a dining car, the latter comparing to a
European or American one as a country pub to a city hotel. It
is time to step aboard. We enter the sleeper, and Europe is behind us. True enough, Moscow itself is not European in the

ordinary sense, but by entering our carriage we have entered a new world.

In the bustle of the departure I see a tall man, dark of complexion with a mass of curly black hair, clad in a black vest with riding breeches, a belt carrying the holster of a gun round his waist. There are many men of yellow skin and Mongol features, nobody speaking a language I know. It was strange enough for me to feel slightly uncomfortable, had I not had a private compartment together with my Russian friend, the leader of the expedition, and another compartment reserved for the two other members of our group, the leader's assistant and a graduate student, a young girl who was to combine a visit to her family with her work in the expedition.

These arrangements seemed to guarantee enough of privacy to banish any feeling of uneasiness. We had our compartments, and therefore we should be among ourselves. These were the thoughts of one who came from America. They were quickly disillusioned. The railway administration has no objection, moral or otherwise, against putting two people of different sex into the same sleeping compartment. But someone in our group had a higher regard for the proprieties: Soon I see my fellow travellers in lively conversation with other inmates of the carriage, whereupon a great moving of luggage set in, with the result that our girl got a female companion, a young Jewish communist, the only other white person in the sleeper, while the assistant was put together with an Uzbek, a native of the country we are to visit. Our isolation was thus broken before the train had left the city.

Meanwhile the train had started on its long journey. The spires and domes of Moscow gradually disappeared; the great adventure had begun. Often in my youth had I dreamed of a journey to the East, of lying in the harbor of Port Said, the gate to all wonders of Asia. This was different. No proud ships, no glamorous Eastern port; a very commonplace car in a drab landscape of stunted firs and sand. And yet I was grateful to fate, who seldom fulfills our wishes quite in the way we expect.

And I was thrilled; I felt the excitement of leaving my native Europe and its civilization on which I am, alas too much, dependent. Though we sat in our compartment, discussing plans and experiments, experiments and theories, I was on my way to Asia, nay, I was in Asia.

Four days we spent on the train: working several hours every day and passing most of the others in the company of our fellow travellers. Late on the second afternoon we crossed the Volga, that river famed in song and lore, grander than any river I had seen, the symbol of a country which is a continent.

When I woke the next morning and glanced through the window I saw the steppe, the steppe which was to stay with me for the rest of the trip, becoming more and more barren and losing its shimmer of green as we went east and south. The train stopped for about an hour at Orenburg, a station as drab and dismal as all on this line. The city, as much as one could see of it, quite un-European: few pointed domes of Russian churches, but many slender minarets; camels and primitive carts.

A few hours later we had crossed the imaginary boundary line between Europe and Asia. Night in the steppe. The sky had become overcast, and in the distance violent thunderstorms were breaking. The train stopped somewhere; nobody knew why. We went to the door of the carriage and opened it. Blackness without; but from this blackness there floated towards us a breath of perfume such as I had never smelled before, wafted on the mild and soft air of the steppe. Suddenly the darkness would be rent, and in the bluish white light of the distant lightning the endless plain was for moments spread out before our eyes. We climbed down the steps of the carriage and walked across the embankment, solitary points in this vast expanse of night and scent, of softness and mystery. What can life be like on these steppes, and what can it mean to us that people are still living their lives upon them, so different from ours?

On the next day we reach the northern tip of the Aral Sea, an inland sea within a desert steppe. Then our train follows the valley of the Sir Darja, the Jaxartes of the ancients which

meanders through the yellow desert. On the next morning we
pass the starting point of the Turk-Sib, the new railway which
connects Turkistan with Siberia. Later in the day we stop for
well over an hour on a high plateau. The line being single-
tracked, we have to wait till a goods train had been brought up
from the other side—and this line is the one link that connects
Russia with Turkistan, the artery over which all transports
would have had to travel had the Czar gone to war with Britain
and tried to invade India.

There are high mountains in the distance which remain in
sight while our train descends. After a while the landscape begins to change. Almost imperceptibly at first, then faster and
faster, vegetation springs up; brown and grey is superseded
by luscious green; soon we are in one huge orchard, we are
entering the oasis of Tashkent, the capital of the Republic of
Uzbekistan.

While things happen outside, other things transpired inside
our sleeper. Soon we knew most of our fellow travellers, sat
with them in their own or our compartments, discussed politics, philosophy, and religion, and toasted each other and the
world revolution. The strongest impression I gained from being
with these different people in the train was the amazing uniformity of their outlook. It was as though all of them, my colleagues included, had gone through the same school in which
they had learned the same lessons, lessons in history, economics, politics, and philosophy.

The fundamental conviction colored their views on all subjects, and this conviction had all the power, but also all the
rigidity of a dogmatic faith. Theirs was the proletarian state
bringing the dawn of real culture, while beyond the Soviet
border bourgeois civilization was still bending all its efforts,
even their science and art, to the profit of capitalism and
thereby perverting them.

That religion was obscurantism, and deserved nothing but
the crudest mockery, was so much a matter of course, that the
Jewish communist girl sang a song about the Virgin Mary, the
blasphemy of which was only equalled by its rawness. I think I

lost my temper a little when this song was faithfully translated
to me. At any rate, I protested violently against the vilification
of what had been, and still was, for many people one of the
sublimest topics.

My outburst produced no irritation in my companions. They
treated it from a purely intellectual point of view, explaining
what the church had been in old Czarist Russia, how it had
served the ruling, and helped to suppress the working classes,
and why it was therefore necessary to remove the people from
its pernicious influence; how half-measures were worse than no
measures, a bourgeois would, of course, not understand this.

The uniformity of intellectual and emotional outlook is one
of the strongest memories I carried away from my six weeks'
visit to the Soviet Union. It has its great side; it gives to the
people a wonderful enthusiasm which is ever willing to make
any personal sacrifice. But for a mind like my own, brought up
in the tradition of the West, it was not only utterly alien but
actually oppressive. It was not that I had to guard my tongue;
on the contrary, I gained the distinct impression that the people with whom I talked liked to get my spontaneous reactions.
Neither do I believe that these people said what they were
"supposed" to say. I believe I should not have felt the oppression quite so much, and certainly not in the same way, had it
been like this. What confounded me was that they all were
honest and yet uniform. Talking to them was like running
against a stone wall. To have built this wall in a relatively
short time is perhaps one of the greatest achievements of the
Soviet government—however negatively one may value it. Of
course I do not want to say that all persons in the Union think
and feel alike. After all, I have met a very small number of
people, and selected groups at that, selected not on purpose to
impress or convert me, but by the very nature of things. Thus
even the passengers in a sleeping carriage on the Tashkent
train are all privileged persons, travelling on official business.

I shall pass briefly over the few days in Tashkent. Our visit
of this capital did not form a part of our scientific program. It
was a matter of courtesy to the Uzbek government which took

an active interest in our expedition by helping us in all possible ways. They secured living quarters, railway transportation and our board, they instructed the provincial administrations to provide us with housing and food, and generally looked after our welfare. The fact that I was the first foreign scientist ever to visit their country evidently increased their zest, chiefly, I should say, from a feeling of hospitality. The wish to show the foreigner that a communistic Asiatic country could make him comfortable was possibly there, but played a very minor role.

To explain the reason why the government took this interest in us requires a word about the purpose of our enterprise. The official task of the expedition, financed by the Psychological Institute of the first University of Moscow and the Pedagogical Academy of Samarkand, was to study the dependence of the mental functions of people upon the historico-economic conditions of their country. And indeed, Uzbekistan offers a rich field for such studies, passing after the political revolution through a period of rapid economic and cultural transformation. Thus it was possible to investigate people who had been to various degrees affected by these changes. I suppose that the Moscow government were willing to spend considerable sums of money on this enterprise because they expected formal proof of the beneficial effects of their policy on the intellectual and moral status of the citizens.

The Uzbeks themselves had still another reason. This emerged on several occasions, in conversations with different men in leading positions, among them the president of the Uzbek Executive Council himself. Under the Czarist regime a commission of psychologists had been sent down from St. Petersburg—so I was told by my various informants—to test the native population with a view to develop an educational system adapted to their intelligence. This commission had reported home that the Uzbeks were of such low intelligence that it would not be worth it to give them any education at all. And now the Uzbeks who were governing their country and bending all their efforts to the spread of education found themselves in this dilemma; they wanted to introduce their countrymen and women to science, which was to take the place of religion, but science had found that their efforts would be futile.

Anyone will sympathize with their hope that a new scientific commission would annul the decree of the first one. Naturally, our expedition did not have such an intelligence test as its aim, being convinced beforehand that the findings of the old commission revealed more about their own intelligence than about that of their innocent victims. But naturally, in our intercourse with the natives we had to get an impression of their intelligence, which, needless to say, did not at all agree with the opinion of the old commission.

Tashkent, then, was for us a city of official conferences and visits. This was heralded by our reception. Our leader, not trusting in the power of his own or anybody's efforts of organization, had been rather doubtful whether as much as lodgings would be prepared for us at our arrival. How great was therefore our surprise when, as soon as the train stopped, one of the highest officials, the Commissariat of Education, a Russian, came to our compartment, offered us a most cordial welcome, and led us to the platform where about twenty men and women, all connected with the capitol's scientific institutions, were assembled to receive us. Four motor cars were waiting for us to transport us and our luggage to the Hotel Regina (!), a dingy shack opposite the magnificent new huge building of the Ogpu [secret police].

In many ways Tashkent, the first Asiatic city I saw, was a disappointment. It simply did not look Asiatic. The streets are laid out as they might be in any city where there is much space, the houses are ordinary low buildings without any style or architecture, presenting a dismal and distinctly uninviting appearance; the ugliness is mitigated only by the beautiful tall and densely foliaged trees which screen the fronts of the houses from the eyes of the visitor who sits in a car. In short, Tashkent, and the same is true of the two other cities I visited, is a Russian provincial city, built for Russian civil servants, officers and soldiers, tradesmen and artisans. In this Tashkent there are numerous Russian churches—today either closed or turned to different uses—but not a mosk [mosque]. Indeed, under the old regime no native was allowed to live in this city, their dwelling place being old Tashkent a couple of miles or so distant. This old city I visited one afternoon, and here I found for the first time the true Orient. This was no more a city built by Europeans for Europeans, but at the time of my visit it went through a period of reconstruction which was quickly turning it into a squalid pile of debris with only a few remaining picturesque spots.

One of these was an old mosk now turned into a "normal school," i.e. a school where adolescents and adults were, within two years, to be transformed from illiterate peasants into regular teachers for elementary schools.

This is in reality much more serious than it sounds. It reveals the determination of the new government to change the cultural level of their citizens by educating them. Education, however, requires teachers, and where are they to be found in a country which before the revolution was 98% illiterate? So they have to be made, and the government begins to make them, and the population responds. Men and women, boys and girls, were sitting in the classrooms surrounding the quadrangle of the old priest school bent over their desks and eager to acquire that most elementary knowledge which European schools teach in their lowest forms.

The top of the dome of this mosk had been made accessible by a wooden ladder which esthetically speaking was completely out of place and which would previously have been considered a desecration. Still I was thankful for it, for this point of vantage afforded a wonderful view of the basin of Tashkent and the high mountains in the distance. There is nothing tropical about this landscape, no palms or evergreens, but a richness of growth, which gives it a color of its own.

We had arrived in Tashkent late in the afternoon on Sunday. We left early on the following Thursday on the train to Samarkand. For a long time it was stifling hot. The best we could do was to lie down and doze, but in the later afternoon, it grew cooler as we approached the defile which is called Timur's gate and through which Timur or Tamburlaine once led his troups on one of his first conquests. In the evening we arrived at Samarkand station from where it is a fairly long drive to the city and the hotel. This was a surprise indeed. A new building of modern architecture with large unbroken surfaces with balconies running along its whole front. After being shown into our rooms we were asked whether we should like hot baths, a question answered in the affirmative, with as much emphasis as astonishment. That ended the matter, however. We waited a long time and finally discovered that the hotel's water system had completely broken down; there is no water system in Samarkand or Tashkent, though it was planned to bring water down from the 40 miles distant mountains. During our week's stay the hotel system was never repaired! [20 September 1934]

reactions to the gathering clouds of war

As early as 1933 Koffka became concerned about events in Germany. Hitler had become chancellor of Germany at the end of January 1933, and by March 23 he had established a Nazi dictatorship. The German government had proclaimed a national boycott of all Jewish businesses and professions to begin April 1. Koffka reported on a letter received at that time from a relative in Berlin.

She writes that things are much better in Germany than they were before Hitler came to power. I can't understand that. I'm afraid it is the egotistic bourgeois point of view that judges merely on the ground of personal safety and order, unconcerned with the ideological forces behind it all, and ignorant of the actual suppression of liberty.

I wonder what her reaction will be to the boycott which is to begin tomorrow. People in Germany misunderstand foreign public opinion as always. They know that the atrocities reported in WWI were grossly exaggerated, largely invented. But they do not see that the physical violence is only a part of the causes which have stirred public opinion in the U.S. and in England. And that the fundamental causes are much deeper, and not done away with by a denial of atrocity stories. It is the discrimination against persons of other creeds and opinions which shocks the world rightly and against which it raises its voice. So in spite of all she says, I'm not sure what I shall

165

do in the summer. World war seems possible in Austria also.
[31 March 1933]

Koffka's alarm grew as Hitler's influence spread. A Nazi coup in Austria on 25 July 1934 followed a year of terrorism in that country. Austrian prime minister and dictator Engelbert Dollfuss was forced to resign, then was shot and killed by the Nazi conspirators.

What do you think of the dreadful Austrian news? It looks ominous. Like July 1914, one shudders when one thinks of the horrible possibilities. It seems that the madness has now reached a climax, when will it lead to a general upheaval. I have no great sympathy for Dollfuss who used force and violence himself, but the Nazi terrorism in Austria is worse than anything that has so far happened. The next few days may bring important developments. [25 July 1934]

In 1936 almost every letter showed his concern:

A special edition of the newspapers has just announced that Germany has thrown troops into the demilitarized Rhineland, and that France has convoked her war council! Does this mean war? What a horrible thought. I am quite shaken. We shall know more when you get this letter. What does the future hold for us? [7 March 1936]

The international situation seems again much tenser. I am glad that Briton [Britain] has somewhat modified her all too compromising attitude. But I am much concerned about the issue. We are living on the brink of a volcano, which may start its devastating eruption any minute. . . . I sometimes wish I was safely back from [the summer visit to] Europe. [13 March 1936]

The clouds are so black on the entire European horizon that a thunderstorm will break unless a miracle happens. Will Germany, Italy and Japan give Briton enough time to re-arm? Or will they strike sooner. I am deeply worried. [25 May 1936]

By early 1938, Harrower had been appointed to the Montreal Neurological Institute and Koffka had begun arrangements to go to England, where he had been invited to work in Oxford with the neurosurgeon Sir Hugh Cairns.* The news from Europe grew more and more bleak. In England, Foreign Secretary Anthony Eden resigned on 20 February to protest Prime Minister Neville Chamberlain's intent to sign an agreement with Italy. Germany invaded Austria on 12 March. The next day Austrian Chancellor Seyss-Inquart proclaimed union with Germany, and on the fourteenth Hitler arrived in Vienna. In Spain, General Francisco Franco's Insurgent forces were overcoming government troops. And in France, Socialist Premier Léon Blum was trying without success to organize a coalition cabinet to cope with the critical international situation.

[KK] The world events are simply terrible. I feel deeply depressed about the whole future. Of course the new British policy puts an end to the slow but steady strengthening of Anglo-American relations. How do you, in Canada, feel about all this? Or are you overwhelmed by the major readjustment to your new life and responsibilities? I am at a loss to advise, for myself, also everything is so uncertain. From [British neurologist] Sir Henry Head's* letter I get the impression that they expect Oxford to make me a permanent offer. But of course he cannot know. [23 February 1938]

[MH] I know how agitated you must be by the European news. All yesterday I hung around the radio. Several of the Fellows came over that evening to listen to the broadcasts from the various capitols. [Martin] Nichols, our Fellow from England is almost ill with excitement. I must say I am frightened, and don't like the idea of you in Oxford. Is there no peace of mind to be found anywhere? I hope you don't think it wrong of me to give you my problems in the face of it all, but it simply sharpens my desire to have a few years of normal life before the general holocaust begins. [14 March 1938, Montreal]

[KK] The European situation becomes more alarming every day. By Monday there may be a sort of war between Germany and Austria, and what then? . . . I am almost unable to think about anything except the European situation. It seems as though nobody may be able to cross to Europe this summer. A visit to Germany, at least, seems more doubtful. [12 March 1938]

Finis Austriae. I believe nothing more will happen at the moment. Hitler never strikes in two places. But the general insecurity has increased and war has been brought so much nearer. God knows what this means for the summer. [14 March 1938]

The situation grows worse with the impending collapse of the Spanish Government. And how can things go on peacefully when thousands volunteer in Britain for emergency work during air raids?

Troops in Austria, the horrible bombardment of Barcelona and the continued success of the Spanish Rebels. The unbelievable stupidity of the French rightish parties, as well as the muddle of the British Government. No ray of hope. What will the world look like two weeks from today? [16 March 1938]

By autumn 1938, Koffka has decided to risk a visit to Germany to see his family. Between 12 September and 29 September, the German-Czechoslovakian situation became critical. Chamberlain met with Hitler at Berchtesgaden on 15 September and returned to England to discuss with French Premier Edouard Daladier Hitler's demand to annex the German parts of Czechoslovakia. On 22 September, at Godesberg at a second meeting with Hitler, Chamberlain conveyed the Czech government's agreement. His refusal to accept Hitler's additional demands aggravated international tensions and led to the Munich Conference on 29 September. As a result of the conference, where Chamberlain represented England, nearly all of Hitler's demands were met. Koffka reported from Berlin:

So much has happened. The days in Berlin were painfully exciting. It is much worse on the spot than outside. The war situation was critical although I was assured on my second day in Berlin that nothing would happen before the Partietag [Nazi party conference]. The Jewish situation is unbearable beyond words.

You know, I presume, that all Jews have to assume the names of Israel and Sarah respectively on January the first. They have special licensed numbers on their cars; they have to use yellow benches in public parks. All Jewish shops have to bear the name of the owners in large white letters on plate glass. This is already in existence. But they are afraid, based on leading Nazi papers, that they will be driven out of their apartments since Jews must not defile houses owned by Germans.

Under these conditions I could only confirm my mother and my brother in their respective resolutions to emigrate to America. This means new responsibilities for me. I must give them affidavits, and must try to find some sort of employment for my brother. He wants eventually to get in with film production, and of course I have no connections with that group.

Incidentally, Kupper [unidentified], the publisher, of whom more later, told me that England seemed to offer much better chances for people who would be able to contribute something to film production, since in England, they had a lot of programs of construction to be started presently. If you happen to know anything about it, please let me know.

The news after a few days' respite was most alarming this morning. It is not impossible that the world will be aflame by the time I arrive back in New York. Although I cannot really believe it yet. However, my reason tells me that a catastrophe is bound to come sooner or later. Things cannot continue to go as they are at the moment. A new holocaust, much more terrible even than the last, may be necessary, and it is the most depressing part of the situation that such a new wholesale slaughter would probably lead to a peace even worse than the last one, and therefore breed new wars. Berlin has thoroughly discouraged me. I can't help agreeing with Gloucester in Shakespeare's King Lear when he says something like this "what flies are to boys, we are to the Gods, they kill us for sport" you will know the quotation. [9 September 1938, Berlin]

While I am writing, Chamberlain is probably closeted with Hitler. I cannot understand this move but I hope it will lead to a permanent solution. A mere "peace at any price," a clear abandonment of Czechoslovakia, would not be that. It would probably only postpone a catastrophe, but make it worse when it comes. This tension is really unbearable. It is Hitler's method, and the world has allowed him to get good results by it. And they could stop him, by firmness and frankness. [15 September 1939, Berlin]

Harrower, writing from Canada:

We have endless discussions here at the Institute as to what is the "best" thing to be done. What appalling responsibilities must rest on Chamberlain. Do you really think that the holocaust is inevitable, sometimes I still feel it is worth attempting to avert it at all costs, at other times I feel that each time it is averted it's only until Hitler gets stronger. I ache for what it all means for you, and how it will affect your plans and those you love. Your news about conditions in Berlin made me feel so sick I could cry. If I can do anything to help your mother and brother you have only to say so. I'll write to the only people in England whom I know that have anything to do with movies and find out. I know nothing firsthand.

These are days of terrible anxiety for everyone. The more acute the closer one's ties are with Europe. Goodness knows when I shall see my home again.

I feel almost ashamed to be living a peaceful, normal life. The only thing that I can say is that I am learning not to waste time, so that my inner conscience is relieved. [16, 17, and 23 September 1938, Montreal]

With Koffka back in Northampton, the discussion continued:

[KK] I agree with the feeling that the catastrophe cannot be avoided. The more one yields to Hitler, the more powerful he will be when he unleashes his forces eventually. If Britain and France allow him to swallow Czechoslovakia, they condemn themselves to be powers of the second rank. Then there will be one power left in Europe and that power will go on suppressing human liberty and dignity.

The news today is difficult to interpret. But I now think that war will not be avoided because the Czechs have courage and idealism. And of course they fight for their very existence, not only as a nation, but as free and respected individuals. It is ghastly to find oneself almost wishing for war. The only justification is that war would at least wipe away German dictators. What else it may bring, nobody knows! I agree it is a terrible predicament. [17 September 1938]

[MH] I know how you will be feeling in these days of anxiety. It is surely one of the most tense and dramatic periods of history that has ever happened. For the radio brings so much to the compass of everyone's thought in such quick succession, that it is almost like a mental newsreel being played off in front of you.

I met yesterday the head of one of the biggest British armament firms, who said it was impossible for France and Britain to fight for six months as the French Air Force had been depleted by sending too many planes to Spain. He received hourly cables from the foreign office, so perhaps his reports may be valid. His feeling was that the news at all times is too extreme in regard to the nearness of war, but finally I wondered if it was not wishful thinking on his part, because of his anxiety about his daughter who lives in Germany.

Did you hear Chamberlain? I thought it was very powerful. Even one of the most skeptical fellows, who has lost every atom of faith in the British altruism and diplomacy in these days, was impressed. [24, 28, 30 September 1938, Montreal]

[KK] I did not hear Chamberlain, though, of course I read his first and second speech. I thought the editorial in the *New York Times* after the Munich agreement truly excellent. A tremendous relief, but what a price! I should feel better than I do if I could believe, as you do, that the British Government had learned a lesson. But I doubt it. Why this completely nonsensical pact of nonaggression with Hitler? A good many people think that Chamberlain's promise to remove causes of misunderstanding may mean that the British press won't be allowed any more to say the truth about Germany. No, Hitler's victory is unparalleled in history, and that at a time when both he and Mussolini were caught in their own ruts, and the whole world was united against them.

Don't think that I am one of those who say that Chamberlain should have at all costs gone to war. In the first place I have no right to think that, being far away from the field of action; and this is equally true of many of these critics. But he should not have given the impression of having done a great and good thing. Hitler is being praised for having yielded on a few, not very important, points. But what about the incredible demands which he made at Godesberg, the ones from which he yielded. The business is utterly depressing.

Chamberlain ought to be turned out as soon as possible and [Anthony] Eden or some person who does not succumb to the "personality" of Hitler put in his place. But of course there is no prospect of that.

Last Saturday there was a most interesting discussion of the situation at the home of Hans Kohn [professor of history and political science at Smith]. You would not have believed how fanatically blind and partial people can be! I even found myself defending Chamberlain. [4 October 1938]

[MH] I don't know what to think. I find one's attitude is partly determined by what the other person thinks. I mean, in discussing so much with one of the Fellows who says what you have said so often, I find myself taking a more pro-Chamberlain attitude than I would when talking to my father for instance. It is that sort of bi-polar social phenomenon again. [4, 5, 8, and 10 October 1938, Montreal]

[KK] What you say about discussing politics is exactly what I feel. I must have told you before how I found myself defending Chamberlain, morally, of course, for politically, I believe, he could have acted more wisely and more successfully. [10 October 1938]

The year ended for Koffka on a pessimistic note, and even the upcoming and much desired visit to Oxford had lost some of its attractiveness:

The German situation is ghastly. I don't even dare to think what may happen to my people, or what may be happening to them in the near future. Of course, I have no direct news. I shall tremble before I open the next letters. Will they be allowed to leave the country? Shall I ever be able to go back? . . . The prospect for the next year of my life is anything but rosy. I listened to Chamberlain's speech this afternoon and altho I cannot yet say what it will mean, it sounded serious enough. I do not believe that I'll be able to go to Oxford. A year in England has for me still the character of extreme unreality, and the events of the last few days have only strengthened this character. I have to write endless letters about my mother and brother. Now I have to give a guarantee that I will reimburse the man who has invited my brother Fritz to England for all extra expenses incurred by him, he also demands that I give Fritz monthly pocket money. I have to concede the point because he won't sign the guarantee demanded from him by the British Government without my assurance. And I can of course understand his point of view. But I worry a great deal, because my mother will cost me much more than heretofore, and how am I to get the money?

So I am not in a rosy mood and do not look forward with any expectations to the year that is to come. [18 November 1938]

The spring of 1939 saw Germany's annexation of Czechoslovakia and Italy's conquest of Albania. By August, when Germany and Russia signed a nonagression pact, Charles Lindbergh had given the first of many speeches pleading for strict American neutrality. That summer, despite a letter from the Oxford authorities asking whether Koffka would prefer to postpone his appointment, he left for London. Germany attacked Poland on 1 September, and two days later England and France declared war on Germany. Soon after his arrival in London, Koffka wrote:

The world situation is growing steadily worse. But I find London absolutely calm. I have heard no discussion in the public conveyances or in the railway stations. God knows how it is going to end. I feel quite weird, having left a home and not yet found a new one. I go to Oxford tomorrow to visit [Hugh] Cairns and discuss plans with him. [21 August 1939, London]

Harrower, continued reporting the impact of the global situation on personal and hospital life in Canada:

My brother cabled me from Australia asking me to try and persuade my parents to come out to Canada. I wish I could get them, I hate the idea of not being able to look after them.

It looks now as if my mother will arrive in August. I'm tremendously glad your mother is now safe in England. Here the same tension. I don't believe it can go on like this all summer, for as our chief neurologist says "the English allowed Hitler to spoil a weekend, but when he threatens to spoil the fortnight at the sea, that's just too much!" [8–18 June 1940, Montreal]

A former student of mine, and her German husband arrived this morning from Germany, and are quite convinced that there can be no war. Very strange to find such an attitude at this time. They say it is quite impossible as far as Germany is concerned. We are all glued to the radio, and my mother now feels she should go back as quickly as possible to my father. Now that the *Athenia* has been torpedoed, the ship she came over on, she blames herself for leaving him, and feels it is unwise to persuade him to take the risk of coming over. So now nothing will stop her going back to him. Things look sinister. What can the British do if Russia and Italy come in against England too? [26 August 1939, Nova Scotia]

The German couple . . . she identifies now with his attitude . . . came over this evening. Their outlook gives one a shock. He cannot disguise the fact that he feels that the Germans are a chosen race, and that they are somehow intrinsically entitled to govern other races. He constantly disparages the Czechs and the Poles. But in the same breath disclaims Hitler's methods. She is obviously torn between loyalties, I don't envy her position.

What do you think about [Charles] Lindbergh's speech. It caused great indignation here. What got into him? [16 October 1939, Montreal]

[KK] What you say about the German couple sounds all too true, alas. The Germans will not learn and cannot learn; of course there are lots of them who don't have to, who are as sensible as anyone else, but I am afraid that they are a minority whose influence now is nil.

Why Lindbergh is making such an ass of himself, nobody seems to know. People here think it is rather ungrateful and ungracious of him after he sought and found sanctuary in England. [29 October 1939, Oxford]

Although England and Canada had declared war on Germany in 1939, America did not enter the arena until December 1941. During 1940, therefore, both correspondents were in countries actively involved in struggle, and each was much concerned with assessing the attitudes of people in the United States. That spring Finland had been forced to negotiate peace with Russia, and Germany broke Norwegian resistance late in April. German troops invaded the Netherlands, Belgium, and Luxemberg on 10 May, the same day Winston Churchill became prime minister of England. The Netherlands fell four days later, and by 17 May German divisions had moved into northern France. Belgium surrendered 26 May, leaving British forces to be evacuated by sea from Dunkirk on 4 June. With the fall of France in mid-June, the Germans intensified their air attacks on England during the summer and fall.

Some sample exchanges early in 1940 dealt with attitudes and prognoses.

[MH] We had the S's over the other night [American citizens temporarily in Canada] with some people from here. It is surprising to find how lukewarm to the significance of an allied defeat many Americans are. The S's are violently against any kind of participation by America, which is perfectly understandable, but it seems strange to me that there can be any doubt in the minds of Americans as to the rights and wrongs of the case. I was tremendously interested at the fact that there is the possibility that you will be invited to stay permanently in Oxford, even if you consider the possibility remote as you think.

What do you really think will happen in Europe? Do you think that the people you talked to in Germany last summer really meant it when they say they wanted war to end the internal situation? How about the "old Guard" in Germany and in Communist Russia, or isn't there such a thing any more? I mean the people who honestly believe that Hitler was an alternative to communism. [13 February 1940, Montreal]

[KK] As to your political question, I am afraid the answer is I don't know. I am convinced that some of my friends in Germany are still hoping that this will free them from oppression which they loathed as much as you or I. But whether they will, or can do anything, I don't know. Probably not. Here, whenever we speak about the situation, we are all agreed that nobody can guess how it is going to develop or when it is going to end. But I have not found anybody yet who is pessimistic about the final outcome. Your letters sounded a bit depressed in tone, but you would lose all that feeling of discouragement if you were here. It is a curious reserved attitude of waiting for something that will finally turn the scales in favor of the only cause that can be allowed to prevail. And there is not a trace of boastfulness in it, nor even hatred. [28 February 1940, Oxford]

[MH] I am just listening to the news which tells of the end of the Finnish war, what an end after their gallant struggle. Can you understand the attitude of Sweden? Don't you think it is a short-sighted policy? Won't they be gobbled up in their turn? It seems as if England has a hopeless task when the neutrals themselves don't seem anxious to be helped to get rid of the menace that hangs over Europe. It is interesting to hear that people in England don't seem depressed. I suppose that explains why my parents will not consider coming to Canada. From here, things certainly look bad, and the American papers don't make anything look better with their independent estimates of the Allied chances. [13 March 1940, Montreal]

Throughout the next months Koffka wrote continually of the optimism of the British people and their belief in a final victory.

I repeat: as far as one can judge from here there seems no reason whatsoever to be pessimistic about the final outcome of the war, even though it may turn out to be a long struggle. I was greatly heartened by a Dutch journalist whom I met at Ethel John Lindgren's [British anthropologist, lecturer at Cambridge] in Cambridge, who was absolutely certain of the Allied victory, and said that the French army was incomparably better than the German. Bad days may be ahead, but the final outcome will be good. [31 March 1940, Oxford]

No letter from you and not much to tell. Of course now the events in Norway and Denmark occupy our minds together with the anticipation of what may come next. You will be

thinking of England, of your parents, your friends and of me, more than ever during these days and weeks. But don't worry, we are perfectly confident of a good outcome. Immorality and brutality will not prevail. But at what a cost to the world.
[14 April 1940, Oxford]

[MH] Our thoughts are turned to the war even more now with the invasion of Norway, and the feeling that the worst is simply not told us. I saw a terrible film yesterday, smuggled out of Poland, taken by a man who was there during the siege of Warsaw. Perhaps it will come to England. These poor defenseless people being shot down in the fields as they tried to get potatoes, and the complete inhumanity and brutality of it all is recorded for all time. It is surely no case of special pleading to feel that this war is different from others in which the blame may be more evenly distributed. [3 May 1940, Montreal]

I have been getting more and more paralyzed with alarm for England, you, and my parents in Cheam in the last few days. Now with all the news this morning it is all I can do not to be sick. How I wish you were "safely" on this side, for is there safety anywhere? Do you think my parents would come over? How can things go well for the allies with the rules of the game entirely different for each side? It is all so awful and one has been lulled into an escape from the obvious pessimism of this distance, by all your, and my family's cheerful assurances. It's so maddening to be able to do nothing towards at least getting them out.

It seems quite silly to talk of our doings: I am speaking to a convention of 2,000 people tonight. Provincial nurses of Quebec. I go to Cincinnati in a week's time, giving a paper on the epileptic personality. I think I'll be startled at the United States attitude, the students are so outspokenly against England, as the arch imperialist etc. It's quite frightening. From the people I've talked to I would find it difficult to live there now. The S's are leaving Canada, because they feel so unsympathetic to Canada, even though he has no job in the States yet. [10 May 1940, Montreal]

Somehow with the news as it is, with England in imminent danger, with the whole of civilization, perhaps, about to topple, I can muster no enthusiasm. I have to give my paper in Cincinnati, but I'm no longer interested. There comes a point when theoretical work simply doesn't hold one, what if epileptics don't have a typical personality! I have been extremely pessimistic and depressed for several months now, I admire beyond words the steady belief that you have that "right" will ultimately triumph. But with all the small countries under the German advance how have we any indication that we can withstand them. They have made a business of aggression and brutality, and it does not seem likely to me that a miracle can happen. However, believe me, my prayers are as fervent as anyone's.

There was a marvelous article by Dorothy Thompson* last night urging the States to keep [Franklin D.] Roosevelt and claiming that the Nazi's trade on just the political indecision which America will shortly be experiencing. She suggested the novel idea of a Republican Vice President, like Wendell Wilkie, who seems a splendid person, and no campaigns or elections, with Roosevelt continuing. [16 May 1940, Montreal]

Koffka continued to write of the British attitude with admiration and affinity.

No news from you for the second week. Transatlantic mails are becoming scarcer. I know how your thoughts are hovering over Cheam, Oxford and England. And you know enough of English people to imagine what it is like over here; a superb control of emotions. Life goes on as usual, people enjoying the unusually beautiful spring, observing the bloom of the different shrubs and flowers, and going into the woods to hear the nightingales. And they even continue to come to my lectures. I had a good audience on Friday, for the most difficult of my four presentations. [19 May 1940, Oxford]

By 26 May Koffka had decided to accept the advice of the U.S. consul and to return to the States on the last available ship. If there had been no complicating factors, he probably would have chosen to remain with his British colleagues. However, he was trying to bring his mother out of Germany, and negotiations for this had to be handled in the States.

[MH] Welcome home. I refrain from commenting on the news, for what's the use! I am trying again to get my parents over, they seem more willing than heretofore. Tomorrow I start on a vacation, but I can't feel entitled to enjoy it. You will probably know what I mean, as much as I have longed for it, I did not get any outdoors or swimming last year. Everything is so ghastly, perhaps you will see now why I have been so gloomy, for from here it has looked as if this would happen [France overrun]. You always spoke of my being pessimistic, more pessimistic than the people in England, but I have only been afraid that just what has happened, would happen. I just could not see that the calm and optimistic view was justified in the face of the relative strengths of equipments and armies.

What do you feel about America? Will she go in, and would it really help if she did? Do let me know people's reactions and feelings. I feel sorry for Anne [Mrs. Charles] Lindbergh, surely she must be torn between her mother's and her husband's point of view.† I find myself lucky in the atmosphere, both in my immediate and wider circles, which is perfectly consistent with my own feelings. Yet I don't really know if I am American, Ca-

---

† Anne Lindbergh's father was Dwight Whitney Morrow, U.S. ambassador to Mexico in 1927. In 1930, he was the U.S. delegate to the London Naval Conference and, in the same year, was elected U.S. Senator from New Jersey. His wife, Elizabeth Cutter Morrow, a noted educator and writer, was acting president of Smith College in 1939–40. Both parents were strongly supportive of the Allied position during the war; hence the comment on Anne's probable conflict of loyalties.

nadian or English. It's so strange that I should come to admire the essentially English qualities of my close friends. I am glad I am in Canada, for though I have no rampant empire-outlook, it would have been hard during these last months to have to meet and cope with isolationist attitudes and opinions. Do you still feel the allies can survive? Even minus the French fleet? [8, 14, 16, 17, 18 June 1940, Montreal]

[KK] When people tell me that I must be glad to be back I cannot agree. I feel very badly that I had to leave England at the most critical time, but I had no choice. I came alone. Quite apart from the fact that my mother would not have been on the *Roosevelt*, she has not got a visa, owing to the inefficiency of the U.S. consulate in London and I have to start proceedings at once to get her a new one. [12 June 1940]

I have to thank you for several letters. I thought I might delay my answer until the fate of France were definitely known, but now news seems to drag and I'd better write. First of all: you were right all along and I was wrong in my optimism, but I haven't learned my lesson yet. I still refuse to believe that Britain and the British Empire will lose this war. Churchill's speech in the house yesterday was masterly. The fight will be joined presently; England will suffer horribly but she will not be conquered.

I have talked with many people here, colleagues and ordinary tradespeople, so far I have found only absolute sympathy with the Allied cause and a determination to fight Hitler. This country has, of course, weeks ago, ceased to be neutral. To declare war at this moment, when the country is so lamentably unprepared, could probably do the Allied cause more harm than good and would play into Hitler's hand by scattering of resources. If America joins the war she will have to do it with her full power all at once and not in dribbles which can easily be beaten and destroyed. But I have found nobody yet who thinks that resistance should cease and Hitler have it all his own way.

I hope you will be able to get your parents out. I had to leave

Oxford in such a hurry that I could not communicate with them any more. But they surely ought to be spared the nervous strain of steady bombings. I feel as though I had run away from the realities of war but honestly I believe that I had no choice and [Hugh] Cairns very much corroborated my opinions.

Please don't lose hope or courage or faith in yourself or what you, what we, are struggling for. We, you and I are together in this, as we have been together in many things before. My thoughts revolve around the same problems as yours; only I have the advantage of having just been in England, and that is why, as you say, I am happier at the moment than you, because I believe in England. It is inconceivable to me that England will perish. You say you have no country. Neither have I. But in a finer sense we have a country, both of us, the house of decency, of good living, of courage and self control, of fairness and tolerance, of this country, England is the largest and oldest province.

In this country are your roots as well as mine, to the survival of this country we must devote whatever power we have. This country, the U.S.A. is another province of our country, and I believe that its citizens begin to realize that now with a new poignancy. I have talked to many people, faculty and just ordinary people in shops, the post office, janitors, and they seem all agreed that if England goes, then goes the bulwark of all those values that make their lives worth living. So far I have heard no word of hostility towards England, not even of smugness or unconcern. Everyone I know, or have talked to is touched and an ardent partisan. Whether America shall enter the war now, that is a different question which I somewhat answered in my last letter. To do as an empty gesture would in my opinion, do more harm than good; and I don't see that at this moment it could be more than an empty gesture. Give supplies to the limit of our ability, repeal the Neutrality Act so that supplies need not be paid for in cash, and build up a terrific Navy, Air Force and Army. I shudder to think that I can write such a sentence but what else can one think today! If America entered the war now, we would have to give help in other ways than those I mentioned, and that would mean a scattering of her resources. Let her first be strong.

If England holds out till Xmas, then America might be, if not ready, at least sufficiently strong to give truly effective help. And that would be the finest Xmas present this country could give to the world.

Did English people feel America should help? (your question) Yes, a good many did, i.e. they thought it a sort of moral obligation. I often contradicted them, partly because I was afraid that such a view, if known over here, would put up the backs of many people who otherwise might be friendly, partly because I cannot admit the justification of the claim. America was not consulted about any of those actions that ended in the present catastrophe. Mr. Chamberlain and his Cabinet made one mistake after another without dreaming of taking the advice of Washington. Therefore it seems to me there is no obligation for the American people to save the British from the consequences of their own mistakes. But, of course, in another sense, there is a moral call: help those who fight and bleed for our ideals and who protect us against a common danger. And so in every word I say about England and my year there I consider the effect it may have on people over here. I am not a propagandist, I just try to tell them what England is like and what a horror it would be if she were lost. [19 June 1940]

In one of his last letters dealing with World War II, Koffka uses a poem written by Harrower for his Christmas greeting:

Here are all my best wishes for Xmas. We know what they are, you have expressed them beautifully in your poem Canadian Christmas 1940 [Harrower 1972, 53–54]:

> Across the earth a giant spectre stalks
> Spectre of famine: not of bread alone
> But of the truth:

Across the sun a dread eclipse has passed
And death lies in the shadow it has cast
Death of man's spirit and integrity.

And locked in conflict those who would be free
And those who would impose this rule of night
Negation, hatred, force and pagan might.
We cannot sing in praise because our land
Is rich, its sun still bright.
Their fight is ours, and thus vicariously
We suffer blow for blow with those who stand
And offer broken thwarted lives for liberty.

But we may praise, and fierce may be our joy
That in past years, which naught can now destroy
We were vouchsaved the chance to work, to strive
The chance to throw our weight against a yoke
The chance to give ourselves to a campaign
That brings no conquest, save of suffering
No subjugation save disease and pain.
And in these vital years of strength and youth
Could burn our candles at the shrine of truth.

My mother sends you her best love. She said today that you
were unique among all the people she knows. And so you are,
my dear. [23 December 1940]

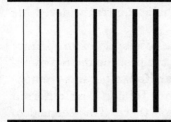

in oxford
the clinician

In the chapters dealing with Koffka's year in Oxford (August 1939–June 1940), his experiences are presented from two perspectives. In chapter 8 there is a close-up look at particular themes. One such theme, that of Koffka in his role as clinician, is almost unknown. Certainly nowhere in his published work does his particular blend of scientist and humanist appear in the same way. In letters dealing with his experiences in the Nuffield Institute, there are many examples of scientific curiosity, together with a concern and respect for the patient-person which was typical of Koffka, himself.

In chapter 9 there is a wider-angled view from longer letters, selected to give more of the flavor of the total Oxford experience. The significance of Koffka's Oxford appointment, however, began long before his arrival in London in 1939.

The Significance of the Oxford Appointment

Koffka's efforts to move away from the Smith College and to obtain another position were not only unknown but would probably still cause great surprise to those who remember him in Northampton. Yet the letters revealed, between 1933 and 1941, six attempts to change his base of operation. There were raised hopes and, as those hopes were dashed, deep disappointment. In 1933, when so many of his friends in Germany were losing their positions and livelihoods, Koffka felt that he could not let it be known that he was interested in relocating. But by 1935, with Wertheimer safely established in New Rochelle, he reconsidered his chances of another affiliation.

Early in 1935 there appeared to be the possibility of an opening in Swarthmore, but for various reasons the position did not materialize (see chapter 1). Later in that year Koffka became tremendously excited about a letter from Edward Tolman* in California indicating the strong possibility of a job there. This seemed to Koffka ideal, but when several months later another letter from Tolman arrived stating "the administration is now looking for a younger man," he summed up his plummeting hopes with an atypical explosion: "LOUSY isn't it."

At this point, Köhler, who had been aware of the California offer, mentioned that Carl Seashore, who was retiring as head of the psychology department at the State University of Iowa, had spoken of Koffka as a possible successor. Koffka's hopes were raised but dashed again.

Then Koffka got news from Goldstein* that Margaret Washburn's* position at Vassar was to be filled by a German. The choice seemed to rest between Heinz Werner, an experimental psychologist at the University of Michigan, and Koffka. The outcome of this was a severe blow. Koffka, according to Köhler, had apparently given too difficult a lecture—the old problem—when speaking at Vassar and had been ruled out on this count.

Shortly after, Koffka was told that Duke University psychology professor William McDougall* had "in retiring recommended as his successor Köhler, Koffka, and Lewin* in that order." Koffka was invited to Duke to give lectures. Harrower warned him against repeating his mistake:

> You will not find them essentially theoretically minded with regard to psychology. I mean, do not expect too much, for you must remember, otherwise you will not get yourself across, that the average person, even the good academically minded person, has not the theoretical-minded-ness that you have. I know you

don't believe me but you would really be surprised at the number of people who say your thought is so difficult. Not in the sense that it is muddled, but that you give so much and take so much for granted in the other person's understanding. [18 February 1939, Montreal]

Koffka promised to take this advice to heart. His lectures were successful, and he was warmly received. But, although he was told, "Well it is all settled. You will be here soon. Your lectures were excellent and a tremendous success," these unofficial reactions did not result in a firm offer.

With this background it becomes clear that, should a definite offer ever come from a large university, it would have great significance, and it would be even more satisfying if the possibility arose of a position in England. Koffka had a deep love for England and the English. He had always received a special welcome from British psychologists, going back to 1923 when the International Congress of Psychology was held in Oxford after World War I. His perfectly modulated English speech and his anything but autocratic bearing always evoked a friendly response.

Thus, when later in 1938 Koffka received a formal invitation from Sir Hugh Cairns* to come to Oxford, he was overjoyed. Cairns, a neurosurgeon, was head of the richly endowed Nuffield Institute for Brain Injury, part of Oxford University.

This invitation, of course, did not come by magic. Various intermediate steps had occurred. There had been an important change in Harrower's professional status. In 1937, she had been appointed to the Montreal Neurological Institute to work with Wilder Penfield* on a Rockefeller Foundation Medical Fellowship. There began a shift in the topics discussed in the letters in the direction of this new and challenging field in which she was working. These discussions brought about an important change in Koffka's attitude to the whole problem of an experimental psychologist working in a hospital situation. He now began to envision himself as able to contribute, from his Gestalt orientation, to the problems presented by patients under special conditions.

A second series of events was set in motion by a formal letter from Dr. Robert Lambert of the Rockefeller Foundation, who advised Harrower, while on vacation in England that summer, to get in touch with Cairns, who, coincidentally, was also a personal friend of her family. Lambert wrote:

> While you are in England this summer I suggest that you meet Mr. Hugh Cairns, neurosurgeon at the London Hospital who is to be Professor of Surgery at Oxford. (You have probably heard of Lord Nuffield's magnificent gift to Oxford which among other things will make possible the development of clinical teaching and research there.)
>
> As Mr. Cairns I believe is contemplating psychological studies on brain cases similar to those planned by Dr. Penfield I'm sure he will be interested in talking with you. I am enclosing my card which will serve as an introduction. [13 July 1937]

At her meeting with Cairns, Harrower mentioned Koffka's possible accessibility. Cairns jumped at the suggestion, so that Harrower wrote to Koffka, "Cairns wants to meet us both in Paris at the International Congress to discuss Oxford possibilities. Please draft a program of what a psychologist could do in a big university and medical center with Nuffield money. It is a tremendous task for someone" [19 July 1937, London].

Cairns and Koffka achieved an instant meeting of the minds, Cairns arranging for both Koffka and Harrower to examine a patient with him in London. Thus, within a few months Koffka reported:

> A letter from Cairns, or rather two letters in the same envelope. The first a discussion of the case we saw together, the second all about my sabbatical. He is "very interested and highly honored" by my proposal, has discussed it with the Regius Professor of Medicine Sir Farquar Buzzard,* a very distinguished neurologist, who thinks my visit could be tremendously stimulating but does not consider a year long enough

and therefore may try to get one-half of my salary from the Nuffield trust. [22 November 1937]

There were, of course, innumerable technical details to work out at Smith before the appointment was official: the question of a sabbatical year, post-sabbatical responsibilities, and the loss of some part of the salary. Koffka saw President Neilson* and reported:

Many details of the situation in Oxford were new to him. He was interested and pointed out that I was expected to return to Smith for another year and, since he would then no longer be in office this would be enforced. I asked whether a refund of half the salary would be considered fair, he replied it would be absolutely correct. Finally I went into details and said I hoped he saw why I wanted to go now and not wait for another year. I explained how everything was being built up and that there might be a chance of their offering me something permanent. It is a slow process, painfully slow, but at least it is a process, something does happen. I owe this Oxford invitation entirely to you. I wanted to say that in my letter yesterday but forgot. But it is never absent from my mind. You made all this possible. [29 November 1937]

After over a year of negotiations, Koffka left for Oxford in the summer of 1939. A month or so after he arrived, he began to write of his clinical experiences.

I got a very good start with [Sir Charles] Symonds* (visiting neurologist from London) through Cairns, who told him that I had discovered a symptom in a patient which had escaped the rest and which interested him particularly, namely a disturbance of intellectual orientation. Symonds knowing the country from which the patient came very well, confirmed my findings beautifully, but he said to me: "It is always easy to confirm what somebody else has discovered." So I think I am not doing too badly: moreover, I have quite a strong human influence on the patients. [22 October 1939, Oxford]

Let me tell you about a woman, a parlor maid in Devonshire where her husband is butler, whom I had examined several weeks after her brain operation, she had a removal of a small tumor, left frontal, and another operation a few days later. She came back from a nursing home for a removal of some necrotic bone from the wound. When I saw her come in quite unexpectedly, I noticed that she was in trouble. So later on I went to her room and talked to her. She was frightened that she would again be paralyzed in her right leg, and would lose all the gains of the last month. And she, a cheerful person, began to cry. In a few minutes I made her laugh and be cheerful and full of hope. She was very well after the operation, most sensible and brave.

There is now the wife of a factory worker from a village in Warwickshire, 58 years old, with an acoustic tumor and according to reports a severe loss of memory. The loss of memory is in reality a matter of recall, of "communication" in my terminology, because she tells me the minutest details of her life in the village and remembers perfectly what we have been doing together at the beginning of our meetings. Also when I left her after my first visit, I told her that when she would see me on the next day she was to say to me King George and King Edward. And she did it! She is a most likeable person and speaks a pure Warwickshire dialect, the vowels like the German or middle English "Hoosband."

I could go on chatting about people like that, but you are too busy to attend to such gossip! I must tell you, though, that little Jocelyn is progressing very well. (The boy with the big fungus.) I was tremendously surprised when a few days ago I applied, more or less by chance, a new test. He has still great difficulties in naming objects and in finding the proper words in general. But when I asked him to name "opposites" he did it

quickly and correctly, even with quite difficult words like
"funny." Synonyms are more difficult.

Referring to the fact that he was working again subsequent to a
heart attack, Koffka wrote:

I am perfectly well, and the new work is a tremendous intellectual stimulus. One of my aphasic patients has been dis-
charged, and I am now trying to interpret the picture in my
own theoretical terms. Very difficult indeed. Two new men
have come, one a farmer, of the Hunting class, with an inoperable wide spread tumor, the other a director of an export firm,
Oxford man, with probably a frontal or parietal tumor.
The first is the empty shell of the squire. He has all the
heartiness, the self reliance, the lingo of his class, but has gone
completely to pieces. His worst features come out, I am told in
the way he behaves to the nurses. He was, in his old days, a
heavy drinker, and I suppose he did his fair share of wenching.
And now the inhibitions are gone.
The other, whom I have only seen once, is one of the finest
types of Englishmen. According to his wife's story he used to be
a tower of strength to his family and friends. He knows that he
is going down. He is wonderfully cooperative and "he can take
it," i.e. when he fails in a test, he does not make evasions or
excuses, nor does he try to laugh it off like the other man. He
just accepts it as a fact. I find Goldstein's stick test very helpful. Also problems like this: get seven gallons with two buck-
ets, one holding five the other three gallons. If one follows this
step by step one gets a real insight into the intellectual defects.
[8 October 1939, Oxford]

That fine man I told you about in my last letter died on
Friday. They made a ventriculogram and found an inoperable
tumor, and gave him a decompression. His death was surely
the best thing that could have happened to him. I saw him for
the last time on Wednesday, when he relaxed a bit and told me
how nervous he was before the operation. "It's like going over

the top." He was a general favorite in the department. [15 October 1939, Oxford]

One of the things that intrigued Koffka most was when an experiment resulted as he had predicted.

Yesterday Dr. Falkoner [Nuffield Institute house surgeon] and I examined a hemianopic patient together, intent on finding some of the Fuchs phenomena—Dr. F. I believe was rather skeptical although he was very ingenious in devising tests and acting as a tachistoscope. (It all had to be improvised in the "field room" without any apparatus.)

The results were tremendously interesting. The blind half "saw" when cooperating with the normal half under some conditions but not under others [typical Fuchs phenomenon]. *And the difference was of course, one of total structure!* I have to devise new tests before the results can be properly interpreted. [26 November 1939, Oxford]

Koffka had particular rapport with the children on the wards.

Have I ever told you of the 7 year old Joyce M. a child from Peckham with a cerebellar tumor? She has been in the woman's ward for many weeks, at first paralyzed with her head thrown back, and entirely cut off from any human intercourse. Now after prolonged X-ray treatment, she takes a great interest in her surroundings. When I come into the ward she calls: "Doctor, come, and speak to me." But these written words don't convey to you the strange appeal of her tiny voice, nor the wistful, almost wise expression of that curiously old face with its big black eyes.

Her contribution to our "conversation" is usually limited to "yes" and a curiously knowing nod of the head. Occasionally, when I am testing another patient the word or "opposite" vs "function" test, (my invention) she supplies the answer. I shall never forget her pathetic little figure. [4 February 1940, Oxford]

The Nameless Patient: Unity Mitford

In an unusual incident, Koffka was asked to interview, and subsequently to treat, the young English aristocrat, Unity Mitford, daughter of Lord Redesdale. She had become enamored of Hitler and the Nazi regime and had gone to Germany in 1933, becoming a member of Hitler's salon. When Britain and France declared war on Germany on 3 September 1939, she shot herself in the head in despair. When Koffka reached Oxford, she had been brought back to her parents' home and was under the care of Sir Farquar Buzzard.*

Mention of her name in a letter from England would probably have involved the censors' wrath, so Koffka, recording his first meeting with Unity, wrote guardedly.

Cairns gave me a small lunch party in a dining room at Balliol. I sat next to Sir Farquar Buzzard and had a very good talk with him. He asked me to let him come some day and watch my methods so when I have a good patient I will call him up.

A fascinating two hours with Cairns yesterday afternoon and a very pleasant and entirely informal family tea. Then an unusual conference which had as its main object a special patient but then branched out into general topics. The most interesting thing, however, was this very patient. If you read the English newspapers you might guess who she is. Sir Farquar has decided that I shall see her and since she stayed in Oxford only for a short visit I spent a great deal of time with her.

It was a combination of organic and mental (functional) symptoms and the sessions were quite exciting to a person not calloused by experience with many similar cases. I have supplied the mother with instructions for measures of re-education and shall see her again at regular intervals, but as it seems difficult to bring her here, I may have to go into the country

only 25 miles away, provided that the patron of our institute
provides the transportation of which there seems to be little doubt.

I have written so much about this; because you will be
pleased to know the mark of confidence which this charge implies. [4 February 1940, Oxford]

On Thursday morning I telephoned Sir Farquar Buzzard to
tell him that I had an interesting patient and that he might
like to see me testing her. So he came and watched for three-
quarters of an hour and then there was a good discussion between him, Cairns and me. Sir F. is a fine old man, and he
seemed truly interested. He also discusses with me each time
spontaneously the case I mentioned in my last letter. I shall see
the patient again on Tuesday when I shall be driven to High
Wycombe in the morning and shall lunch with the family. It
seems rather soon, but apparently the family wanted it so, because Cairns and I had decided to leave the choice of the date
up to them. [11 February 1940, Oxford]

Harrower queried from Canada, "By the way, is Unity Mitford
chez vous. As you know, Lord Tweedsmuir* [governor-general of
Canada] is here!" [11 February 1940, Montreal].

Koffka began to report on his weekly visits to the home of the
special patient.

Now about myself. . . . A visit to High Wycombe on Tuesday.
An excellent chauffeur who went 65 miles an hour! A very interesting examination and a pleasant dinner à trois, the father
being in London. My services are actually required, not only by
the girl, but also by her mother. The girl wanted me to come
back "tomorrow," but even the mother demurred when I suggested a fortnight, and said that they had hoped I might be
able to come at least once a week for a period of about 6 weeks,
after which time they are planning to go to a small island
which they own on the west coast of Scotland. So I have to go

next week, but probably I shall go there again tomorrow. Even before my last visit it had been decided to consult a psychiatrist, a decision which was only strengthened by my report. T. A. Ross [psychiatrist] has agreed to see the patient, he has a cottage nearby, and wants to see her tomorrow in consultation with Cairns. And Cairns, who will drive over, asked me to come along. [17 February 1940, Oxford]

Because of delays in transatlantic mail, Harrower reacted to the first account: "I am thrilled by your account of your special patient and would like to hear everything about it some day. I suppose there's no chance of getting a Rorschach" [19 February 1940, Montreal].

[KK] You will have guessed that the patient whose name I did not mention was Unity, so you will have answered your question yourself and will know that I am still seeing her regularly, my last visit was made yesterday. I have now lunched three times with the family, but the father has been away and I shall probably see him again next time. I have met two sisters, Nancy the oldest, who is married, and Deborah only 19, who is the only girl I have seen here who looks like an American girl, so well groomed and with that independence and assurance of manner which I like so much.

My patient is definitely getting better, though she has still plenty of symptoms, notably an extreme fatigability, or shall I say satiability. We are on very friendly terms and on my next visit I shall bring her a copy of the *Harzreise* (Heine) for educational purposes. She said she would like to have it, although of course she would not like it. So I bought a very poor edition, the only one they had at Blackwells. [28 February 1940, Oxford]

On Tuesday I was in High Wycombe as usual. I gave a lift to Deborah the younger sister 19 years old. She looks very much like an American student, but her only interest, as far as I can

make out, is "huntin". My patient is showing real improvement. She is translating Heine's *Harzreise* as an exercise. I call
that an achievement! [19 March 1940, Oxford]

After dinner I had to go to a German psychotherapist, a
funny little man who is trying his best to become acquainted
with me. Nothing has happened this week except my regular
visit to High Wycombe. My next one may be the last, but I may
go once or twice to a cottage they have near Bunford in the
Cotswolds. The patient was much better than the week before.
She said it was a great pity that I did not know the real U.M.
and when I suggested that the next time the real one might
put in an appearance, she promised to do her best. [21 March
1940, Oxford]

Of what appeared to be the last meeting, Koffka wrote: "I went
this time to Swinbrook. The cottage is tiny, really part of the village pub; one living room and a kitchenette dining room. The patient was little changed, she talked much about herself" [28 April
1940, Oxford].

When face-to-face contacts ended, Unity kept in touch with
Koffka by letter. (Two of her letters, reproduced here, show interesting changes in handwriting and subject matter.) Back in
Northampton, Koffka wrote Harrower of these changes, once
after six months and then the following year.

A letter from Unity showing much improvement. She tells
me with much humor of an alleged German bomb which was in
reality "an electric mine made in poor England." It exploded
the moment that her mother was writing to her sister in America how awful London was but how peaceful was Swinbrook!
[2 December 1940]

Then I had a nice and sensible letter from Unity. She says:
"Well I am, at last, myself again or practically. I can read well,
write fairly well but chiefly, *think!*" The last word, plus her ex-
clamation mark, may have some significance. I had written her

9 September
1940

Dear Professor Koffka,

I really did mean to write to you ages ago, but somehow all of my time was taken up, and I put it off.

You will be glad, I think, to hear that I am, at last, really well.

Yesterday, all the Cairns's came over to tea, six of them! Professor Cairns now wears a Uniform! It is really a <u>lovely</u> Uniform, with red on the hat!

I have read three whole books. That is lovely for me, as I wasn't able to read at all.

Well, I'm afraid this letter isnt very interesting but our life here isnt very fascinating now.

Yours Sincerely,

Unity

---

20 August
1941

Dear Professor Koffka,

I was just about to write to you, when I got your letter, this morning. I am so sorry about your heart, I didn't know it was bad, how bad is it?

Well, I am, at last, myself again, or practically. I can read well, write fairly well, but, chiefly, think! In fact, I am really well, & can even — since last week — drive again! I wish you were here, & could come over —— you would hardly recognise me!

My mother sends you her love.

We have had various troubles since you were in England, but have got over them! One of my cousins was killed, but not in the war!

Yours Sincerely,

Unity Mitford

Letters from Unity Mitford.

from Wakefield [hospital] but it was nice of her to reply so
promptly and cordially. [22 September 1941]

Formulating the Psychologist's Role in a Neurological Institute

In the summer of 1939, Harrower was approached by the program
department of the Canadian Broadcasting Company to give a series of lectures on psychology over their national network. Her
book, *The Psychologist at Work*, had recently been published in
Canada and had been favorably reviewed as highly readable and
directed toward the "intelligent layman," a term much used by
English publishers at that time. Thus it seemed to lend itself as
the basis for some nontechnical talks. Harrower had sent Koffka
in December a summary of the projected topics (chapter 9) and, in
planning a second series, wanted to include some reference to
Koffka's ideas on the emerging role of the psychologist working in
a neurological institute. Koffka replied by sending the introduction to the book he was working on, *Psychology for Neurologists*.
(The unfinished manuscript is in the Archives of the History of
American Psychology.) The original draft was edited by Harrower
at Koffka's request and, in its present form, is still forty years
later a pertinent answer to the question of the psychologist's role.

Probably a neurologist, when he sees the title of this book
and gives it some of his attention, will be puzzled as to its contents. So not to raise any false expectations, it seems wise to
tell him that this book is neither an "Abnormal Psychology" as
this term is now currently used, nor a manual of tests in the
accepted sense of this term, although it will include a discussion of many abnormal phenomena, and will describe many
methods, or tests, by which abnormal phenomena can be studied. In short, neither Freud nor Binet and Simon [French psychologists Alfred Binet* and Theodore Simon, developers of the
Binet-Simon intelligence test] are the patrons to whom the following pages can be dedicated. Instead they are intended for
the neurologists, who are concerned with organic disturbances

of the nervous system and the effects of such disturbances on behaviour.

If we agree that psychology is the science of behaviour in its broadest sense, then the neurologist is, of necessity, a psychologist, whether he knows it, or wants it. Every routine neurological examination tests a number of psychological functions like sensitivity, memory, concentration, judgment and reasoning, speech in its various aspects, and the emotional and volitional behaviour of a patient. If localization of the disturbance were the neurologist's one and only interest, then a mere empirical correlation of certain test results with certain organic defects might be sufficient for his needs, provided that such a simple correlation could be discovered.

But a patient may, in a particular test, exhibit a certain symptom, while the same test, applied under *different conditions*, may fail to elicit it or bring to light a new and entirely unexpected one. The literature on the symptoms of frontal lobe lesions, to give but one example, is full of such apparent contradictions (Goldstein, Rylander [Scandinavian psychologist Gosta Rylander]).

I need not dwell on such facts, for there is an even more radical objection to the idea of a mere empirical correlation between psychological symptoms and localized defects. The tests by which symptoms are demonstrated have not been chosen at random in a blind trial and error fashion, but were the outcome of systematic theoretical considerations. Conceptions of what language, or thinking, or even perceiving is, have guided the development of methods and thereby also the discovery and systematization of symptoms, and thus the neurologist who applies psychological tests cannot be indifferent to the psychology that has produced them.

Not that I think that he *wants* to ignore these theories, for, important as the localization of an organic defect is for the neurologist, he wants to learn more than that from his examination. He wants to get a picture of his patient, i.e. he wants to understand his *behaviour* as it results from his injury. Far from being satisfied with a list of symptoms, he tries to find a link that connects as many of them as possible, preferably all, in such a way that they appear as manifestations of a few very general features which have been modified by the injury.

One neurologist has even gone so far as to say "that different symptoms can be regarded as expressions of one and the same basic disturbance" (Goldstein, *The Organism*, p. 29). Whether this extreme statement is true or not is of no significance for our present argument. Whether the symptoms manifested by each particular defect can be derived from one general cause, or even whether symptoms of every kind of brain injury are indications of one and the same general disturbance does not affect the fact that we need to order the rich array of symptoms, that is, that we need to reduce them to a more general and fundamental modification of organic-behaviour.

The neurologist, then, is not only interested in symptoms, he is even more interested in the *connection* of symptoms. And thereby he is, willy nilly, a psychologist; his task has become that of understanding the behaviour of his patient, his task is to deduce from the total behavioural pattern, the change in the structure and function of the nervous system which is responsible for it.

Such an insight is the basis on which his therapeutic procedures can be based, be they surgical operations or methods of re-education and re-adjustment. But such an insight presupposes an understanding of all behaviour, normal as well as abnormal, i.e. an acquaintance with psychology which tries to reach such an understanding.

Neurologists and psychologists are agreed on one fundamental assumption, namely, that all behaviour, be it accompanied by consciousness or not, *is dependent upon the neuro-muscular structure of the organism*. This assumption, simple as it seems, is ambiguous: its meaning depends on one's conception of the neuro-muscular structure itself. One may, to put the difference in the form of two catchwords, regard it as a "machine," however complex, or as a "physical system" with a greater degree of freedom.

Viewed as a *machine* the whole structure can be resolved

into a large sum of separate and essentially independent, part-structures which through summation and interference will determine behaviour. The penny-in-the-slot machine exemplifies the summative aspect: drop your penny in one slot, and you receive a match box, in another a cigarette, in a third a piece of chocolate. Less crude would be the picture of a network of dial telephones. Common to all machines is the feature that their effect is completely determined by the interconnectedness of their various separate parts and *totally independent* of the result to which their action leads. Once the switch has been thrown, for example, the train will proceed on a determined track, no matter whether it leads to the intended destination or to a catastrophe. The work which the forces in a machine can do, is completely determined by the rigid constraints of the machine.

None of these statements are any longer true when we turn to the consideration of physical *systems*. Here any motion will result from the interplay of the forces themselves, and the final result will influence the action only inasmuch as is compatible with the state of equilibrium.

For example, take a glass of water, move the glass, and the water will ripple, but, provided we leave the system—glass and water—alone for a short time after having disturbed it, the surface of the water will have returned to a smooth horizontal plane, although there are no restraints comparable to telephone wires or rails to produce this result. We should add that a system is no less subject to the laws of nature than a machine, and therefore, an explanation of behaviour in terms of a physical system is no less a casual explanation than one in terms of a machine.

Having explained our two catchwords we must decide which of them is to serve us for a model of neuro-muscular structure. Without hesitation we shall choose the second alternative and refuse to treat our physical bodily structure as a machine.

If we regard the neuro-muscular structure as a non-machine system, the relation of normal and abnormal behaviour is easily defined. Neurologists have long ago discovered that in-

jury of the nervous system does not affect behaviour merely
by diminution, by the elimination of some part-functions originating in the injured centres, for all these, and ever so many
more modifications, can be fitted into the same explanatory
frame as "normal" behaviour if the nervous system be viewed
as a physical system.

We must now expect that a change in one part of the system
will, to a greater or smaller extent, modify *all* processes that
occur within the system. The degree and kind of modification
will depend upon the nature of the system before the injury,
and the extent and locus of the defect. And since it is extremely
unlikely that any two injuries are exactly alike, and still less
that the pre-morbid structures were identical also, we cannot
expect two identical clinical pictures.

More important than this conclusion is the next: Normal and
abnormal behaviour follow the same laws, both are reactions of
physical systems to sets of conditions that upset their existing
states; different systems will react differently, and that not because a locus, responsible for certain part-functions, has been
destroyed, but because, through destruction of tissue in one
place the systematic characteristics of the whole system have
been altered.

We started out by referring to the neurologist who tests the
separate functions of the organism, and enumerated several of
the psychological functions thus tested. Now we see that the
functions of the organism cannot be separated in this manner
because as reactions of the whole system they are *interconnected*. There is no reason, of course, why we should not use
terms like perception, memory, concentration, intelligence, etc.,
provided we beware of two errors.

In the first place we have to remember that most of these
terms derive from ordinary language and have therefore a very
complex meaning in which the *accomplishment* (or performance) rather than the *function of the organism* dominates. To
explain the difference between these terms it is only necessary
to remind the neurologist that the results of many of his examinations are expressed in terms of failures, of what the patient

cannot do. A patient sees badly; he cannot orient himself in space, he forgets his chores and errands, and so forth. In other words, the patient is judged by a standard of *accomplishment.* Such a procedure, though it is justified for a *first* survey and for a decision of measures of re-education and adjustment, can be no more than a beginning.

We want to know *why* the patient is less efficient than a normal person, what his actual functions are which result in his reduced level of accomplishment. What does a hemianopic person see, *how* is a patient's phenomenal space constituted if he lacks an orientation? How are his mnemonic functions modified when he cannot remember his tasks?

In order to answer such and similar questions, very different concepts will have to be introduced, concepts that refer directly to functions and not to accomplishments. For the relation between accomplishment and function is by no means simple or unambiguous. The same accomplishment may be due to different functions, and what may seem simple as an accomplishment, may in reality presuppose a complex interplay of different functions, so that a modification of an accomplishment may be due to the disturbance of different functions.

When a person gives a correct answer to the question: How much is 8 × 7? he may *either* automatically reproduce a part of the multiplication tables which long ago he learned by heart, *or* he may "multiply," or his response may be a combination of the two factors. If the patient gives the same answer as we do, we still do not know whether he is capable of both these functions or only one. This is not a fictitious example as has been shown in an investigation of the arithmetical procedure of a patient by Benary [German psychologist W. Benary], where an even more fundamental difference between arithmetical functions was brought to light.

In the second place we have to remember, when we use those ordinary psychological terms, that the different functions denoted by them, are not independent faculties or processes. Let me illustrate this by pointing to the interdependence of perception and action: Perception depends on action, and action depends on perception. I need not remind the neurologist of the fact that movements become uncoordinated when the afferent impulses resulting from the movements are eliminated as in locomotor ataxia. Or take the difference between walking in the dark and normal walking as a further example.

It is no more difficult to illustrate the dependence of perception on movement or action. Stationary objects appear at rest when we move our eyes, but they appear to be in motion when one of our eye muscles is paralyzed, or again, the localization of sound depends on head movements with their sensory effects.

This last discussion has indicated the task for the clinical psychologist. It is he who must call attention to the functions of the organism which account for its accomplishments, and thereby introduce the neurologist to a systematic neuro-psychology.

The study of abnormal phenomena found in neurological disorders is connected with a systematic psychology in two ways. On the one hand, it will show what functions will take the place of normal ones, in consequence of organic defect. On the other hand, it will throw light on the nature of the normal performances themselves.

The first will be the neurologist's interests, the second the psychologist's. But inasmuch as both require the same kind of research, there is no essential difference between neurology and psychology in this field. A thorough investigation of abnormal behaviour has revealed, even more poignantly than that of normal performances the interaction of psychological functions. The reason we discuss functions as separate is because there is no other way of doing it.

We have to start our analysis by artificially separating functions from their context, both in actual experimentation and theoretical deduction. There is no danger in such a procedure as long as we keep this methodology in mind, but its artificiality must always be remembered.

These three terms, perception, memory, action, contain the key to a psychologist's work. *Perception* supplies the organism with the environment in which his behaviour takes place, and through action he maintains himself in the environment. Neither perception nor action are immune to modification by "experience." Rather the past in many different forms pervades both environment, behaviour, perception and action.

If then we divide psychology, like Gaul, into three parts we seem to follow a scheme quite familiar to the neurologist who distinguishes in the nervous system receptors and afferent nerves, effectors and efferent nerves, and central structures and association fibres. But it would lead to grave mistakes if our psychological division were correlated bit by bit with the neurological one. The central structures, far from being the domain of memory alone, are essential for perception and action quite apart from their mnemonic components. Moreover, this division tends to give us a false understanding of action: for, thinking in terms of reflex arc, the receptor-centre-effector sequence, we are apt to envisage actions as reactions and to choose as standard instances such behaviour as the "menace reaction" of the eyelids or the startle reaction. The term action, as I feel psychologists should use it, has a much broader meaning, a meaning which applies to the whole variety of human behaviour. Most human actions defy the simple reflex-arc schema; they originate not in a sensory impulse but in wishes, decisions, plans, or demands arising from a complex intellectual or social situation; and as often as not they are preceded, accompanied or followed by various emotions, In short, we should use "action" as a short-term to connote all striving, meaningful, connative behaviour. It is clear that in this sense it cannot be correlated or identified only with the outgoing part of the reflex.

That our schema is not totally satisfactory appears from the fact that it has no proper place—as yet—for thinking and imagination, that is for modes of behaviour which are neither perception nor action, nor typically mnemonic function. But the world of thought is not really so different from the world of perception. Thinking may be the first step in acting, thinking utilizes as a rule that which is preserved by memory.

in oxford
the year unfolds

There was much more to Koffka's Oxford experiences than can be recorded in terms of his clinical opportunities with the neurosurgeons, his unusual "patient" Unity Mitford, or the emerging views on a psychologist's role in a clinical situation that he had begun to formulate. The full flavor of his year in Oxford may be seen best in larger excerpts from his letters, covering many topics.

Koffka arrived in London in August 1939 during one of the critical months of World War II. England would enter the war a week later, on 3 September. On arrival he wrote:

I know you will be worried about me and no doubt it is as serious as it can be. The bombshell of the German-Russian pact burst on the day I went to Oxford where everybody took a very serious view. Cairns was extremely nice—his family are in Sussex, his wife is expecting another baby. I had hardly lunched when I was taken into a brain operation, in white gown, cap and mask, for in the London hospital there is no such elegant visitors' gallery as in Montreal's Neurological Institute. I stood for awhile close to Pennybacker [Joseph B. Pennybacker, brain surgeon and first assistant to Hugh Cairns] who did the operation, and could have touched the brain! Several good talks and an interesting ward rounds where I made a few suggestions. I shall go to Oxford whatever happens, Cairns was quite empha-

tic about wanting me to stay if I did not mind. In fact I should
have gone there already if the Dundee meeting [the British Association of Sciences] had been cancelled, but it has not, so I
shall go on Thursday provided war has not broken out.

The people are marvelous, perfectly calm and confident, and
they will not believe that war is coming. The worst thing one
can do under this condition is to do nothing. I felt much better today when I jotted down my final notes for Dundee, and I
should have preferred to go to Oxford and begin my work now.
Germany is of course out of the question, even if the worst is
avoided for the moment [Koffka had planned to make a brief
visit there]. I'll be all right, and I shall have an active and interesting year. I forgot to say that according to Cairns, Balliol
[College] is going to offer me its hospitality; the Master there
seems to have a good opinion of me!

All good wishes, I wish you were here—no I do not mean here
now—but in Oxford during a quiet year of work. I am glad you
are where you are, out of harm's way. [26 August 1939, London]

Wednesday was the official opening with Sir Albert Seward's
presidential address. On Thursday the meetings began: I attended the physiology section to hear a quite interesting presidential address on evolution, and then went over, quite far away,
to Section J—Psychology—where I got in on the tail end of a
not particularly good discussion of films.

After a solitary lunch, I had reported my presence to the section president R. J. Bartlett, the London Bartlett [as distinguished from F. C. Bartlett,* professor at Cambridge], but had
not met any of my friends, so I returned to Mrs. Tosh's [his
hostess for the British Association meetings in Dundee] for a
rest. Then the reception given by the City of Dundee. Here I
spent all my time with the Bartletts, Walters [University of
Reading professor of psychology] and Mrs. [Richard C.] Oldfield
with whom I even danced. But it was a rather dull time, discussions on pacifism and factor analysis don't go with tails, and
sounding brass bands.

Bartlett had told me that their committee had made me a

vice president for the time of the meeting, and asked me to attend the committee meeting that evening. During the committee meeting we heard of the invasion of Poland by Germany. At 10 Bartlett gave his presidential address, Aveling [Francis A. Aveling, professor of psychology in London University] in the chair. I followed him at 11, and had a fair success.

Naturally people's minds were concerned with other matters! Aveling had given me a nice introduction, expressed the thanks of the meeting to me. Rex Knight [Aberdeen University professor of psychology] was there and I went to lunch with him. Also Julian Huxley [biologist and writer] had come, the *Times*, which gave an account of the meeting, mentioned my paper.

I returned to the meetings after lunch, heard a rather uninteresting paper by Philip Vernon [later Glasgow University professor of psychology] on prediction of psychological aptitude and a somewhat more interesting paper by Stephenson [psychologist at Oxford] on physical activity, sports, etc., which was read by Rex Knight.

I even said a few words in the discussion. Then I had had enough. So I left, got myself a gas mask, went to headquarters, waited for the decision of the General Committee, which came about 4 p.m. to the effect that the meeting would end as of that night.

Made arrangements for my departure that same night, attended a sherry party given by the president of the association for foreign and dominion guests, had to wait for Mrs. Tosh's car, packed in a deuce of a hurry, had dinner, said good-bye and got to the station which was porterless, and practically dark, with only a few blue lights shedding a ghostly light. Without the chauffeur I should never have got on board.

However, the train left punctually and I found in my compartment the Oxford physiologist, Le Gros Clark, and a young chemist from Oxford. Endless stops at all stations. In the morning I found R. J. Bartlett in the same train, also Julian Huxley. War had not been declared yet, and people were so distrustful of [Prime Minister Neville] Chamberlain that they thought he might avoid it again. "He'll be in Berlin tomorrow morning" is what one man said. We got to Oxford three hours late.

I rested, lunched, and then went on a long expedition. First to the infirmary where I reported my arrival to Cairns, and from there all on foot to the police station, beyond Christ Church, coming back by bus. After dinner I got into a long conversation with one of the other boarders here who has been often in the U.S. which he loves, reading poetry aloud, chiefly to schools. I retired at 11:40. And all this had been too much for me. All of a sudden I felt the pressure in my heart which did not subside when I lay down. I fell asleep, but when after three hours I woke, it was still there. So I decided to take a nitro-glycerin tablet which, alas, I had never done before. This helps most people, but some are intolerant of it, and unfortunately I belong to that group.

So I had a pretty lousy night. The next morning I telephoned Cairns, who at once sent me a consulting physician, came himself a little later, and sent me plenty of books through one of his women doctors. The consulting physician, Dr. Cook, sent me a practicing physician the next day, a Dr. Hoey, who found me in very good condition, "tolerance test" absolutely normal. But the two of them have decided that I have to get an electrocardiogram, and before that I am to do no work.

Now I told you all this because I promised, but there is nothing to worry about. Moving two flights down to the other room will make things much easier, although I don't experience any difficulty in coming upstairs.

I feel awful not doing any work, but it may be a saving in the long run. I am, however, working at my Bryn Mawr lectures, but find it, or rather them, very difficult, much too difficult for me [Koffka 1940]. Your paper sounds perfectly fascinating. If you could send me a carbon copy, I could tell Cairns about it, and use it in my own work. [7 September 1939, Oxford]

Harrower's letter of 11 September arrived on the twentieth; an excerpt explains some of Koffka's comments:

Yesterday I saw the Chief [Wilder Penfield] and applied via him for a National Research Council Fellowship, for wartime activities, possibly discovering incipient neurotics or unstable personality structures before they are subjected to positions of undue psychological stress. I feel rather tired and much in need of a holiday, but the real holidays are over, both in weather, and in one's mind. How are you: I wish I were with you, even if you wish me out of harm's way! [11 September 1939, Montreal]

[KK] As I came home a few minutes ago from my first afternoon at the infirmary I found a letter from you and one from your mother. I am so glad to know she is safely back in England. She tells me of the marvelous time she had with you.

As for you, of course I wish you were here. But of course it is much better that you are on the safe side of the ocean. And I find every possible help and cooperation, I shall try to do as much as I can to help the regular staff of doctors to get through these busy times, and by giving examinations that would have to be given anyway.

How far has your article gone [Harrower-Erickson 1940a, 1940b]? Would it be possible to let me have a carbon copy before it is published? I have mentioned it already at the Radcliffe Infirmary and people there are *much* interested.

I hope you get the National Research Fellowship for your program. My dear, I wish I had your imagination which makes you always see the demand of the hour and the best way for you to comply with it. But do relax. Don't let the protracted strain get the better of you!

I should have written much sooner, but I expected every day to hear some news about the condition of my heart. The electrocardiogram was taken exactly a week ago, and it is only this morning that the doctor heard the results. On the telephone this morning the doctor told me it was good. I went to see him this afternoon and he read me a short note he had received from the consulting physician, saying that the record showed a

Perhaps the only formal photograph of Koffka (probable date 1938).

few slight abnormalities but revealed that there were no gross defects. So I might be allowed to get about by degrees.

And so I went to the Radcliffe and had my first patient, a charming boy of eleven years, son of a musician, who has a beastly protrusion of the brain through a large opening, which was made to remove an extradural abscess. I worked on his speech. So far I'd say a light case of verbal aphasia. I'm sure I can help him along.

The weeks of enforced laziness were not entirely lost. I

finished my Bryn Mawr lectures and shall have them typed tomorrow. I shall send them directly to Rhys Carpenter, who is
the editor of the whole volume, without submitting them to
you; too much time would be lost. I'd feel much safer if you
could have passed judgment on the manuscript.

I also made some calls, had tea with the Zimmerns [Oxford
political science professor Sir Alfred Zimmern and Lady Zim-
mern], called on the Master of Wadham, to whom Morwitz
[personal friend in Germany] had given me an introduction,
and visited J. Z. [John Zachary] Young in his lab. He is the
man with whom I had had dinner the evening before I wrote
you last. Tomorrow I shall dine with him in Magdalen. On the
12th I dined with Cairns and with Sir Farquar Buzzard.* The
men had to go to a meeting, and I stayed on a little while with
the family. John, a lad of about 16, put on records, a nice boy,
and good records. I stayed for the first movement of the Emperor concerto.

Then I walked home through the black and blacked-out
night. It was really not so bad, but it is a strange experience to
walk through streets that are absolutely pitch black. It is only
about five minutes walk from here to the Cairns.

My mother is still near London, and my brother will leave
the house of a friend who got him by signing a guarantee for
him, so that I now have to support him too. So I am rather hard
up. However, that is the least important trouble in the world
of troubles.

I don't know what to think about the situation. You may
know more about than we, particularly if you get the U.S.
newspapers. We can do nothing but serve and wait. And, lest
I forget, don't ever reproach yourself for having got me here.
This was entirely my responsibility. You see, I might have left
when war came. And I didn't. And in this decision you had no
share. [20 September 1939, Oxford]

I dined at Magdalen with J. Z. Young and had a long discussion afterwards in the rooms of Wildon the philosophy tutor,
a very amusing and clever young person who had read my
book. . . . Called on the Master of Balliol, and on the White-

heads, great friends of the [Erwin] Schroedingers*. . . .

My work in the infirmary is fascinating. I saw another operation. Cairns came down to tell me that in 10 minutes they would have opened up, Pennybacker doing the preparatory work and Cairns taking over. So I saw him cut the dura and insert two brain needles. The result of the exploration was that he decided not to operate.

I am learning a lot, not only about brain lesions, but also about people. Talking with "general" and parlor maids, with stokers and bus drivers definitely broadens your horizons. My darling Jocelyn, the boy with the big fungus, has now got meningitis, but the doctors are rather optimistic. He is waiting for my visits every day, and I go and talk to him, even though for two days I have not worked with him. Such a nice and bright kid.

I have been asked to give a lecture to the Oxford University Medical Society, a student organization. They had asked Cairns' advice about the choice of lecturers, and he had told them about me. He, and, I am afraid, the whole Nuffield Department are going to come. Their first speaker is Sir Farquar Buzzard.

The Bryn Mawr lectures typed and corrected . . . at the moment I don't think they are too bad.

. . . About me you need not worry at all. I am perfectly well and at the same time taking good care of myself, with a break in the middle of the day and early to bed at night.

Life is very much as it was. I am afraid it will change a good deal once the German peace offer has come to naught. But sufficient for the day. I am feeling fine, do not worry. . . . you can do nothing better to preserve the years of our working together than what you are doing now. [1 October 1939, Oxford]

In letters arriving in Oxford on 8 October, Harrower briefed Koffka on her recent activities in Montreal:

Today I was awarded a National Research Fellowship, $1800 for me, $1,000 for an assistant, and $200 for expenses! I am thrilled at last in having my own department in a job I feel I've finally equipped myself for. It will be largely "weeding out the unstable," and preventing the wrong appointments. There is a great field and I will be "helping" in some way. Our war work will be staying here in the face of good U.S. offers, and postponing a family for a year or so.

Yesterday the Chief [Wilder Penfield] returned Part 1 of my article to me with the comment "Interesting and well constructed." Since he is a severe critic and none too bright where psychology is concerned, I need hardly say it was a pleasant surprise. I had a good talk with him about assistants and the work for the coming period. I feel at long last that he has "passed" on me, something I have never felt before. I delight in the idea of building up even a small department. By the way, the Chief wants my articles published in the *Archives of Neurology and Psychiatry* [Harrower-Erickson 1940a, 1940b], and will pay for the illustrations and graphs to go in. I am staggered by that! Incidentally, Eric [neurosurgeon Theodore Erickson, Harrower's husband] has two articles recently published, one in *Brain* on the hypothalamus, and another in the *Archives of Neurology and Psychiatry* on cardiac activity during attacks. He has two more accepted for publication, and the work on the book is nothing short of staggering. I'd be interested to know what Cairns thinks of the two recent articles which he has probably seen.

[KK] Your two letters have just reached me. My most delighted congratulations. A National Research Fellowship, that does mean something! And money for an assistant to boot. Simply marvelous. I am so glad for you, that you are being given the chance of doing really good research work. What you indicate of your plans seems most interesting. Even after my very limited experience I am struck by the influence exerted by the patient's personality on the effects of a brain operation.

So you can imagine with what expectations I am looking forward to your new article. How grand that the Chief approved of it in such flattering terms.

Supper with Cairns, the only other guest was Professor

Jefferson [Sir Geoffrey Jefferson] the neurosurgeon in Manchester. His wife is a doctor too. Cairns told me she studied with Sir
William Osler, and had read my book.

I expect to see the Schroedingers in Oxford during the weekend. I decided to go to the Radcliffe Science Library to do some
reading. Well, first of all I behaved like a silly ass. I walked
through the park, and discovered I had left my specs at home!
[8 October 1939, Oxford]

This has been a rather uneventful week. On Monday after
ward rounds I had lunch with Cairns and took the opportunity
for telling him about your fellowship, your work and your husband's publications. He had read the one on the hypothalamus
and thought it very good. On Wednesday I went to the Institute
of Human Anatomy, invited by Professor Le Gros Clark, the
man with whom I had traveled from Dundee. He is apparently
quite an important person, F.R.S. [a Fellow of the Royal Society
for the Advancement of Science], he always comes to our Monday ward rounds, having a very high opinion of Cairns. I am to
have dinner at his house Tuesday evening. Well, he simply
showed me his whole place from cellar to roof, it was my first
sight of a dissecting room—rather ghastly.

[Richard] Oldfield* very kindly sent me his copy of Gelb's*
posthumous lectures, published in the *Acta Psychologica 1937*,
Vol III. He gives a very concise and lucid statement of his and
Goldstein's views. You might enjoy reading it. [15 October 1939,
Oxford]

In letters arriving in Oxford on 20 October, Harrower chron-
icled an event which interested Koffka.

Eric has just returned from the Mayo Clinic, where he was
unofficially offered a job. It's to be head of research in neurophysiology but he can't make up his mind if, if he were offered it, he should desert Canada at this moment, and desert
neurosurgery. It's a pretty big decision. It would be much safer
to take this type of job because of his old lung lesion, but I

suppose the biggest prizes of satisfaction and achievement lie
along clinical and surgical lines, rather than research. But he
is good, and I am thrilled.

[KK] I have your two letters. . . . I cannot allow you to give
me anything like a gramophone for Christmas, but the book by
Weisenberg and McBride, if it is not too expensive, on aphasia,
would be wonderful.

. . . Unfortunately your second letter says nothing about the
decision regarding the Mayo Clinic. I can absolutely understand how difficult the decision is. To lay aside the marvelous
tool of surgery which so often restores health, for pure theoretical research is a piece of resignation unless one has very special ideas, hypotheses so fundamental that, if verified, they will
give a big push to human knowledge.

You will be at work now with your new assistant! How marvelous to think of you as having one and cooperating in work of
your own choosing.

Now a report on my week. Cairns came late on Sunday to
fetch me for the Balliol dinner. No wonder: it was a thick fog.
Driving was a nightmare. When we arrived the Common Room
was deserted, and so we sneaked into the hall for a delicious
dinner. After dinner in the Common Room the Master sat next
to me and we had a very good talk. When he left, the senior
tutor, a fellow of All Souls, came over with whisky and soda
and started a long political discussion. He is a modern historian. A very strange discussion it was too. Cairns told me two
days later that he had felt badly about it and had even wanted
to apologize. But I assured him that I had taken the manner
of the discussion rather as a compliment, as though he had
treated me as "belonging" and I had replied in the same spirit.
Cairns said: "You have been magnificent."

Yesterday when Cairns examined a patient I had an idea.
The woman indicated that she felt touch and prick more vividly on the ipsilateral side than on the counterlateral one.
While the anatomical possibilities of this were discussed it occurred to me that possibly her whole body schema might be

asymetrical, one side being the dominant side. So in the afternoon I tested her appreciation of position and her touch localization (on the hands) and a clear asymetry, of the ipsilateral
side was the result, a young doctor who helped me was absolutely convinced. I was quite thrilled and during the night
thought of more experiments, but she was already in the operating theatre when I came to the infirmary in the morning. I
went up later and watched for 2½ hours, an acoustic tumor.
Cairns had a little stool put up for me directly behind his left
shoulder and on several occasions explained the details to me.

This shows you at the same time how well I am now: 2½
hours with a mask on mouth and nose! I got home late for
lunch and decided not to go to the infirmary in the afternoon,
but to work on my material here. Then one of Cairns' secre-
taries telephoned, could he, later on, call for me and take me
home for a discussion of a paper by Oldfield. So we had, in the
late afternoon, a very good discussion over some glasses of excellent sherry. He very kindly said that he was afraid that they
would get more out of me than I out of them; of course I know
that this is not true, but it was so nice to hear it. . . .

On Tuesday I have my lecture. It seems that the rumors of
this have spread, so that in place of a relatively small student
audience I shall have a fairly large one composed of all sorts of
people. The whole Nuffield Department wants to go, including
Hortega [Spanish neurologist Don Pio Hortega], to whom I
have of course been introduced, but with whom I have exchanged no other word than "how do you do." Dr. Riddoch
[neurologist George Riddoch] will be down and will attend, as a
matter of fact Cairns would have asked me to dine with him
and Riddoch had I not been the guest of the student society
who are arranging these lectures. And Dr. Symonds
[neurologist Sir Charles Symonds*] left a message that he
would come from London for my lecture!

Well all this is rather frightening. I had not bargained on
this when I accepted. However, I'll have to go through with it
and hope to be able to give you a satisfactory report next
Sunday.

Harrower in 1940.

Meanwhile I am waiting for your paper. [29 October 1939, Oxford]

[MH] These long pauses between mails make correspondence difficult. . . . I am delighted that your work continues to be interesting, you will probably be able to amplify and expand my tentative ideas concerning the interaction of physical and psychological handicaps.

I am enjoying beyond words my work with Dr. Ross, a wise man indeed with a very fine medical and psychiatric knowledge and an open-mindedness and saneness towards his lack of instruction in psychology that makes him a joy [Donald Ross, M.D., appointed as a member of the newly developing psychology department to provide a close liaison with medicine]. He had outstanding recommendations and is a thoroughly fine person. I am sure that the partnership with him will produce some interesting things.

Eric is in charge of things for a week or so, other people being away. This means interrupted nights, late meals, and the general air of time not being one's own. In a way it does not matter so much now, but I am thankful we had a year and a half of normal living, for there is no question that these completely irregular comings and goings introduce a strain into a household.

I had a letter from Toronto today about my [radio] broadcast talks. They ask permission to publish them!! I don't suppose they will do me any good, but it is a compliment to have them want to do it. I suppose, like the Ford Sunday Hour, they will say "copies of Dr. Harrower's talk will be sent to you free to all who care to have them!"

Tomorrow we have a Halloween party of 24 people, I hope they will get into the apartment! It is supposed to be fancy dress. We have cut out two huge pumpkin faces with candles inside for decorations in the dark stairway.

A few nights ago we went to [physiologist] Helga Malloy's where were collected some ten other people including a Hungarian biologist Hans Selye. The object of the visit was to inaugurate a club, apparently the first of its kind in this benighted university, after the order of your Monday Club. In fact, my proposals based on your Monday Club finally were the only ones universally accepted. We shall not have a dinner, but a bier abend at someone's house, and a speaker, guests appropriately chosen. I hope it will work, the idea was for interdepartmental connections.

. . . I can't tell you how I wish you were safely over here, but I do see that there must be compensations and I think it is wonderful that you are managing it despite everything. Let me know if there is anything I can do. Love as always. [29 October 1939, Montreal]

Another letter from you today. I had one yesterday; that was a grand surprise. You don't know how all your very real and obvious success elates me. I always hoped that it would prove just the intellectual stimulus that it is proving; I hope you will publish much and often.

I find two assistants most stimulating, but hard work, for they are both fiends of energy, and must be supplied with activities all the time. I have got the profile-vase cards under way; when three more requests came in, I decided that something must be done about it.†

You will be glad that the arms embargo has been lifted. An interesting letter written to the Chief by Cushing [Harvey Cushing,* one of the first outstanding American neurosurgeons, died in 1939] a few days before he died, contained the state-

† An ambiguous figure can be so constructed that it is seen either as a vase or as two profiles looking at each other. The Harrower series consisted of seven pictures, one an ambiguous figure, three that enhanced the profiles, and three that enhanced the vase. These drawings, on large cards, were presented one at a time to normal subjects and brain-injured patients. While normal subjects can switch easily from one perceptual experience to another while looking at the ambiguous figure, brain-injured patients require progressive enhancement of the vase (or profiles) in order to overcome the first perception (Harrower, 1939).

ment that he wished the American Navy could be placed exclusively at the service of the British immediately. He probably represents one extreme, but it is interesting to have that on record. There is no question at all of where the U.S.'s sympathies lie; in Eric's part of the country (midwest) the feeling is quite different from what it was in the last war.

I am just waiting to get my chest X-rayed. A routine performance, and means nothing, but breaks up the morning. We go on our quarterly trip to Saranac tomorrow, that is always great fun, and involves a picnic lunch in a lovely spot in the Adirondacks.

I wish you could see Wendy [cocker spaniel] these days, she is so exquisitely graceful and gracious.

The broadcast talks cast rather a shadow over my life, the first was so successful that it puts a greater responsibility on me than I like. Well . . . I'll let this go. Thanks more than I can say for keeping me up-to-date in all your doings. You know how I love your letters . . . as always. [3 November 1939, Montreal]

[KK] No news from you but quite a lot to report from here. I had a letter from Mrs. Geraldine Head, Henry Head's cousin who now manages his house for him. Henry Head * [British neurologist] is very well, was delighted to hear from me and would very much like to see me if it was at all possible. So Cairns may some day drive me over. It was an awfully nice letter and the good news about Sir Henry was confirmed by Riddoch when I saw him.

Riddoch had accompanied one of his patients to Oxford, and in the afternoon he came to see me. We had a very long and most delightful talk. When I first saw him, I thought he was Jewish, then when he spoke, I heard that he was Scottish and when later he called himself an Aberdonian, I asked him about your family. He knew your grandfather John Forbes White [art collector and critic] and knew your Uncle John Harrower. From the very first, I felt perfectly at home with him, as though we had known each other for years. Of course Cairns had done a lot to prejudice him in my favor. He had told him of several

things I had done, among them the investigation I mentioned
in my last letter, the schema test.

Now about my lecture. When we arrived, shortly before
eight, the room was filled to capacity. Every seat taken and a
few people sitting on the floor. About 200 in all. Cairns, Riddoch and Symonds in the second row and practically the whole
Nuffield Department scattered among the audience. Then after
some society business had been dispatched, I gave my lecture
"Elementary Conceptions of Gestalt Psychology and Some of
Their Applications in Medicine." I spoke for about 55 minutes,
very elementary and almost entirely on perception in a larger
biological context, not wanting to overload the short period.

You know that I truly dislike this kind of lecture, because
one cannot do anything at all within the short period. How can
one explain problems of psychology and of Gestalt Theory to a
mixed audience in which the majority has no pre-existing
knowledge. Add to this the presence of a great neurologist—
and I believe [Oxford psychologist] William Brown was
there too!

Well, afterwards there was a discussion lasting a good half
hour. Someone in the audience sent up a note suggesting that
Dr. Riddoch be requested to say a few words. Riddoch made a
very nice speech trying to give some more examples of Gestalt
function from his own observations. Then there was the ubiq-
uitous commentator who wanted to know whether Gestalt Psychology had improved the conditions of the working classes! At
last it was over. Cairns had told me that he would drive me
home or take me to his house for a chat with Riddoch and Symonds if I did not feel too tired. Symonds said literally it had
been the most lucid exposition of any subject he had ever
heard. Well, that did please me.

Then I was beleaguered by so many students who wanted to
speak to me. Cairns told me the next day that it had been "a
magnificent show" and that Symonds had said he would not
mind coming to Oxford every week from London for such a
lecture.

On Thursday Cairns cut off the fungus of my little boy patient. I watched for one and a half hours. The boy seems quite well now but he has not spoken yet to his mother or to me. Though he did say a few words to the nurses. I hope he will pull through.

The next day, R. C. Oldfield and Oliver Zangwill [subsequently professor of psychology in Cambridge] came for conferences with me and Cairns. I talked with them for several hours during the afternoon, giving them my criticism of a paper written by them jointly. [Oldfield and Zangwill were junior members of the Psychology Department at Cambridge when Koffka was writing.]

I forgot to say that Cairns suggested that I publish my lecture in a medical journal if the writing up does not mean too much work. But I'm afraid it would since I spoke from notes which gave the framework and improvised in accordance with the situation. Besides, it is so elementary that I don't think it should be done.

I had a nice letter from your mother. You evidently told her about my heart attack and I set her mind at rest. She asked me to lunch with her when I came to London.

A few more things about my work. I might have told you in my last letter that my range of patients has now been so broadened to include a Jewish boy from the east side of London where the father has a small jeweler's shop. He had a cerebellar tumor removed and suffered from hallucinations afterwards which I tried to explore. He has a stammer caused apparently by a fright which he got when he was five years old. He is now 16. Probably a trained psychotherapist might find out a great deal. But I was afraid of meddling. The Rorschach test would be interesting in this case.

Then there is a Miss Campo, 53 years old with a nominal aphasia, due either to a temporal hemorrhage or a neoplasm. No operation is considered. I have a great amount of material from her. I am trying systematically to test all sorts of avenues that do or do not give access to language traces: naming of objects, opposites, functions, (glass—to drink from), parts of a whole, etc. The "function" test gives naturally the best results because it is this process which she uses when in object naming she cannot find the proper word.

Well, yesterday she produced the following response: "piano"—"sing, no, er, how do you call it when you play? ah play." Marvelous, isn't it? I find things a good deal more complicated than would appear from Gelb's brilliant but oversimplified presentation. I must stop. You have no time to read whole books! But I enjoy writing to you so much that I can find no end. [5 November 1939, Oxford]

Very little happened during the week. On Sunday night I dined in the huge hall of Christ Church among the students and had port in the buttery and sat for a short while in the Junior Common Room. It was again a vile night, dark and raining. On Monday, I found a very cordial note from Stephenson inviting me to dinner at Corpus on the preceding Sunday. We have now fixed it for a week from today. Meanwhile I have visited him at the Institute of Experimental Psychology. This has worked out well and is pleasantly established.

Yesterday morning Cairns telephoned to tell me that the Jeffersons were here from Manchester and would very much like to talk to me. You may remember that I had met him once in Cairns' house and that she was a student of Sir William Osler and also a psychologist. I had a splendid talk with them. Pennybacker and a man from Edinburgh were present part of the time. I showed them some of my case records, explained my methods, and some of the ideas which guide me. Mrs. Jefferson took many notes for her own use. Then I took them to see little Jocelyn and demonstrated certain things I had spoken about. They are awfully nice people. He has, I believe, a very high reputation as a neurosurgeon, about equal to that of Cairns. And they asked me to stay with them for a few days in Manchester.

During Christmas shopping I had a nice experience. I was in a large second-hand book shop. The owner was a man with real knowledge and love of books. He said: "May I ask you a very impertinent question?" I said: "Certainly." So he asked me

whether I was the author of the *Principles*. And when I told
him I was, he told me his son, a biologist, had a great venera-
tion for me and had been strongly influenced in his thinking
and even in his planning of his career by my book! You will
understand what real satisfaction one gets from such news.
[12 November 1939, Oxford]

Your two letters, October 29 and November 3 arrived on Sunday morning.

My congratulations on your success on the wireless! I'm very
curious to see the printed report, because I cannot imagine the
kind of material that can be presented to a radio audience nor
the form in which it can be done.

I hear that Schroedinger* is now in Dublin where De Valera
[Irish prime minister Eamon De Valera] plans to build up a
research institute like the Princeton one. At the moment
Schroedinger seems to be just an ordinary professor, but De
Valera attended his inaugural lecture.

I hope your Halloween party was a great success. I am sure it
was lots of fun. I told Cairns of Cushing's letter to Penfield.
Naturally he was very much pleased.

. . . I greatly enjoy the give and take in my professional in-
tercourses, particularly as so far I have not found a trace of
antagonism against the psychologist outsider—which would
have been quite understandable. I am to dine with Sir Alfred
Zimmern in New College and in two weeks, with William
Brown at Christ Church. I had an extremely friendly note from
him. I had supper with Cairns on Thursday to meet a Mr.
Sumner, a historian at Balliol. A very charming person with
the hands and face of an artist or poet.

On the wards a really dramatic incident when a patient succeeded in understanding a connection of relation after a series
of seemingly endless failures. The patient enjoyed it as much
as I did. I will try the same with little Jocelyn when I am to see
him together with Dr. Symonds whose patient he was
originally.

I am staying at home most afternoons to keep my records in

order. Tabulating the results in different ways takes an awful
lot of time but it is absolutely necessary. [19 November 1939,
Oxford]

[MH] Last night I simply had to send a cable to you for I feel
that it is untold ages since I wrote and even longer since you
received a letter from me . . . can that be, yes, I suppose so! I
got your letter of November 12th yesterday, and have had several others which I have not answered, so I decided that today
must have as its prime concern a letter to you. It is not that
your letters are any less eagerly looked for or devoured, but
these weeks have been quite exceptional.

They have been perhaps the most satisfying of my time here,
partly because we have become organized into a real department, partly because, with an assistant working for me, things
got done which would otherwise have piled up, and partly because we are on the scent of a really interesting discovery of
neurotic personality types which may cut across the accepted
psychiatric delineations in an interesting way.

But most of all I think, because at long last I came to grips
with the Chief instead of skating along paths of completely different thought. The business with the Chief arose with my
pages in the manuscript Part II [Harrower-Erickson 1940b]
concerning their case K. M. He was very angry with my first
presentation which quoted from the case history instead of
their MS which I had never, and could never, have seen! This
led to my writing out in great detail my point of view, which I
think I mailed to you, and his very decent and very generous
comment in answer.

On the heels of that I had to address all the neurologists in
Montreal, in his room, to tell them of the use of the Rorschach
in this particular war situation (a short survey of which I will
send you sometime). This was very successful, so much so that
he wrote me a note from New York telling me my presentation
was "excellent." An unheard of thing; and asking that I do his
Rorschach! This means at long last I need not have my "inferiority complex" with the Chief, and it is a great relief!

I am delighted that you had such a good time with the Jeffersons. I loved your story of the bookseller's question. I am sure your Rorschach will be different when you come back from Oxford, you have established so many different types of relationships with people. I love to think of you working there! It has been, as you know, one of the really greatest desires of my life to have you productive in a realm where it will tell. While I am apprehensive about you in England in wartime, I still am delighted that the thing did come off, and very anxious to see what they will do when the idea of your leaving has to be faced.

What else is there to tell you? We lead a very quiet though busy life. No decision has been needed with regard to the Mayo Clinic yet, as it was a feeler on their part. I do not think that Eric will really want it, even though the chance of research, which one sees extinguished in all but the very greatest surgeons is very tempting. In many ways, all the selfish ones, I would like an ordered life better than a clinical one. With no financial worries, I mean the steady salary which means one could forget money, rather than the endless collecting bills from patients, and the knowledge that at least part of your life was your own. It is hard to face the idea of being so completely at the mercy of important cases. On the other hand, I think the really good brain surgeons are fewer than the good physiologists, so it is more of a challenge. However, I think I can adjust to either when the time comes. I wish you could hear the Saturday concerts which Toscanini is giving . . . all the Beethoven symphonies. They start at 10, so we go to bed in a most restful manner. As ever. [26 November 1939, Montreal]

[KK] No letter from you and a rather uneventful week. Dinner at Corpus last Sunday was particularly nice. I had a long talk with a very charming President Livingstone [Sir Richard Livingstone, president of Corpus Christi College], and an extremely interesting one with the philosopher Paton [Oxford professor of moral philosophy Herbert J. Paton].

On Wednesday I attended a lecture which Harold Nicolson [English diplomat and journalist] gave on the diplomatic background of the war: a very well prepared and delivered lecture. Very pleasant to listen to though not particularly new in content. [26 November 1939, Oxford]

[MH] I am sitting up in bed listening to Toscanini play the 9th. There have been a wonderful series of concerts on Saturday evenings and this is the climax. . . . My thoughts will be with you during the Andante.

Unfortunately just an hour ago Eric had to leave for Vermont on an emergency call, he will travel all night and bring back the patient with him. I managed to write you a long letter last Sunday, which I hope reaches you safely, I also sent off a little parcel. The manuscript left some time ago, as did the Profile-Vase cards.

I give my last broadcast talk this week; I've had fan mail from all over Canada, from Manitoba to Nova Scotia!! [2 December 1939, Montreal]

Yours of November the 19th has just come, at a marvelous moment. There are no ward rounds today as the Chief is away, and I don't have a patient for an hour. . . .

I agree with you about the Binet, it's of very little value [for reflecting certain types of brain damage]. I argued against it in connection with the Hebb and Penfield article, but got into hot water [Hebb and Penfield 1940]. About the radio talks, there have been five in this series. Since I don't know when you'll see the reports I'll tell you the subject matter.

1. What psychology is *not*. Examples of experimental situations, [Tamara] Dembo on anger, the association test for detecting thieves, the psychogalvanometer [comparable to a "lie detector"].

2. Learning, remembering, forgetting. Learning to type, plateaus, slow motion study.

What we want to forget. Substitution of another activity. The talk loaded with examples.

3. Child psychology. Developmental studies beginning with a

paraphrase of you! "In fact a famous psychologist once began
his book on Child Psychology by admitting that at heart every
mother feels she knows more about her child, than any scientist, no matter how learned, can ever know. And instead of
telling her in ponderous terms that what she knows is of no
importance, this author sensibly admitted that the knowledge
of the mother, and that of the scientist are different in kind,
both necessary and both important in our ultimate understanding of human beings." Some of [Arnold] Gesell's studies, bodily
and behavioral stages. Huang's "tooth pick" example showing
mental stages.

4. Child again. Nature, Nurture, Johnny and Jimmy. The
environmental influence in studies like [Kurt] Lewin's* on
Dictator-Democratic groups, showing aggression towards the
scapegoat.

5. This week's not yet given. "Social psychology." Political
opinion swung by emotional attitudes, inconsistency prejudice.
Mechanisms of self deception. Unreliability of testimony.

I jog along in a chatty way. People who matter seem to think
they are really good. Eric and my assistant always see them
first and criticize.

Eric is back from Vermont, bringing the patient. He asked
$10 for the consultation, but they gave him $50. He can't get
away from the fact that these things should be done because
they need to be done, and he can do them. I wish you knew
him. [4 December 1939, Montreal]

[KK] On Monday your cable, then your letter to Penfield,
your manuscript and the Harrower pictures. Thank you for all
of them. I think your letter to Penfield is extremely good. I do
not trust crude intelligence scores at all for the question of
whether an operation, say, has changed a person, or not. The
raw score is made up by summation of so many unanalyzed
items, that an improvement in score—perhaps the more superficial ones—may overcompensate a deterioration in a few more
important ones. I am now no longer speaking on purely the-

oretical grounds, but I have now some experience to substanti-
ate this claim. To me no test result that is not analyzed means
anything for the individual diagnosis.

Your three papers are frightfully interesting. I gave them to
Cairns together with an offprint of your article. He will be
reading them now. If he is sufficiently impressed he may want
the Rorschach Technique introduced here. Naturally I could
not do it, it is a whole time job, and would make it impossible
for me to do the work I am most interested in. But perhaps we
might get somebody else for this.

The Harrower pictures arrived at a very good moment. I
have used them twice, first with a woman of high intelligence
who has an inoperable deep-seated tumor of both frontal lobes
involving the corpus callosum, and other parts. It is frightfully
difficult to find any defects in her behavior. So far the only very
clear indication is the lack of understanding of jokes. The
Baker joke is extremely useful in this regard. [The Baker joke
was used by Harrower in her doctoral dissertation (Harrower
1932).]

She behaved quite normally with regard to the Harrower pictures except that she said of Vase 3 she saw "a vase with a fish
in it or worms." How would you, with your experience judge
that? Also when she saw Profile 3 she said "You have changed
them into women. They were all men before." This hardly
seems normal does it?

The other case is also frontal with some speech disturbance.
He acted typically in not being able to change from one aspect
to the other.

When I saw Cairns to show him your "figures" he asked me
about my dinner with Stephenson at Corpus. This gave me the
chance of telling him that S. had asked me whether I should
not like to become attached to Corpus. I had replied I should
like to very much indeed, but that I felt under some sort of
obligation to Balliol. When I told Cairns he was delighted. He
said that Corpus was an excellent college, its president Sir
Richard Livingstone the best type of Englishman, the finest

product of Oxford, and that I could not do better. Corpus, incidentally, was the college of [William] MacDougall* and [Ferdinand] Schiller. So I wrote Stephenson a note and got a very enthusiastic reply.

From Corpus to New College! I had a very pleasant evening with Sir Alfred Zimmern. It was a perfect night, a full moon, and no cloud in the sky. . . . I talked to a number of interesting people, as a matter of fact in the Common Room old Joseph, Schiller's arch enemy, allowed himself to be drawn into a philosophical discussion, to Sir Alfred's surprise. Afterwards we were asked by the Warden, the grand [historian and statesman] H.A.L. Fisher to his house where we listened to Chamberlain's very good speech and had some political discussion. Fisher told some interesting stories from his experience in Lloyd George's Cabinet.

These Sunday evenings in college are the highlights of my life here, except for the thrills in the infirmary. Tonight dinner at "The House" [Christ Church] with William Brown. I could write much more about my work . . . but I have to prepare a test for my frontal lobe patient. [3 December 1939, Oxford]

Dinner at The House last Sunday was pleasant. I sat next to the Dean, and finally met Professor Lindeman, the physicist who had been chiefly responsible for getting Schroedinger his appointment in Oxford four or five years ago, but who now has considerably cooled towards him.

. . . I may go to London for Christmas, though I don't see how I can afford it. If so, I'll be in touch with your mother, of course. Oh! I got an invitation to lecture to the Cambridge Psychological Society sometime in February, and stay during my visit with Thouless [Robert Thouless,* psychology lecturer at Cambridge]. Of course I have accepted, although that too will mean extra expense.

. . . The week started with a letter from Professor Paton, vice president of Corpus, telling me that I have been elected a member of their Common Room for the duration of my stay in Oxford. I was at first very pleased, but my pleasure was somewhat dampened when I hear that this is quite an expensive business. However, there is nothing to be done about it now. I shall dine in the hall on the first Sunday of the new term.

. . . The only other event worth reporting was that Mr. Little, that medical student, retired officer, who sometime ago had asked me for dinner, came to the Radcliffe to ask me for tea. It was a very interesting time because he told me a lot about himself and his family. He had a hard time and was once near complete collapse, but was helped by a practicing psychologist and seems now well adjusted. A very interesting story, much too long to tell.

. . . I was tremendously thrilled by the naval action off Montevideo,† and am now waiting, like everybody else, for the sequel, which will be ancient history when you get this letter.

A happy New Year to you . . . and loads of love and affection. [10 and 17 December 1939, Oxford]

Look at the address! [70 Gloucester Place] Not very far from your lodging in 1932–33 when you lectured at Bedford College! Now a boarding house for refugees, where my mother is staying, a nice place in what must once have been a very beautiful house.

. . . First to acknowledge your letters of the 21st, 26th, Dec. 2nd and 4th.

. . . I am thrilled at your success with the Chief. I have read your short article, it may interest Cairns very much, and probably Symonds still more, because he is particularly keen on a test that discriminates organic function and malingering cases. I shall give the paper to Cairns next week and when I have supper with him discuss your other papers. They are all definite contributions, but you will know that they fail to satisfy me completely because of their purely empirical basis. I am

---

† The *Graf Spee*, a German ship preying on British merchant ships in the Atlantic, was cornered by British cruisers in the neutral port of Montevideo, Uruguay, in 1939. When forced to leave the harbor, it was scuttled by the German crew.

hoping for more psychology, and eventually I am sure you will supply that.

Your wireless talks seem to have been grand. That is the kind of thing I could never do.

I spoke to your father yesterday. I shall go to see them on Wednesday afternoon and stay for dinner, so in my next letter I will give you a full report.

My mother sends you her love. I am so grateful that you are happy in your work and in your home. [25 December 1939, London]

This is to be a Cheam letter [Harrower's old home, where her parents lived]. I took the train from Victoria Station, and since it was still light when I got to Cheam, I tried to find my way to the cottage, but instead of turning right at the first traffic light I went straight ahead and so got lost. However, eventually I met a postman who directed me, and when I came to the corner of your street I saw an old gentleman coming from the opposite direction. It was your father who had been to visit his sister in a nursing home.

He was very cordial and when we entered the house asked me for my bag, they had expected me to stay overnight, which I had not been aware of. They offered me pajamas and all other necessaries, but it seemed simpler to return by the last train.

Your mother looks better and younger than I have seen her for years. She was lively and in very good spirits. Proudly she showed me the two cables from her children, from Canada and Australia. Your father also is amazingly well. He took a lively part in the conversation and asked me a good deal about Germany, explained why he liked English Gothic better than French, and discussed your brother's career with me. There were hundreds of Christmas cards all over the drawing room. We sat for a long time over an excellent tea, and when I went upstairs to wash and came down again, your father poured out the sherry and your mother appeared in a black dress with her beautiful Venetian lace. Then a royal dinner, soup, pheasant, and the best Christmas pudding I have ever had. Your mother telephoned for a taxi and the man came a little ahead of time so that my visit to the kitchen to see Catherine had to be curtailed.

Then home in an unlighted and unheated train. A very pleasant afternoon and evening, it was good to be in Cheam again and during dinner to look at your portrait and to see how amazingly good it is. Your parents could not have been nicer. As I said, your mother has not been so well for a long time, and your father though he is an old man, does not show any signs of being an invalid.

. . . On Thursday I was to have dinner with Riddoch, but his secretary telephoned to say that to his great regret he had to cancel the engagement because of an urgent case. Yes, doctors are never masters of their time. I left London on Friday for Oxford. The train was full of soldiers on leave. I telephoned Cairns and shall have supper with him tomorrow to discuss your papers. I'll bring him your last one.

. . . It is so cold, I now have to turn on my electric stove. I shall probably be alone when the New Year enters tonight, and then I shall think of you, and of old times. [31 December 1939, Oxford]

I am afraid that this letter will be late for your birthday! Even so it carries all my best wishes to you. I have just been in town to have a small parcel dispatched to you, a very modest present indeed, a book which may interest you. I shall think of you on the day as you know.

. . . I had supper with Cairns and a long discussion and talk with him, frightfully pleasant, on your articles among other things. He had not read the last one, he is terribly busy. He is not yet quite convinced that your tumor results are significant. Could they not, that is his argument, be indicative of exhaustion, rather than of the specific causes of exhaustion. I did not remember the articles well enough to answer this criticism, but he suggests that a number of Rorschachs be given to patients who are exhausted for different reasons, i.e. pneumonia. What is your reaction to that?

The articles will be shown to Symonds, because of their potential importance for war work. Cairns does not see that he can afford a special person at Radcliffe to do just Rorschachs, particularly since he is convinced that you will take care of the research side. I cannot take it up, and Oldfield does not want to do so without some special training. But it may well be that Symonds will want somebody for his war hospital which is to be opened before very long.

Then Cairns asked me if I would give a series of University Lectures either in the next, or the last term. I said I would be delighted, and suggested the final term. He agreed for many reasons, one being that the lectures would come in the evening and that it would then be much less of a strain for the lecturer and the audience to attend them when the days were longer. I am quite thrilled at the prospect, and I know you will be pleased.

With loads of love . . . and all good wishes for a fruitful and contented and peaceful new year. [12 January 1940, Oxford]

I was much distressed to hear about [Kurt] Goldstein* and I hope that [Leonard] Carmichael* will call him to Tufts. I did not know that the Montefiore appointment had a time limit. I wish I could do something for him but I don't see what I could do. [Harrower was able to report later: I have just heard from the Goldsteins that they have been appointed to Tufts. I am so glad. I wish Alan Gregg [of the Rockefeller Foundation] would fix you up somewhere in the same vicinity. The Goldsteins wrote such a nice letter to me about the "active way in which I had proved my friendship during the winter."]

Your advice about the Rorschach appointment will be taken. I discussed the problem with Oldfield and even then we had decided that it would probably be wisest to consult C. J. C. Earl [Rorschach expert in England] if a Rorschach person were wanted here. I wrote to Earl, and got a very nice reply from him. Cairns has been away and therefore your papers have not yet been given to Symonds, who seems much interested. Things go slowly, I am sorry to say, but eventually something may develop. In the very unlikely event of your coming to England, I am sure you would be welcomed here with open arms.

Tonight I shall dine in Corpus, the first time as a member of the Common Room. The uninterrupted cold is quite a strain, particularly as the dining room is freezingly cold. However, I am perfectly well. But I do wish that the thermometer would jump above the freezing point.

Your broadcasting success is stupendous: speaking to the Rotarians, and being broadcast on the National network, that is real fame! As to Oxford: only yesterday I told you that Lady Zimmern wants me to stay, but that is a pious wish and quite unofficial. Still I don't say that there is no possibility of my being asked, or at least the chances being discussed. You see, last night at Corpus the Vice President, Prof. [Herbert] Paton, a philosopher, spent the whole evening with me; after having sat next to him at dinner, he asked me to sit with him in the Common Room, and had coffee and smokes served there instead of going up to the smoking room, we found ourselves in thorough agreement about matters philosophical, and he asked me whether I could give some philosophical lectures in Corpus next term. I accepted of course, but turned it into a seminar on Köhler's book on value [Köhler 1938]. He seemed very pleased. So in the Trinity term I shall give University lectures and have a college seminar. What I shall do if there is a question of something more permanent raised, will depend on conditions. I am also bound to return to Smith for at least one year, unless I refund them the half salary they are paying me this year. However, I shall cross that bridge when I come to it, and quite honestly believe that during the war the chance, though perhaps not zero, is very small. [21 January 1940, Oxford]

No new letter from you. So I can continue a part of my last letter, i.e. make comments on your Rorschach papers. On Wednesday I found them all on my desk with a message from Symonds that he wanted very much to discuss them with me on the following day. So we met for an hour and talked things over.

He was tremendously interested and very much impressed by the quality of your work and the clarity of your presentation. But he said that in order to be fully convinced he would have to work at the test for a considerable time. I argued that there could be no doubt about the accuracy of your results, that both your own standards and Penfield's great caution were sufficient guarantee for that. He was particularly impressed when it transpired that Earl was the Rorschach expert in this country, because, so he said, Earl would never take up anything phoney.

Nevertheless, nothing will be done at the moment. But if he encounters a man among his many neurological collaborators who has experience with the Rorschach he will take it up again. At the same time, admitting the validity of your findings, Symonds had the same feeling of dissatisfaction about the lack of insight we possess about the relation between the undoubted success of the test and its actual data, the same thing which we have discussed so often.

I re-read your three papers carefully on Wednesday afternoon in preparation for my conference with Symonds, and made a number of notes, some of which I shall refer to later. But again, I had the same feeling of insecurity. Why, so I asked myself again and again, has so little truly psychological work been done about the test. If you reply that such work has been done and that I simply do not know it, an answer that may be perfectly true, I should have to ask: why do you not utilize or even mention such work in your papers! By this I mean, e.g. what is the contribution of the individual cards to the total score?

I have seen what a total score means in the Stanford Binet, and am thoroughly distrustful of it, therefore I am not willing to accept a Rorschach total score without criticism.

Similarly: considering the enormous importance that is attached to the color responses, why just those colors and no others. Surely scientific method demands an independent verification of different variables, in this case: the same shapes in different colors and different shapes, and the same colors.

I see tremendous scope for true Rorschach research, but

without such research I do not feel too comfortable even about your results, or rather their interpretation. [4 February 1940, Oxford]

[MH] Did you know that His Excellence (Lord Tweedsmuir)* died last night? So the place is gradually returning to normal this morning. Everyone looks very weary and black under the eyes as everything possible was done to save him. I saw the X-ray photo this morning, an enormous shift of the ventricle, only one filled. I shall see the brain later today. It is very unusual for a thrombosis to cause such swelling apparently. The various operations were to relieve pressure. The first removal of fluid from the ventricle, the next a subtemporal decompression, and the last to cut the tentorium. He was much beloved here, and it's a great loss.

. . . Eric feels that I have been working under rather a strain lately and he wants me to rest up a bit. [12 February 1940, Montreal]

The Rotarians brought me two more lectures, but after that I have promised to refuse all invitations. But the two I have received from the Chamber of Commerce and the St. James Literary Club, the oldest organization of its kind in Montreal, are supposed to be things one ought not to miss. Both have asked for the same talk, so that it can hardly be considered a strain. [13 February 1940, Montreal]

Your first question, what is the contribution of the individual cards is rather easy to answer. They were each evolved to call out certain specific types of "perceptions" or "perceptual determinants," not only individually, but in relation one to the other. Rorschach experimented for almost ten years until he finally selected from the thousands of blots those which facilitated or gave the opportunities he wanted in the sequence. I quote: "Not every picture obtained in this way can be used, as there are several conditions to be fulfilled. For one thing, the shapes must be relatively simple."

I started a long Rorschach reply to your criticism which you will eventually get, but it is the kind of thing that the more I think about it, the more there seems to be. Added to this, I have really so much extra writing to do, lectures, and the chapter for the Penfield-Erickson book [1941], and now finally a plea from the psychology students in McGill for me to give a big evening lecture on the Rorschach, despite the Psychology Department's attitude! This is perhaps the most formidable thing so far, they wish to open it to the University at large. When all that is over, March 12th, I still have Atlantic City and Cincinnati but hope very much to get away for 10 days or so in late March or early April.

I am surprised, however, at how much fun I really derive from thinking and writing these days. I really prefer an evening in which I can work even after a hard day at the Institute. As a sort of hobby I am taking up graphology, a thing I have always been interested in, actually it is more complicated than the Rorschach, it is a real discipline with endless detailed and minute observations to be made, but I am sure rewarding finally. Today Ross speaks to the Fellows Society on Psychology in the Service of Medicine, I am looking forward to that. The other night the Chief who is in hiding for three weeks, had Eric and [neurophysiologist] Herbert Jasper* and me out to hear part of the book and offer criticisms. He was dealing with the type of experience, dreams, hallucinations, and evoked memories which arise as the result of stimulation of the temporal lobe. He now speaks of underlying neural patterns of memory which are set off together with a recorded electric discharge, in certain areas. All very fascinating. How I wish you had been there to give some really pertinent suggestions. All we did was to prevent him from getting in wrong, and spoiling his work in the eyes of some people by too laymanlike use of certain psychological terms. I wished it could be done oftener, I mean discussion of that kind. [19 February 1940, Montreal]

[KK] On the eve of my departure to Cambridge, I met Alan Gregg, and O'Brian (of the Rockefeller Paris office) at the

Cairnses' where Oldfield and I had been invited for supper. Gregg began to speak about you spontaneously, and told how you got your fellowship, and how he had had his little joke about it with Lambert [also with Rockefeller], knowing that you simply could not be turned down. He also said that he is going to visit me in Northampton in the fall. He seemed to mean it and I am curious to know what he wants to discuss with me. A very pleasant evening. Cambridge: I stayed with Thouless,* who was extremely nice and hospitable and made life as easy for me as he could, but the house is rather primitive and it was fairly cold.

. . . Whether the people at the meeting liked my paper I have no idea. There was some discussion, and Thouless said that it had been the best he had heard in that society for a long time. . . . I saw lots of people, and sat next to the Master, Sir William Spence, the Civil Defense Commissioner, for the whole district. . . . Yesterday I heard our Chancellor, [British statesman] Lord Halifax, lecture in the Sheldonian, a rare and exquisite pleasure. It would have been fun, and good propaganda, to have his voice and that of Hitler and Goebbels [Nazi propaganda minister Joseph Goebbels] on the same record! What a contrast, what a difference in level!

I saw [Sir Frederic] Bartlett* for 20 minutes in the lab. He is very busy and he explained that he was so tired in the evening that he did not go out. So he did not come to my paper that evening. I can't help feeling that there is more behind it, particularly when I compare Adrian's* [Edgar Douglas Adrian, British physiologist] cordial behavior here in Oxford with Bartlett's correct but definitely not expansive attitude. [28 February 1940, Oxford]

[MH] Your last letter was full of interest. I am disturbed about Bartlett. I found his letter which you forwarded, most constrained, very strange. But far more strange is not going to hear you speak. I can only conjecture that it is a hangover from his violent German prejudice or that of his wife, combined with the fact that he is jealous of your Oxford success, and that

Oldfield has gone over there to work with you. I know that
Miss Harvey's [English psychologist Margaret Harvey] going
over to work with you was a blow to him, she herself told me.
But it still seems outrageous that he should not have treated
you as the honored guest that you are. About your meeting
Gregg, I am more than delighted, and his Northampton visit
sounds just what I would like. About two years ago he asked
me if there were other psychologists in England, other than the
Cambridge group I mean, whom he might consider giving aid
to. [13 March 1940, Montreal]

Harrower's suggestions seemed to make sense to Koffka, who
concluded the topic in a subsequent letter.

Your analysis of Bartlett's behavior interested me very much.
As an added piece of information which fits somehow into your
pattern, I tell you this: During the half hour or so I talked with
him, he suddenly said he wanted to ask me a confidential question: What did I think of Oldfield. I told him that I had a very
high opinion of him, that he did good work in Oxford, and that
Cairns liked him and his contribution very much, to which he
replied that he was glad to hear it, but that Oldfield had better
look out, this was the last chance that he, Bartlett, was giving
him; if he again changed over to something else as he had done
constantly in the past, his Rockefeller fellowship would be
withdrawn. I reiterated that I did not see the slightest reason
for believing that Oldfield would not persevere in this work
which seemed to be his real interest, and the matter was
dropped. I told nobody of this conversation, not even Oldfield, I
tell you because it seems like a piece in the jigsaw puzzle for
you to place. [31 March 1940, Oxford]

Reports of work continued from Montreal and Oxford.

[MH] There is really so much to answer and say that I am
almost swamped. Days ago I started to write a reply to some of
your Rorschach criticisms, I find part of it now, which I enclose

. . . but work has been so pressing that I just had to let it go.

I have one more rather important speaking engagement, that is to the psychology students. One boy came saying that they felt that they had "prejudiced dead wood" at the head of the department and would I not speak to the group of them on what I was doing. This has grown into a big evening lecture in the McGill ballroom! and will be quite a task for I have to give a bird's-eye view of the method and scoring and then show some results.

I enjoyed greatly my talks before the Board of Trade and the St. James Literary Society. I have now quite got over the worst aspects of stage fright and answered questions in both places for over an hour. In one place I had to get up and answer directly, in the other I had pencil and paper and was given time to reply to them all at the end.

Both experiences quite new to me. I particularly enjoyed the St. James Society, of which Tweedsmuir was Patron, for their questions were more philosophical than the very practically minded Board of Trade.

. . . Later: Another hectic day. We are about capacity as far as cases go. I have just been asked by the leading endocrinologist, J. S. L. Browne to cooperate on a very fascinating study. Testosterone being given to dwarfed children, who show marked personality changes. A psychological Rorschach, study before-after treatment. I have just been appointed to the Royal Victoria Hospital on the staff, as far as I know the only non-MD ever to get such an appointment. I'll do some theoretical thinking on the Rorschach; for the time being I have to keep it on this level! [7 March 1940, Montreal]

[KK] You need not have worried about me because of the cold. The pipes here did not burst, we had hot water every day. Though the dining room was at times at freezing, there was an electric fire in the lounge, and a small electric stove in my room. I am terribly sorry for your people in Cheam, it must have been awful for them, and I am only glad your mother is recovering from the effects of that extended cold spell.

This week with Ribbentrop [Nazi foreign minister Joachim von Ribbentrop] in Rome seems to be frightfully important and pregnant with all sorts of possibilities. By the time you get this letter we shall know what it led to. I shall be very glad to see your friend Dr. Cone when he arrives here.

There is one truly sad piece of news: I heard yesterday that Duncker [psychologist Karl Düncker, a student of Köhler's] had committed suicide. I knew that he had another breakdown, the Köhlers had taken him into their house, and the crisis seemed to have passed when the catastrophe happened. I was badly shaken, an unusually gifted man, whose tragedy was perhaps that he was a German, and, as such could not find the connection between reality and the ideal. Psychology has suffered a great loss, of that I am certain.

I have been invited to be the official guest, together with Pieron [French psychologist Henri Pieron] of the British Psychological Society at their extended meeting in Birmingham from April 4–8th. So of course I shall go. They will pay all expenses. Very generous indeed. There I shall meet Earl.

Your letter of Feb. 29th arrived two days ago. I was thrilled to hear of the different engagements you had and the joy you derive from reading and writing psychology. Graphology, if intelligently done, should be a mine of fruitful research. I hope that in the stress of all your various occupations you won't forget to give me full accounts of your various lectures, papers.

All my very best wishes. Last night I dreamed that you had come on a visit to England. [10 March 1940, Oxford]

Back from Birmingham. Apart from the cold weather it was very nice and very successful. It started with a great gesture! On the first evening, I was elected an Honorary Member of the British Psychological Society! The papers were in part lousy, but some were good, and after Pear's [Thomas Pear, Manchester University psychology professor] I started a long discussion which was continued on Sunday night and lasted till almost midnight. Pear spoke on the Trivial and the Popular in Psychology, defended his own publications on non-trivial subjects, like war, against criticism and attacked the lab psychologists. I made a long speech which under the circumstances was rather difficult, and to my great surprise I not only got loud applause but had several other speakers on my side, among them Thouless who declared that much as he regretted having to desert his old teacher, he had to agree with me.

When the discussion was continued last night, Stephenson made a very personal attack on Pear, to which Pear attacked equally aggressively. Then Walters who is the ideal chairman called a pause for tea, and after that interval the sea of emotion had calmed down. Toward the end I made another, conciliatory speech, never had there been any rancor between Pear and me, and after two more speakers, Walters summed up, "passing sentence" on the prisoner in the dock (the man whose paper was discussed had to sit in an armchair next to the chairman) and although he was most amiable to Pear and full of kind and pleasant humor, took sides very definitely with the point of view I had defended. It was a masterpiece of tact and formulation and was enthusiastically applauded. My own paper went extraordinarily well, I had tremendous applause and a very good discussion without any attack.

Even Spearman [C. E. Spearman,* professor of psychology, University of London] who on Sunday evening, speaking about another paper, referred to me, was very polite and only asked a question to be answered in the future. I had a talk with him afterwards. Of other papers I mention [social psychologist] Maria Jahoda, an Austrian refugee, who spoke on Some Socio-Psychological Problems of Factory Life, having worked in a factory for several months with the purpose of making this study on Group Spirit, based on actual studies in several American students' work camps (definitely good) and Thouless on Education in Reasoning.

Of the people I saw and talked to I mention: Myers, with whom I had a long talk on Saturday in the morning, he explained to me why [Sir Henry] Head* had broken with him, to his, Charles Myer's* infinite regret. Miss [Beatrice] Edgell* who came late and left early, Rex Knight, J. C. Flugel [John

Flugel, University College psychologist], Alec Mace [Birbeck
College psychology professor] and of course, Earl. He had a paper on the Clinical Use of Mental Tests, after which we went
for sherry. He invited me and Miss [Margaret] Harvey for
lunch on Sunday coming for us at 11 a.m. and showing us his
big institution. One of the most amusing and charming men I
have met, thoroughly Irish! When he repeated, or rather re-
enacted a conversation between Yeats and [Irish poet and fiction writer] James Stephens in which the latter called the former a bloody liar, in all friendship, one had to roar with
laughter.

But there was no discussion of the Rorschach although I
tried a few times to get him on to that topic. The Cambridge
people, i.e. from the Lab, were not represented.

Walters invited me to come to Reading for some talks. We
agreed tentatively on the 21st May, when I am to speak to his
students in the afternoon and to a group of (apparently similar
to my Saturday and Monday clubs) in the evening. When this
is settled I shall write to Head to arrange a visit.

. . . So I send you loads of love. It would have been nice if you
had been in Birmingham, and you would have liked it. [8 April
1940, Oxford]

That same evening there was a debate of the Oxford Union
Society on the question: That in the opinion of this House German aggression has left us no place for neutrality. A fellow
lodger had got me a ticket for the gallery and so I watched the
proceedings of this famous assembly for the first time in my
life. Harold Nicolson and Beverly Baxter [both English jour-
nalists] spoke for the motion which was introduced by a student and a Dutch journalist, substituting for the Romanian
minister who cancelled his engagement at the last moment, together with two students who were against it. As a debate, it
was poor, every speaker arguing about something different
from everybody else. But there were some fireworks and a good
deal of cleverness. . . .

. . . Yesterday I saw for the first time an operation almost from the beginning; i.e. the latter part of the turning of the skin flap and the whole of the turning of the bone flap. Eventually they did no more than a decompression and the patient was astonishingly well the next day, so that he could speak about his experiences under local anesthesia. There were moments of intense pain, and he said that he had missed something he might compress in his hands to steady himself, like an India rubber ball. Have you got such reports and do you supply your patients with such devices? I shall mention it to Cairns when I have a chance to talk with him.

. . . Friday was the great event: the first of my 4 lectures at the Nuffield Institute. I had supper at the Cairns before going over. When we arrived the absolutely charming lecture room, octagonal with alternating long and short sides, was filled to capacity, it seats about 60 people, people carrying chairs, several had to stand, others sat on the floor. St. Hughes [women's college] was well represented, our department at the Radcliffe, the German colony was there, including the Nobel prize winner [Otto] Loewi, Mrs. [Geoffrey] Jefferson had come from Manchester, with a psychologist. It seems to have gone well. How good these lectures may have been, you may have a means of judging for yourself, for Cairns told me he wanted to see them published. . . . Cairns is due in about half an hour.

. . . Don't be impatient and don't worry about the [war] news from Norway. Things are bound to move slowly and initial reverses have to be counted on. What will you do in the summer? Just think the academic year is almost over! [28 April 1940, Oxford]

The ordinary and pleasant aspects of the week are naturally overshadowed by the happenings in Holland and Belgium [invaded by Germany 10 May 1940]. Exciting weeks are ahead, and one does not feel like talking about one's little private affairs. The blow fell on Friday, the day before my second lecture, Cairns called for me in his car and said he expected a small audience. Actually, the hall was almost as full as the week before, a marvelous sign of the people here who carry on and are willing to forego the evening news to listen to a theoretical lecture on memory! Mrs. Jefferson had come again, this time by train, a 6 hour journey, she had to report the lecture to lots of people in Manchester. And Cairns told me there was someone in the audience to report the lectures in the *Lancet* [British medical journal].

I am frightfully busy. Two lectures have been given, the third is prepared and the notes on the fourth just started. Then I have to give the two talks in Reading, one of which has still to be prepared, and then the four lectures have to be got into shape for publication. [12 May 1940, Oxford]

I had a good audience on Friday, the most difficult of my four lectures. Jefferson himself had come with his wife, and again we went afterwards to the Cairns for drinks. He, Jefferson, came to my room yesterday for a long and very good talk. He is a very fine person besides being one of the leading men in his field. I believe that the Jeffersons have become real friends of mine.

My fourth and last lecture is all written out. Therefore if the University Press are willing to publish the volume I shall start at once to get all four lectures into shape. Except for the last there is nothing, or practically nothing that can be considered new, but if medical men were really to buy them, it might give a new interest in psychology. That is the reason why Cairns is keen on publication. I have forgotten to tell you that after my first lecture in which I had shown two of your Harrower figures, Nichols spoke to me [Martin Nichols, a research fellow at the Montreal Neurological Institute]. He had just come to St. Hughes [women's college turned over to the armed forces in World War II]. I reminded him that we had had tea together at the Institute when I visited there. [19 May 1940, Oxford]

I have your cable from Cincinnati, and your letters of May 3rd and 10th. You will, first of all, want to know what I have decided to do. Well I shall go to London tomorrow to see the American Consul, have a new passport issued, mine expired a few days ago, and ask his advice about the future action. If he tells me to go home on the *President Roosevelt* I shall do so, and I have a feeling that he will. So probably you will have heard from me before this letter reaches you. I shall be very sorry to leave, but I don't see what else I could do if this was the last assured chance of getting home.

People here understand perfectly, but they are far less pessimistic and excited than you seem to be on the other side. But things are in a turmoil, no doubt about it. Still life goes on very much as usual, as will appear when I tell you of my work.

I went to Reading on Tuesday and talked to a small group of faculty men friends of Walters' at a dinner club like my Monday Club, except that they met at the university since the war, as they can no longer drive. On Wednesday at 11:15 Sir Henry Head's car arrived for me to take me to Hartley Court where I met Mrs. Geraldine Head. Sir Henry has gone down during the last 3 years, his memory for recent events and not so recent as that, has gone. He remembers all the details of our first meeting in Oxford in 1923, but did not know whether I had ever been in Hartley Court. Still he is the same grand person. The neurologist who observes the patient, Henry Head, he told me interesting things about the beginnings of aphasia in himself. Thursday my class in Corpus, very enjoyable, and the next day my last lecture to a good though somewhat depleted audience, I conflicted with the King's [George VI] broadcast. Cairns made a nice speech afterwards, very embarrassing for me, and I spent the rest of the evening with Mrs. Jefferson, who had again come from Manchester. . . . I am due to give a lecture at the Institute of Experimental Psychology but I doubt if that will come off. If I have to leave I shall have no time nor the necessary peace of mind.

These have been trying weeks but they have added to my affection for and admiration of English, or British people. They will come out on top yet. [26 May 1940, Oxford]

epilogue.   koffka's core values and beliefs

Every now and again Koffka's letters reveal what might be called his core values, the vital needs that remain despite changing circumstances.

Recuperated from one of a series of heart attacks, Koffka became somewhat self-evaluative:

> Often during these weeks in bed, I have thought about my life, examining my actions from my early youth. And the final verdict was that I have been a great fool, that I did not utilize ever so many opportunities, that I might have done infinitely better. Not that all along there have not been beautiful things in my life, things to whose beauty I contributed. Also I was not altogether lazy and inefficient. A few times in my life I worked fairly hard and with great enthusiasm. In thinking about my life and its vicissitudes I played with the idea of writing a true and uncensored story of it. Of course, I shall never do it. Quite apart that the wish would not be strong enough my gifts do not lie that way. [22 January 1937]

Although Koffka was self-critical and at times depressed, these moods belie the essence of his positive orientation to life. No one endorsed more heartily "the everlasting Yea," no one could be more positive of the triumph of meaningfulness. In his own personal crises and those of others, his faith in the emergence of what might be called the good gestalt of life was unshakable, and he expressed this faith in various ways. Much of his feeling went into these paragraphs on poetry.

It is impossible to express the Universal, apart from one's own emotions, before one has experienced and expressed the universal *in* one's own emotions. One cannot at an early age contribute to the solutions of the great questions of mankind, but as a person matures, as they gain true access to the eternal problems, there is less of the immediate and the local. The Self becomes representative of the universal struggle, the universal assertion, the everlasting YEA.

But the tragedy is that poetry that expresses the crying needs of the hour, even if they are the crying needs of millions and millions, directly, is apt to be bad poetry, some process of transformation must take place. The needs of millions must become the needs of the poet, and at the same time, say, the needs of God, before a real poem can result. [7 April 1933]

There were, for Koffka, intrinsic laws governing the deepest human relationships.

A real union demands to be exclusive to a point. It does not demand that no partner have his or her individual friendships. It does not demand that all experiences should be communicated to the other partner. But it does demand the most intimate relationships be unique. Please do not misunderstand me at this point. I do not mean that in order to have a real union one must promise to the other partner or impose upon oneself certain abstractions. Such promises are sure to be broken, such impositions sure to produce grudges. My meaning is much deeper. One must feel that one is free to do not only what one wants oneself, but also—and that is more difficult—what ought to be done for some other dear and valuable person.

This sacrifice, as I mean it, must be demanded by the living reality of the union and must for all its painfulness be a source of deep satisfaction. [September 1937]

Koffka was not religious in the ordinary sense of the word, but one letter reflected his attitude.

God is no longer a short cut, but a task. One may pray for his existence, and work for his existence. Does not "God" really mean that the world is not only chaos, or chance combinations of separate, coherent systems, which clash and interfere with each other and destroy each other, but that there are seeds, or beginnings, at least in the Universe of greater meaning and significance, seeds which tend to unfold and impress their order and significance on the rest? That there is a possibility of a real, universal development?

And does belief in God not mean that we feel individually that we are part of this beginning, and that we bend our efforts so as to help this development, however small our individual contributions. That we crave a God as a background, a guarantee of continuity, this is the most difficult of all questions. How can continuity be realized? Without which the greatest achievements lose much of their value. I agree that the immutable church does not solve the difficulty. Again I think the solution must be within, not without, but how to envisage this correctly I do not know, except that we are to some extent, all of us, what the great minds of the past have made us. [11 April 1933]

Speaking of his most important personal goals, he stated that what he wanted was "a fine and close relationship with people. Very close with one or two. This is to me the most important thing in life! More than anything it gives me zest and joy" [7 January 1940, Oxford]. "To have gained and kept such closeness is ever so much more important to me than having written *The Principles*" [7 January 1937].

In the months before he died, Koffka wrote (4 August, 9, 10 September 1941):

I have had a magnificent life, have achieved more than could be expected and have lived through periods of happiness which cannot be surpassed. I have loved in my own way. I could not play-act or pretend to be what I was not, nor really wanted to be.

I'd rather be dead now than have missed any of the things of deepest meaning to me. Rather go out in a great flame when I still have the vitality to throw caution to the winds than drag on an old hypochondriac who thinks of his health before everything else. Marvelous years: They cannot be erased from the scroll of time.

appendix a.   biographical sketch: koffka

Kurt Koffka was born in Berlin on 18 March 1886 and died at Northampton, Massachusetts, on 22 November 1941. Despite a heart condition which had caused him to modify and restrict his activities for several years, he continued to teach until a few days before his death and had been working with vigor on various experimental projects, theoretical papers, and the manuscript of a new book up to the last. There is no question that his death left unfinished much that would have been among his more important contributions to psychology. At least he was saved the more complete invalidism that might have been his, and he died in harness as he would have wished.

As a boy, Koffka attended the Wilhelms Gymnasium in Berlin from 1892 to 1903. On leaving school, since he came from a family of lawyers, his career might well have followed along traditional lines, but his mother's brother, a biologist, had aroused his keen interest in science and philosophy, so that he decided to study the latter.

Before entering the University of Berlin, however, he spent a year at the University of Edinburgh, where he came under the influence of several outstanding British scientists and scholars. This student year abroad, in addition to perfecting his use of the language, brought him in close touch with English-speaking people and laid the foundation for the international scientific recognition that was to be his.

After returning to Berlin in 1904, Koffka spent three years at the university there, giving up his idea of studying philosophy because he "was too realistically minded to be satisfied with pure abstractions" (Koffka 1935a) and turning to psychology. His activities included research in W. A. Nagel's physiological laboratory. It was from this laboratory that his first published work appeared in 1908, *Untersuchungen an einem protanomalen System* (Investigation of a case of red-green color deficiency), a study of his own color weakness. In this work he was first drawn to consider the problems of color contrast, the interrelation of brightness and color, the difference between colors of long and short wavelengths, the questions of figure and ground—problems that were to captivate him in one way and another for thirty years to come.

Also in 1908 he received his degree of Doctor of Philosophy, presenting as his dissertation *Experimental-Untersuchungen zur Lehre von Rhythmus* (Experimental investigation on the theory of rhythm). In view of the subsequent development of Gestalt theory with its birth in 1912, this work is of particular interest. Koffka spoke frequently of his readiness to receive Max Wertheimer's* theory when it burst upon him in their discussions in 1910, and how he had let it grow on well-prepared soil. The extent to which he had actively prepared the soil is evidenced in his dissertation, for many of the questions raised in it, the type of experimentation, and the terminology might have been expected subsequent to a formulation of Gestalt theory rather than prior to it.

Immediately following his doctorate, Koffka spent a semester in the physiological laboratory of Johannes Von Kries at the University of Freiberg. From there he went to the University of Würzburg where he worked first under Oswald Külpe,* and, after Külpe left, as assistant to Karl Marbe.* During this period, in 1909, Koffka married Mira Klein. In 1910 he spent three semesters as assistant to Friedrich Schumann at Frankfort a. M. This year was, in his own words, "of special importance in my scientific development . . . with Köhler* as Schumann's other assistant and Wertheimer working on the perception of motion in the laboratory. Thus we three who knew each other slightly before were thrown into the closest contact which resulted in lasting collaboration" (from a personal communication).

In 1911 he was appointed Privatdozent lecturer at the University of Giessen, presenting as his Habilitationschrift, an inaugural dissertation, part of an experimental study done in Würzburg, *Über Vorstellungen*. These experiments, while reflecting the type of problem that sprang readily from the Würzburg soil, differed in a characteristic way, reappearing to be developed further in Koffka's theory of memory in his *Principles of Gestalt Psychology* twenty-five years later.

Koffka remained in Giessen until 1924, in 1918 becoming ausserordentlicher professor. During the years of World War I, he worked with Professor Sommer at the Psychiatric Clinic in Giessen on patients with brain injuries and especially on aphasics. Later he was engaged on problems of sound localization, first with the army and then with the navy.

This period saw the birth in 1921 of the Gestaltists' journal, *Psychologische Forschung*, with Wertheimer, Köhler, Koffka, Kurt Goldstein,* and Hans Gruhle* on the original editorial board. There was also the publication of Koffka's *Die Grundlagen der psychischen Entwicklung* (1921), later translated by R. M. Ogden as *The Growth of the Mind* (1924), with other editions in Spanish, Russian, Chinese and Japanese. Koffka and his students put out a steady flow of experimental studies. Eighteen articles appeared as "Beiträge zur Psychologie der Gestalt" (Contributions to Gestalt psychology) in the newly founded *Psychologische Forschung* together with half a dozen shorter experimental papers.

In 1922 there appeared in the *Psychological Bulletin* Koffka's first paper written in English: "Perception: An Introduction to the Gestalt Theory." In a systematic and thought-provoking manner, reflecting many of the characteristics that would recur in longer discussions in *The Principles of Gestalt Psychology*, the experimental studies on which Gestalt theory was based were made available for the first time in English.

In 1924 Koffka came to America, spending successive years as visiting professor at Cornell University and the University of

During World War I, Koffka (standing center) worked on sound localization for the army and navy. Disliking his military rations, he claimed he lived on Albert biscuits sent by his friends.

Wisconsin. In the next three years he published articles in English, French, and German. These, with one exception, were theoretical papers. He discussed, from the point of view of the Gestalt psychologist, such questions as introspection as a method, the mechanistic-vitalistic dilemma (see Harrower 1937, chap. 1, and Koffka 1935, chap. 1), the implications of isomorphism, and the unconscious. He had not concerned himself before with such broad issues, and the new articles did much to extend the implications of Gestalt theory.

In 1927 Koffka was appointed William Allen Neilson Research Professor at Smith College. This position was in effect a five-year plan, when no publications were demanded, no teaching involved. Again the majority of experimental projects undertaken by Koffka and his students lay in the field of visual perception. These publications appeared again in the *Beiträge*, which at the close of the period numbered twenty-five, and they were also published as *Smith College Studies in Psychology* (1930–34) which ran to four volumes. The year following the Smith appointment, 1928, marked Koffka's divorce, then his marriage to Elisabeth Ahlgrimm.

In 1932 Koffka joined an expedition originating in Russia, to Uzbekistan in Central Asia. In his own words, "The official task of the expedition was to study the dependence of the mental functions of a people upon the historico-economic conditions of their country, and indeed Uzbekistan offered a rich field for such studies, passing after the political revolution through a period of rapid economic and cultural transformation. Thus it was possible to investigate people who had been to various degrees affected by these changes." His experiments were unfortunately never published, and indeed the expedition had anything but a happy conclusion, for Koffka contracted relapsing fever and spent many difficult days before he could be brought out of that primitive country.

Interestingly enough, it was during this illness and under very trying conditions that the first draft of the first chapter of *The Principles of Gestalt Psychology* was conceived and written. On his return from Asia he began serious work on *The Principles*, admitting reluctantly that the exhaustive study into which he was led could not remain the book for the layman which he had first envisaged. Published in 1935, *The Principles of Gestalt Psychology* is so well known, and its contribution to psychology has been so thoroughly assessed by reviewers, that it is out of place to comment on it here. Watching it grow, however, as was my privilege, one could not but be impressed by its relentless thoroughness and Koffka's determination to be honest and systematic at all costs. In this book he took stock of himself and his own position, forcing himself to recognize gaps, inadequacies, and inconsistencies in Gestalt theory as he saw it, thinking through and integrating within this framework his astonishingly detailed knowledge of experimental problems.

After writing this book, after he had taken stock and had seen where he stood, Koffka permitted himself, as a psychologist, to be concerned with many wider problems. He had always been intensely interested in art, music, and literature, and in general social and ethical questions, but he had argued that, as an experimental psychologist, he had no right to be concerned with them. His "Psychology of Art" (1940), his various lectures on tolerance and on freedom (see Appendix D), his dialogue on the "Ontological Status of Value" (1935), all show that he had now extended the province in which he felt the psychologist had a right to participate. To all these more general topics he brought the same vigor of thought, the same careful avoidance of loose generalization, that characterized his intensive work in experimental problems.

In 1939 Koffka revived one of his old interests: he spent a year as visiting professor at Oxford University, working at the Nuffield Institute with patients with brain lesions, and at the Military Hospital for Head Injuries, where he helped to develop tests to bring out defects in judgment and comprehension. These tests are now in use. During this year he gave a series of lectures in the university entitled "Gestalt Psychology and Neurology." At the request of his neurological colleagues he had started to incorporate these lectures and much valuable case material into a book which he called, provisionally, *Human Behavior and its Modification by Brain Injuries*. This book, unfortunately, he was unable to complete.

appendix b. major dates: koffka

1886	Born 18 March, Berlin
1892–1903	Wilhelm Gymnasium, Berlin
1903–4	In Edinburgh as student
1904–7	University of Berlin
1908	First published work
1908	Doctor of Philosophy; Dissertation: *Experimental Untersuchungen zur Lehre von Rhythmus*
1909	Marriage to Mira Klein
1910	Meeting with Wertheimer and Köhler; discussions relating to the emerging Gestalt theory
1911	University of Giessen
1914	Privatdozent
1918	Ausserordentlich professor; during World War I worked for Navy on sound localization and in the Psychiatric Clinic on brain-injured aphasics
1921	Birth of *Psychologische Forschung*: original editorial board, M. Wertheimer, W. Köhler, K. Koffka, K. Goldstein, H. Gruhle
1921	Publication of *Die Grundlagen der psychischen Entwicklung*; trans. 1924
1922	First paper written in English: "Perception: An Introduction to Gestalt Psychology"
1924	Came to United States; visiting professor at Cornell

	and Wisconsin; English translation of *Die Grundlagen* as *The Growth of the Mind*
1927	Appointed William Allen Neilson Research Professor at Smith College
1928	Divorced from Mira Klein; marriage to Elisabeth Ahlgrimm
1932	Expedition to Uzbekistan in Central Asia; work with Alexander Luria; began to write *The Principles of Gestalt Psychology* while ill in Russia
1935	Publication of "The Ontological Status of Value"; publication of *The Principles of Gestalt Psychology* in England and America
1939–40	Appointed to the Nuffield Institute in Oxford, headed by Sir Hugh Cairns, to work with patients with brain lesions
1940	Publication of "Art: A Bryn Mawr Symposium"
1940–41	Returned to United States
1941	Died 22 November, Northampton, Massachusetts

appendix c.   major dates: harrower

1906	Born 25 January, Johannesburg, South Africa
1918–24	Godolphin School, Salisbury, England
1924–25	Ecole Vinet, Lausanne, Switzerland
1925–27	Bedford College, London University, London, England
1927–28	Associate editor of *Psyche*
1928–30 ⎫ 1931–32 ⎬	Smith College, Northampton, Massachusetts, research associate in psychology
1933–34 ⎭	
1930–31	Wells College, New York, instructor in psychology
1932–33	Bedford College, University of London, senior lecturer in psychology
1934	Ph.D. from Smith College; dissertation: *Organization in Higher Mental Processes*
1934–37	Douglass College, Rutgers University, director of students
1938	Marriage to Dr. Theodore Erickson, divorced, 1945
1938–42	Montreal Neurological Institute–McGill University; chief clinical psychologist, lecturer in psychology
1941–44	Josiah Macy, Jr., Foundation, grantee
1944–67	Independent practice, psychodiagnosis, consultation, and therapy

Part-time consulting positions

1947–50	Department of State, psychological consultant
1947–52	U.S. Army, psychological consultant
1948–51	Air Surgeon's Office, member of Technical Advisory Committee
1951–52	Children's Bureau, consultant in psychology
1955	Marriage to Mortimer Lahm; deceased 1967
1957–62	Johns Hopkins Hospital, consultant psychologist

Part-time research and lecturing positions

1952–54	Manhattan Children's Court, research director, Court Intake Project
1953–57	University of Texas Medical Branch, visiting lecturer, Department of Psychiatry
1959–64	Temple University Medical School, professor, Department of Psychiatry
1964–67	New School for Social Research, New York, visiting professor of psychology
1967–75	University of Florida, professor of clinical psychology
1975–	Professor emeritus
1980	Award: distinguished contributor in clinical psychology, American Psychological Association, Division of Clinical Psychology
1981	Honorary degree: Doctor of Humane Letters, University of Florida

appendix d. a note on the koffka papers

1. Unpublished Lectures Classified Under the Headings
   Used by Koffka (Harrower 1971a)

   (a) Gestalt Theory
      1. New School for Social Research
         Start & Goal of Gestalt Theory 2–12–29
         What a Gestalt is 2–19–29
         Psychological Dynamics, 2–26–29
         A Gestalt Psychologist's Outlook on Social
            Psychology, 3–5–29
      2. A Brief Outline of Gestalt Psychology
         (8 lectures) New School for Social Research, New
            York, Jan. 9th to Feb. 27th, 1931
      3. Ideas and Aims of Gestalt Psychology
         N. Y. Chapter of the International Philosophic
            Society, New York, Feb. 14, 1931
         New School for Social Research as "Gestalt
            Psychology" Nov. 3, 1932
      4. Die Überwindung des Mechanismus in der
         Modernen Psychologie Mosken, May 29, 1932
      5. Gestalt Psychology
         Rand School of Social Science, New York, 12–5–32
      6. Untitled series of lectures in 12 parts as indicated:

I   Introduction (p. 1–9)
II   Psychology of Perception (p. 10–14)
III   The Law of Precision (p. 15–21)
IV   The Nature of Gestalt (p. 22–26)
V   Action (p. 27–32)
VI   Learning (p. 33–36)
VII   Thinking (p. 37–41)
VIII   Applications (Sociological) (p. 42–48)
IX   Applications to Physiology & Psychopathology
(p. 49–56)
X   Application to Biology (p. 57–65)
XI   The Philosophy of Gestalt (p. 66–73)
XII   Conclusion (p. 74–81)

7. Personality from the Standpoint of Gestalt Psychology
Hartford, Conn. 1–27–32

8. The Problem of Action
University Club, Madison, Wisconsin

9. Untitled Lecture
Saturday Club, 10–16–37

10. On the Organization of the Ego
Harvard Psychological Colloquium, 3–29–33

11. The Ego in His World
University of Chicago, 2–4–38
Duke University, Durham, N. C., 2–27–37

12. On Group Behavior
Saturday Club, 11–10–34

13. The Ego & the Group
Rand School of Social Science, New York, 2–5–34

14. Zur Psychologie der Gruppe
Cincinnati, Ohio, 3–27–27
Repeated in English to Arden Club, Madison,
Wisconsin, 4–17–27

15. How We Behave
Holyoke College, 4–23–29
Smith College, 5–24–29
Channing Forum, Berkeley, Calif., 7–28–29

16. Behaviour in Gestalt Psychology

Stanford University, 8–7–29
Vassar College, 11–5–29
Wells College, 2–28–31
Repeated in German at Academy in Samarkand,
6–5–32

17. The Application of Gestalt Theory to Behavior
Problems
Columbia College of Physicians & Surgeons,
1–24–31

18. The Psychological Field
Talk to Wakeman Class, 1–22–32

19. Modern Developments in the Study of Personality
Graduate School of Education, Yale University,
7–10–33

20. The Self from the Viewpoint of Gestalt Psychology
2 lectures delivered at Pennsylvania School of Social
Work, 2–17 and 2–24–36
Repeated under title The Ego & the Group, Geneva
School of International Studies, 8–24–36

21. Wertheimer Seminar
1–14–38

(b) Perception

1. Some New Experiments on Visual Contrast
Meeting of APA Washington, D.C., 12–29–24

2. The Perception of Movement
An instance of experimental method in Gestalt-
psychology.
Annual meeting of National Academy of Sciences
Washington, D.C., 4–27–25

3. Perception of Movement. An Experimental Problem.
Psychological Laboratory of the University of
Illinois, 3–23–25

4. Form & Colour
Cornell University, 1–17–29

5. Example of the Way in Which Gestalt Experimentalists Work
Journal Club, Smith College, 1928

6. On Space Perception
   Talk to physicists from Smith, Amherst, Mass. Ag.,
      Mt. Holyoke 4–22–30
7. Three Lectures on Perception
   Smith College, March 10, 11, 13
8. Excursion into the World of Space & Colour
   Smith College, 4–20–32
9. Some Aspects of Visual Organization
   New England Ophthalmological Society, 4–12–38
10. A Talk to Olive Larkin's Class on Art Appreciation.
   3–17–41

(c) Lectures Philosophical
1. The Contribution of Psychology to Science &
   Philosophy
2. Machines, Life, & Gestalt
   Brown University, Providence, R.I., 2–20–29
   Columbia Psychology Club & Institute of Arts &
      Sciences, 4–3–29
   American Association of University Women in
      Boston, Boston Univ., 4–24–29
3. The Significance of the Gestalt Theory
   Dartmouth College, 1–11–29
4. Matter Life Mind
   University of Wisconsin, 5–10–27
5. Philosophical Aspects of the Gestalt Theory
   Philosophy Club, University of Chicago, 7–2–25
6. General Aspect of Gestalt-Theory
   Harvard Philosophic Club, 12–10–24
7. The Contribution of Psychology to Science &
   Philosophy
   New Jersey College for Women, 12–3–34
8. The University of Sciences
   Syracuse University, 12–17–35
   Smith College Philosophical Society, 3–21

(d) Lectures in Oxford 1940
1. Introduction to Harrower's class in C. C. C., 4–25–40
2. On Isomorphism

A talk at the University of Reading, Dept. of
Psychology, 5–21–40
3. 57 pages of untitled lecture (IV)
4. Untitled page No. 21
5. Some Traits of Human Behavior as Revealed by the
Study of Brain Injuries
Read to Extended General Meeting of the British
Psychological Society at the University of
Birmingham, 4–7–40
Repeated with additions to Saturday Club, 10–19–40
6. Notes on Intellectual Functions
7. Elementary Conceptions of Gestalt Psychology & Some
Applications in Medicine, Oxford Medical Society,
10–31–39
(e) Language
1. Problems in the Psychology of Language
New England Modern Language Assn., Holyoke,
Mass., 5–9–31
2. The Psychology of Learning with Reference to the
Acquisition of Language
National Council of Teachers of English,
Washington, D.C., 11–30–34
(f) Child Psychology & Education
1. Mental Development—Instinct, Training, and Intellect.
Princeton, Dec. 3, 1924
Smith College, Dec. 13, 1924
2. The Growth of the Mind of the Child
University of Wisconsin, 3–30–25
From same notes: Federation for Child Study, N.Y.,
4–8–25
3. Mental Development
Clark University, 4–29–25
Wellesley College, 5–4
Repeated With Modifications, Wells College, 5–12
University of Chicago, 7–16–25
4. The Nursery School and Psychological Research
Nursery School Conference at Vassar College, 2–6–28

(g) Body & Mind—the Structure of the Unconscious—The Ego
  1. On the Structure of the Unconscious
       Read at Symposim of the Illinois Society for Mental Hygiene, City Club, Chicago, 4–30–27
  2. Body and Mind.
       Lecture at Stanford University, 7–20–27
  3. The Ego in His World, Read to Section T of British Assoc. for Advancement of Science at Dundee, 9–1–39

(h) Introduction—Book
  1. Introduction & Survey
  2. The World We Create & How We Create It. Chapter I
  3. The Past in the Present—An Analysis of Memory & Experience, Chapter II

(i) Lectures on Learning
  1. The Question
       1–21–25
  2. The Psychology of Learning
       3 lectures Harvard, 12–10, 12, 1924
  3. Perception and Experience
       Lecture at Yale Philosophical Club, 1–10–25
  4. On Problems of Learning
       Read at Miami University, Oxford, Ohio, 1–15–27
       Smith College Seminar, 3–5–27
       University of Cincinnati, 3–26–27
       Stanford University, 7–20–27
       The Miss. of California, Berkeley, 7–25–27
       Yale University, 12–6–32
  5. The Intelligent Chimpanzee—a study of Productive Thought
       Lecture at Swarthmore College, 3–3–32
  6. Learning & the Theory of Traces
       Talk to Psychological Colloquium of Clark University, 1–20–34
  7. On Association
       10–22–34

8. On Memory
   Talk at Physics Journal Club, 12–10–34
9. Three Lectures on Learning
   (a) An Analysis of the Problem of Learning
   (b) What we know about Traces
   (c) Learning & the Ego
      Pennsylvania School of Social Work,
         Philadelphia 3–8–15, 22, 1937
10. The Psychology of Learning as Seen by a Psychologist
    William & Mary, Williamsburg, Va., 4–24–36
11. The Problem of Learning as Viewed by a Psychologist
    Lectures at University Hall Ohio State University,
       7–20–39
12. On the Problem of Learning
    Talk at Yale, 11–4–35
(j) Lectures on Gestalt Psychology I 1925–29
1. The Organism in the World
   3 lectures delivered at University of Illinois, in Ur-
      bana, Ill. Commerce Hall, 3–24–26–27, 1925.
2. Psychological Theories
   Lecture delivered at Hobart College, Geneva, N.Y.,
      4–17–25
3. My Creed
   University Club, Madison, Wis., Oct. 1926
4. Why I am a Gestalt Psychologist
   Psychology Club, Madison, Wis., 11–9–26
5. Gestalt Psychology
   Talk given at University of Cincinnati, 3–26–27
6. The Gestalt Theory of Psychology
   Lecture to Child Study Assn. of America, New York,
      2–7–28
7. Ideas and Aims of Gestalt Theory
   Smith College, 2–17–28
8. Some Misconceptions of the Gestalt-Theory
   Yale, 4–24–28
9. Ideas & Aims of the Gestalt Theory

Lecture to Woman's City Club, Cleveland, Ohio,
1–30–29

10. The Dilemma of the Psychologist
11. Note on Stimulus Response ⎱ Fundamental catego-
Instinct-Habit ⎰ ries of Behavior

(k) Unpublished Papers (1)
1. A note on E. M. Von Hornbostel, A. Gelb
2. Review of the Natural History of Mind
A. D. Ritchie, 1936
3. The Law of Effect in Learning and its Interpretation.
Manuscript and typewritten copy, paper submitted
presumably for the International Congress mailed to
Madrid in 1936.

(l) Unpublished papers experiments (2)
1. Machines life and gestalt
2. Paper beginning "The Psychologist ought to be a
happy and contented person."

(m) Lectures on the Psychology of Art
1. Problems in the Psychology of Art
Two lectures at Bryn Mawr College, 4–17–19, 1939
2. Psychology of Art
Rough notes for lecture
Manuscript pages 1 through 15
This folder is also labeled: Chapt. 12
3. Actors & Acting

(n) The Place of a Psychologist Among Scientists
Three copies: 1 manuscript, 1 typed, 1 published

(o) Lectures: Historical
1. Beginning of Gestalt Theory
New York Branch American Psychological Assn.
Columbia University, New York, 4–18–31
2. Recent Developments in Psychology
Smith Alumnae College on Germany since 1870,
6–20–34

(p) Folder called "Problems"
(q) Hypotheses, Tentative suggestions, short summaries.
(r) Miscellaneous

1. What I was Told in Russia
2. My Summer in Germany
   10–26–36
3. Some Remarks on the Psychology of the Dog
   2–28–38
(s) Experiments in Memory
(t) Notes on Social Psychology
   Seminar 1934–35
(u) Reflections of a Psychologist
   (This turned out to be Koffka's last lecture.)

2. Koffka's Collection of His Own Reprints (Harrower 1971a)

This includes the following articles of Koffka and those which he published with his colleagues and students (The Beiträge). There are also 10 of his book reviews. It should be remembered that this list of reprints *possessed* by Koffka is not necessarily identical to his complete bibliography which has been published in the *Psychological Register* and brought up to date in 1942. (5) Some items are missing, as for example, the Smith College studies.

(1)   *Untersuchungen an einem protanomalen System.*
      Zts.f.Sinnesphysiologie, *43*, 1908. Ss. 123–145.
(2)   *Experimental-Untersuchungen zur Lehre von Rhythmus.*
      Zts.f.Psych. *52*, 1909, Ss. 1–109.
         (1.und2.Kapitel, 1, Abschnitt, Dissertation, Berlin,
         1908 Ss. 1–71.)
(3)   *Über latente Einstellung.*
      Bericht über den IV Kongress f. experimentelle Psych.
      in Innsbruck 1910. Ss. 239–241.
(4)   *Zur Analyse der Vorstellungen und ihrer Gesetze.*
      X.u.3928. Leipzig, 1912.
(4a) *Über Vorstellungen.*
      Habilitalionsschrift, 1911. Ss. 1–109.
         (s.auch 4, Kapitel 2.)
(5)   *Ein neuer Versuch eines objekitven Systems der
      Psychologie.*

(Betrachtungen zu L.Edingers' Theorie der nervosen
Zentralorgane) Zts.f.Psych. *61*, 1912. Ss. 266–278.

(6)   Beiträge I.

(7)   *Psychologie der Wahrnehmung.*
"Die Geisteswissenschaften", *26*, 1914. Ss. 711–716. Ss.
796–800.

(8)   *Zur Einführung.*
Zus.mit W. Stahlin. Archiv.f.Religionspsychologie, *1*,
No. 81–1914. Ss. 1–9.

(9)   Beiträge III

(10)   Beiträge IV.

(11)   *Probleme der experimentellen Psychologie.*
I Die Unterschiedsschwelle.
"Die Naturwissenschaften", *7*, 1917. Ss. 1–5, Ss. 23–28.

(12)   *Probleme der experimentellen Psychologie.*
II Über den Einfluss der Erfahrung auf die Wahrnehmung. "Die Naturwissenschaften", & *7*, 33, 1919. Ss.
597–605.

(13)   Beiträge V.

(14)   *Die Grundlagen der psychischen Entwicklung*
VII 2788. 1921. (Ziekfeldt, Osterwick am Herz)
a) do. 2. Aufl. VIII 299S. 1925.
b) English translation by R. M. Ogden.
1st Edition XVI 383 pp. 1924.
(Kegan Paul, London)
c) do. 2nd Edition XIX 427 pp. 1928.
d) Spanish edition.

(14a)   *Ein besonderer Fall von Farbenschwäche.*
Ber.üb.d. VII. Kongress f.exper. Psychol. in Marburg,
1922. pp. 139–140.

(15)   *Zur Theorie der Erlebnis-Wahrnehmung.*
Annalen der Philosophie, III, 1922. Ss. 375–399.

(16)   *Intelligenz von Tieren.*
"Klinische Wochenschrift" *1*, Nr.25, 1922.

(17)   *Über die Energie der Konturen.*
Psych. Forschg. *2*, 1922. Ss. 145–147.

(18) *Die Prävalens der Figur.*
      Psych. Forchg. *2*, 1922, Ss. 147–148.
(19) *Über den Lindeschen Kreisbogenversuch.*
      Psych. Forschg. *2*, 1922. Ss. 148–153
(20) *Perception: An Introduction to the Gestalt Theory*
      The Psychol. Bull. 19, No. 10, 1922. Pp. 531–581.
(21) *New Experiments in the Perception Movement.*
      Report of VIIth Internat. Congress of Psych. Oxford,
      1923, pp. 369–373.
(22) *Über die Untersuchungen an den sogenannten optischen Anschauungsbildern.*
      Psych. Forschg. *3*, 1923. Ss. 124–167.
(23) *Über die Messung der Grösse von Nachbildern.*
      Psych. Forschg. *3*, 1923. Ss. 219–230.
(24) *Feldbegrenzung und Felderfüllung.*
      Psych. Forschg. *4*, 1923. Ss. 176–203.
(25) *Théorie de la forme et psychologie de l'enfant.*
      Journal de Psychologie *XXI*, no's 1–3, 1924. pp.
      102–111.
(26) *The Perception of Movement in the Region of the Blind Spot.*
      A report of experiments performed in the Psychological
      laboratory of the University of Giessen.
      Brit. Jour. of Psych. *XIV*, part 3, 1924. pp. 269–273.
(27) *Psychical and Physical Structures.*
      Psyche 1924. July. pp. 80–85.
(28) *Some new experiments on Visual Contrast.*
      Report on Amer. Psych. Asso. Washington, 1924. pp.
      16–17.
(29) *Introspection and the Method of Psychology.*
      Brit. Jour. of Psych. *XV*, part 2, 1924. pp. 149–161.
(30) *Psychologie.*
      Lehrbuch der Philosophie her. von M. Dessoir, *II*, 1925,
      Berlin. Ss. 497–603.
(31) *Mental Development*
      The Pedogogical Seminary and Journal of Genetic Psy-

chology. *XXXII*, No. 4, 1925. pp. 659–673. and in Psychologies of 1925, pp. 129–143.

(32) *Psychologie der Wahrnehmung.*
Symposia, Gestalt Wahrnehmung. Internat. Psych. Congress 1926, Groningen, Ss. 82–88.

(33) *Die Krisis in der Psychologie.*
Bemerkungen zu dem Buchgleichen Namens von Hans Driesch. "Die Naturwissenschaften", *14*, 1926. Ss. 581–586.

(34) *Die Überwindung des Vitalismus. Gestalt Psychologie.*
"Vossische Zeitung" no. 114, Mai 1926.

(35) *Über das Sehen von Bewegung.*
Bemerkungen zu der Arbeit von Higginson. Psych. Forschg. 8, 1926. Ss. 222–235.

(36) *Bemerkungen zur Denk-Psychologie.*
Psych. Forschg. 9. 1927. Ss. 163–183.

(37) *On the Structure of the Unconscious.*
The Unconscious, a Symposium, 1927 (New York) pp. 43–68.

(38) *On Gestalt Theory.*
"The Smith Alumnae Quarterly", Feb. 1928. pp. 142–147.

(39) *Some Problems of Space Perception.*
Psychologies of 1930 (Worcester, Mass.) pp. 161–187.

(40) Beiträge XIX.

(41) *Die Wahrnehmung von Bewegung.*
Handbuch der normalen und pathologischen Physiologie, *12*, 2. Hälfte, 1931. Ss. 1166–1214.

(42) *Psychologie der Optischen Wahrnehmung.*
Handbuch der normalen und pathologischen Physiologie, *12*, 2. Halft, 1931. Ss. 1215–1271.

(43) *Consciousness.*
Encyclopaedia of the Social Sciences, Vol. IV.

(44) *Gestalt.*
Encyclopaedia of the Social Sciences, Vol. IV.

(45) Beiträge XXI.

(46) Beiträge XXII.

(47) Beiträge XXIII.

(48) Beiträge XXIV.

(49) Beiträge XXV.

(50) *Les notions d'hériditaire et d'acquis en psychologie.*
Journal de Psychologie *29*, pp. 5–19, 1932.

(51) *A New Theory of Brightness-Constancy: A Contribution to
a General Theory of Vision.*
The Physical and Optical Societies Report of a Joint
Discussion of Vision, June, 1932.

(52) *Why Things Look as They Do.*
The Smith Alumnae Quarterly, *24*, pp. 144–148, 1933.

(53) On Problems of Colour-Perception. Acta Psychologica *1*
1935, pp. 129–134.

(54) Principles of Gestalt Psychology, XI & 720 pages. New
York 1935.

(55) The Psychology of Learning, with Reference to the Acquisition of Language. The English Journal, College
Edition, *24*, May 1935, pp. 388–396.

(56) The Ontological Status of Value. In "American Philosophy Today and Tomorrow" ed. by S. Hook and
H. Kallen.   New York, 1935, pp. 275–309.

(57) Purpose and Gestalt: A Reply to Professor McDougall.
Character and Personality, *6*, March 1938, pp. 218–
238.

(58) The Law of Effect in Learning and its Interpretation
Onzième Congres International de Psychologie, Paris,
1938, pp. 57–68.

(59) Problems in the Psychology of Art. Art: A Bryn Mawr
Symposium. Bryn Mawr Notes and Monographs IX
1940, pp. 179–273.

appendix e.   koffka's letter to sir arthur eddington

Interdisciplinary conferences are now commonplace. This interdisciplinary exchange between two outstanding scientists, however, occurring in 1935, was highly unusual, perhaps unique. Sir Arthur Eddington was well known to the reading public through such books as *The Nature of the Physical World* (1929). Koffka, one of the three founders of Gestalt psychology, had just published *The Principles of Gestalt Psychology* (1935), a book which was the first comprehensive text and exposition of the Gestalt theory.

For Koffka, the Gestalt concept, however, was much more than a new movement or a new school in psychology. It was an approach to life, a belief, a new gate opening on stalemated problems. Stimulated by Eddington's *New Pathways in Science*, just off the press, Koffka's impulse was to share with him the possible Gestalt implications in such areas as the materialistic-dualistic dilemma, the principle of uncertainty, entropy, and other major theoretical concepts which Eddington had discussed.

The idea to write a personal letter to Eddington required some reenforcement, for Koffka was by nature modest about his own contributions. Here are the steps in his correspondence in 1935.

[KK] I finished Eddington's book yesterday. . . . a grand book, much more difficult than *The Nature of the Physical World*, and not the solution as I see it, in however vague a form. But a grand piece of work, honest, thorough and in a way an attempt to reach the same goal I am striving for. May I keep it a few days longer? I am playing with the idea of writing to him about it, but that would require a lot of time. [23 September]

[MH] Keep Eddington on condition that you write him a letter and tell him also of your book. If you don't, I shall write and send him a copy! [29 September]

[KK] Yesterday I started the draft of my letter to him. It is a difficult job and will take me much longer than I expected. But I want to do something that is consistent and constructive. I'll send it to you for your comments. [4 October]

Here is the draft of my letter to Eddington. Please read it and correct it at your leisure, but send me an acknowledgment of receipt at once because this is the only copy I have and it cost me a whole week to prepare it. Please correct all the mistakes in grammar, and idiom, but take your time, don't let this interfere with your duties. As soon as I get the draft back I'll type it. If you would like a copy, I'll make two carbons. [10 October]

[MH] I got your stupendous letter for Eddington! I'll correct it over the weekend. [12 October]

[KK] Thank you for correcting the Eddington letter. From your comments at the end I gather that you think I should send it and, therefore, I shall begin typing it and shall make the extra carbon for you. [15 October]

The letter was mailed, dated 21 October. Eddington's reply reached Koffka on 3 December 1935. The original was missing from his file at the time of his death in 1941, but the gist of it was luckily preserved in Koffka's letters to Harrower written at this time.

I have just received a long letter from Eddington, four sheets in fairly small handwriting. He explains several points, accepts many of my statements but makes it clear that his system is much more dualistic than mine. At the same time he begins with these words: 'It is not often that I receive (amid a rather unmanageably large correspondence) so profound and clear sighted a letter as yours. I cannot reply adequately.'

And he ends on an even nicer note: "I have read your letter with great interest. On pp. 9 through 12 there are some points I think I might argue against; but as a whole, even where it criticizes my own view, I recognize that your ideas are profound and am quite prepared to believe you may be right."

I discovered another nice feature about Eddington's letter. My letter to him is dated October 21st, his bears the date on the top of the letter, November 3rd. But the post mark is November 21st. So he must have begun writing almost immediately after receiving my letter and must have returned to it again and again.

21st October, 1935

Dear Sir Arthur,

Your Book *The Nature of the Physical World* had given me so much intellectual enjoyment and had so largely enriched my knowledge and understanding that I grasped the first opportunity of reading the *New Pathways in Science*. The impression the new book made on me was even greater than that of the old one; you had in the meantime clarified your philosophical position to such an extent that your new theory is a challenge to everyone who thinks seriously about the meaning of science and reality. While I was reading the book I felt again and again the desire for long conversations with you, which are unfortunately out of the question. It never occurred to me that I might write to you. However, after I had finished the book your ideas gave me no rest. I had to think continually of the problems you had raised and the solutions you had proposed. You had shaken my intellectual equilibrium, and I had to do something to regain it.

So eventually I conceived the idea of writing to you and telling you the points about which I could not possibly agree with you.

I am not sure whether it is right to send this letter, because it imposes upon you a sort of obligation of reading it. I know you are a very busy man, probably engaged at this time in some difficult piece of concrete research far removed from the general philosophical considerations of your book. And I certainly do not want to disrupt your plan of work. Everybody ought to be able to decide what he wants to work at; nobody ought to be at the mercy of odd correspondents. Therefore I shall perfectly understand if you refuse to look at this letter now. Perhaps you might then take it up in later years when you prepare a new book. Whatever you do, I want you to know that I am grateful for what you have given me in your two books. My letter is not meant as negative criticism, but as an honest attempt to reach greater clarity about the most fundamental problems.

To facilitate the discussion I am using several quotations from your books. Simple page references refer to *New Pathways in Science,* while the addition of NPW marks the quotation as coming from *The Nature of the Physical World.*

I shall first state the points in which I am in full agreement with you: (1) Our conception of the universe must be such that truth, value, beauty, have a real place in it; i.e., a final philosophy can neither bar these entities as human illusions nor admit them as mere luxuries which might just as well have been left out. (2) A dualism of the ordinary kind, a mind or spirit breaking through the laws of nature is inadmissible. Your brief discussion of this position on p. 87 is excellent. (3) The deterministic view of Omar Khayyam or Laplace is inconsistent with the first requirement—whether *any* deterministic view conflicts with the first postulate seems to me not so easy to answer; I defer the discussion of this point. (4) The only material we have for gaining a conception of the universe is the world of our direct experience or mind. To become intelligible it requires the construction of a non-experienceable external world which must always remain a construct, although we are convinced of its reality. Your discussion of "New Realism" on pp. 281ff seems to me absolutely justified. I have never been able truly to understand this doctrine, and I have always believed "that there is a tendency in modern philosophy to adopt a view which is scientifically untenable" (p. 5). Perhaps I ought to add (5) Our conception of the universe must also have a proper place for science—this lest you might think that the requirements of science were less important to me than others.

Thus I hope you will agree that we are in harmony about the fundamental aims, the starting point, and certain solutions which we find unacceptable. As to your own solution, I have the greatest admiration for it and consider it a very positive contribution to philosophy that it has been developed with such clarity, breadth, and profundity. My failure to accept it as final (for our time) derived from the fact that my striving for unity is even greater than yours. I am not convinced that science will have *forever* to be satisfied with a small part of reality, and that other, if anything more important, parts shall remain the exclusive domain of other human attitudes and efforts. Being a psychologist, I am concerned with "the story teller and his story" (p. 1ff); his responsibility towards truth belongs to my subject-matter as much as the story he tells me. I have to include both in the system of psychology, if this system is to be adequate; and therefore I must hope to catch the will for truth in my scientific net or give up my job. I am of course keenly aware that the scientific net with which the will for truth can be caught is not any existing scientific net. It is not even yours, since you make yours such as to incapacitate it for catching this fish.

Such a definition of my aim will mean very little to you. You claim to have shown that my goal cannot be reached by its very nature. Therefore I will take up another aspect of psychology. It is of course concerned with the story teller's story, and it has, particularly during the last twenty years, discovered a good deal about the relation between the story and the external world which sends the messages. Now I believe that these discoveries have a great deal to do with our problem. I shall later show that the assumptions which you make, plausible as they seem, are not correct, and that they lead you to a fiction about the nature of the scientific observer which is as illegitimate as the fiction of a mass which exists and moves with uniform velocity alone in the universe. It is my contention that the abandonment of this fiction will contribute to that kind of unification which I have in mind.

I propose to begin my discussion as it were in the middle, analyzing one quotation and proceeding from there in both directions, to the starting point and to the goal. (pp. 90, 91)

Suppose that I have hit on a piece of mathematical research which promises interesting results. The assurance that I most desire is that the result which I write down at the end shall be the work of a mind which respects truth and logic, not the work of a hand which respects Maxwell's equations and the conservation of energy.

If the mathematical argument in my mind is compelled to reach the conclusion which a deterministic system of physical law has preordained that my hands shall write down, then reasoning must be explained away as a process quite other than that which I feel it to be. But my whole respect for reasoning is based on the hypothesis that it is what I feel it to be.

I do not think we can take liberties with that immediate self-knowledge of consciousness by which we are aware of ourselves as responsible, truth-seeking, reasoning, striving.

The dilemma stated in this quotation is of fundamental importance, and the negative conclusion you draw from it seems to me absolutely correct. An explanation of the solution that you write down in terms of the Maxwell equations [1]† or the conservation of energy [2], applied either to the muscles of your body or to the processes in your brain, would not be an explanation because it would miss the point. Reasoning cannot be explained away, because on the one hand it is an observable fact and on the other hand it is the basis of all explanation. But your positive conclu-

---

† Explanatory notes about certain technical terms will be found at end of appendix.

sion is not equally clear to me. You see in reasoning the manifestation of spirit; but this description alone does not help me. In the first place I find that you define spirit only through such manifestations, so that no new insight is gained by calling them spiritual, apart possibly from the claim that they are essentially different from the physical world; and in the second place I do not see how this description solves the dilemma, since you do not accept a spirit that interferes with natural law. Even indeterminism cannot give any aid. For the writing down of a solution involves without the slightest doubt billions of atoms, so that your own argument of p. 88 applies; the uncertainty would be so small as to be practical certainty.

I should conjecture that the smallest unit of structure in which the physical effects of volition have their origin contains many billions of atoms. If such a unit behaved like an inorganic system of similar mass the indeterminacy would be insufficient to allow appreciable freedom. My own tentative view is that this "conscious unit" does in fact differ from an inorganic system in having a much higher indeterminacy of behaviour—simply because of the unitary nature of that which in reality it represents, namely the Ego.

Incidentally, I was tremendously pleased by this argument, which should once and for all put an end to superficial conclusions drawn from the uncertainty principle [3] with regard to the freedom of will.

But let us return to the argument. I do not see how you can refute an opponent who claims that nothing in physics is incompatible with the assertion that the writing down of your solution is in principle explainable in terms of physical laws. Indeed I see only two alternatives, uncertainty having been excluded: either your action is derivable from physical law or it necessitates the introduction of an outside agent, a spirit, a vital force, an entelechy. Unless I misunderstand you completely, you refuse to accept this alternative, but I fail to see how you escape it. Of course my lack of understanding may be to blame and not your theory. In that case it would help me greatly if you would point out my misapprehension.

But as far as I understand you at the present moment, the dilemma still exists; we have to decide which of its horns we choose. I apply your method of exclusion: the second alternative, a spirit breaking through natural law, must be excluded as long as science has not proved conclusively that without such an outside agent it remains incomplete, i.e., unable to cope with all the facts which properly belong to its domain. But if I exclude the second alternative, I must accept the first, although only a short while ago I seemed to join with you in a rejection of it. I shall retract nothing, instead I shall claim that my rejection of the explanation in terms of Maxwell equations and conservation of energy is not equivalent to a rejection of the first alternative. In short, my tentative solution is as follows: natural law is such that it manifests itself as well in the solution of a mathematical problem as in the planetary system, or the vagaries of atoms; if natural law is of this kind, then physical law, the laws found and expressed by physicists, must contain this characteristic also if they are adequate maps or pictures, or symbols of natural law. Very clearly the ordinary laws of physics as usually interpreted do not satisfy this condition, and therefore it seems absurd to explain the discovery of a solution in terms of Maxwell equations. But instead of saying: Therefore I must accept laws of a different kind which cannot be assimilated to natural law (NPW 345).

We cannot assimilate laws of thought to natural laws; they are laws which ought to be obeyed, not laws which must be obeyed; and the physicist must accept laws of thought before he accepts natural law. "Ought" takes us outside chemistry and physics.

I say: Let us therefore see whether physical law, *if viewed differently*, does not contain at least the germ of those characteristics which we need in order to apply them to the *rational* or logical workings of our minds. If we could answer this question in the affirmative, then our dilemma would cease to exist.

I am quite aware that as it stands this suggestion is open to the criticism of philosophical "anticipations" which you give in your first chapter and to which I wholeheartedly agree. The philosopher can indeed become "an officious spectator who bothers the workman by handing him tools before he is ready to use them." (p. 25) But you consider this statement yourself as one-sided and revealing only a part of the truth. Besides, the problem which occupies us both is to look beyond the present state of knowledge towards an ideal condition in which we should understand everything. Nevertheless, it is rather humiliating to feel that one sees a possibility of progress and yet to be unable to make this feeling so clear and concrete that it can be translated into mathematical equations which would be significant for further research. I wish I had sufficient training in mathematics and theoretical physics and sufficient ability to attempt such an undertaking.

Unfortunately, all I can do is to give you a few more indications of my ideas, outlining the direction physics might take in order to fulfill the task I am assigning to it. These indications follow suggestions contained in your own writings; they are all centered in the concept of organization. I have found on page 312 of your new book, the statement "that it is not sufficiently recognized that modern physics, theoretical physics, is very much concerned with organization." Other than this the only direct mention occurs on pages 55, 56 in connection with the second law of thermodynamics [4], but without a general analysis of its implications for physics.

On the other hand there is a very significant passage about it in NPW on pp. 103–104, where you say that the inventory method "misses any world features which are not located in minute compartments. We often think that when we have completed our study of *one* we know all about *two*, because 'two' is 'one and one.' We forget that we have still to make a study of 'and.' Secondary physics is the study of 'and'—that is to say of organization." Now it seems to me that I take this proposition much more seriously than you take it yourself; for neither in NPW nor in your new book do I find any attempt to study *organization* as something real. On p. 106 of NPW you say, presenting, I believe, not your own opinion but current physics: "In so far as arrangement signifies a picture, it is lost; science has to do with paints, not with pictures. In so far as arrangement signifies organization it is kept; science has much to do with organization." I must say that it has not become clear to me what in this context the term "organization" adds to the concept of arrangement. I see the difference between mere (geometrical) arrangement and "picture," but I do not understand the meaning of the third term as different from either the one or the other. Nor does the end of this section in NPW help, for there you abandon the picture concept for the physical world and fall back on our personality. I wanted to ask: But what has physics to do with organization?

Of course your procedure is not arbitrary. You introduce organization in connection with entropy [4] and therefore your concept of organization is bound up with your conception of entropy which since Boltzmann [4] has been connected with probability. I have just quoted you as saying: "Secondary physics is the study of organization." Some time before you say that you define the "secondary laws" as laws which exclude certain events because they are too improbable. Here, then, is the connection between organization and probability in your system, as far as I could find it. Am I wrong in concluding that organization as anything besides "geometrical arrangement which differs by more than a small magnitude from thermodynamical equilibrium" [4] is *not* a special concept of your system? And yet, as I shall point out later, you seem to me, in a different and wider context, to employ concepts which contain the idea of organization at least implicitly.

But at the moment I must follow up your theory with regard to organization in its relation to entropy. I feel very uncomfortable in doing so, because I have to speak about a very difficult subject in which I am no more than an rank amateur, i.e., the statistical interpretation of physics. As far as I can see, the fundamental position can be stated as follows: We consider a closed volume containing a great number of particles (mass points) and we assume that each particle can do what it likes. Then we calculate all possible distributions of coordinates and momenta of these particles and exclude from this array all those which do not fulfill the condition that the total energy of our closed system must remain constant. Thus we have a distribution plane in phase space [4]. Then we find out which regions in this plane are such that they differ from thermodynamical equilibrium first by $\pm\delta$ then by $\pm2\delta\pm3\delta$, and so forth, and we find that the greater the deviation from thermodynamical equilibrium the smaller the regions in the distribution plane, according to Boltzmann's logarithmic law of entropy [4]. From this we conclude that, although any particle can do what it likes, the total effect will with an enormous probability be that the distribution will increasingly approach thermodynamical equilibrium [4], because the particles in their perfectly random migrations have the more territory at their disposal the closer they come to this equilibrium. I know that this is not Boltzmann's method, who derived his law under the assumption that each particle obeys the laws of mechanics; I think this is historically true and admitted by you on p. 300, where you contrast the "practice which used to be followed" with the procedure of Schrodinger, Heisenberg, and Dirac [3]. Now I have to admit that I do not know, and should be unable to understand, the scientific papers of these three authors; but I have read Schrodinger's last popular book and I had many discussions with him this summer in Oxford before I had seen your book; and although it is largely due to Schrodinger's explanations that I could state the case of statistical physics as I did, he must not be held responsible for any errors or inaccuracies of my statement.

As it stands this statement seems to me unsatisfactory for various reasons. My first point is that the relation between what is and what is probable is not really elucidated in this theory. To borrow an argument from Schrodinger (again on my own responsibility): A scientist finds a system in a certain condition which is not thermodynamical equilibrium. Then he will predict with enormous probability that as soon as it changes it will approach this equilibrium, and he will base this prediction on the theory which I have just tried to express. But he might apply exactly the same theory to an inference about the past, and then he would say: Since in comparison with our system there are so many more distributions nearer the thermodynamical equilibrium than further remote from it, it is highly probable that our system, before it reached its present state, was nearer this equilibrium, i.e., that it had a greater entropy in the past than it has at present. If I understand you correctly you solve this difficulty by considering, not without a certain uneasiness (cf. NPW p. 77), the law of entropy as an independent law of nature, the law by which nature carries an arrow of time [4].

At the bottom of all the questions settled by secondary law there is an elusive conception of "a priori probability of states of the world" which involves an essentially different attitude to knowledge from that presupposed in the construction of the scheme of primary law.

If this is so, does not this view exclude the assumption that a particle may do what it likes, since this assumption can be used to derive that $ds/dt < 0$ [4], as I have just tried to show?

My second point: In the theory as I understand it, the distribution plane which alone we have to consider is a small fraction of all possible distributions, selected by means of the law of conservation of energy [2]. Again I can express this by saying: This condition limits each particle in its freedom of action; it can do what it likes only as long as its behaviour does not lead to a distribution that has a different energy content from the one the system has at the observed moment.

Thirdly, it seems to me that Heisenberg's law of uncertainty [3] has also to be applied to each particle with the result that its freedom is further restricted. It cannot move in such a way that the product $\sigma_p \cdot \sigma_q \leqslant h$ [3]. I have not found this argument in the few books I have consulted, and therefore I feel that I may be wrong, although I cannot see where my error can lie. If my argument is correct, then the uncertainty principle, instead of increasing the freedom of events would limit it.

The three preceding points all seem to me to reveal that the statistical view, as I have stated it, is based on an assumption the truth of which it denies: it presupposes that a particle may do what it likes, but it limits the freedom of the particles so that they cannot do what they like.

My fourth argument refers to the concept of freedom or uncertainty itself. You emphasize again and again that the law of causality is an hypothesis, not an observed datum. But is the assumption of complete or partial freedom anything else? Observation reveals within the limits of the uncertainty principle a combination of p and q. So *post* factum we know that the particle has moved in such a way as to have now these momenta and coordinates. Causality theory claims that it could not have had any other, and noncausality that it might—within limits. You have tried, and I think successfully, to defend yourself against an argument which is similar to this one (pp. 84f.); but the difference seems to me sufficient for claiming that your refutation of the determinists' claims does not affect my criticism. I will elaborate: I suppose that at the moment t_0 we do not know, i.e., we cannot predict, the p,q of a particle at the moment t_1. At t_1 we know these p,q. Then the determinist says: the particle has at time t_1 the properties p,q, because it *had* to have them, because it *could not* have had any others. The indeterminist says: this is a mere assumption; it might *for all I know* have had p',q'. The danger of this second statement lies, in my opinion, in the concept of possibility. At t_0 I could not say which p,q the particle would have at t_1. The p,q it actually shows at t_1 appear at t_0 as a member of a class, the class of the *potential* p,q. Where, then, is the potentiality to be placed? The determinist places it entirely within the mind of the ignorant physicist, the indeterminist at least partly within the particle itself. I cannot say that either claims more than the other; but to me the concept of a potentiality inherent in a particle is essentially unclear, and therefore

I cannot connect any definite meaning with your statement
on p. 83:

> The future is never entirely determined by the past, nor is it
> ever entirely detached. We have referred to several phenomena
> in which the future is *practically determined*; the break-down
> of a radium nucleus is an example of a phenomenon in which
> the future is *practically detached* from the past.

It seems to me that the more science strives to stick to the observable the less place it should have for the potential (in an
objective sense). Determination and freedom seem to me to be
not two opposites within the same universe of discourse but to
belong to two different universes of discourse.

I proceed to a brief analysis of the principle of uncertainty itself. I cannot help feeling that though it is a principle of uncertainty (of knowledge), it is not a principle of indeterminacy (of
things). And I am basing this feeling on your own presentation.
If you write: "There is a double consequence; the interaction
starts a signal informing us that the value of a certain symbol q
in the system is q_1 and at the same time *it alters to an unknown
extent the value of another symbol p in the system*" (p. 100), does
not the clause underlined by me imply that before the interaction the symbol now altered *had* a definite, though unknown,
value? I do not see how you can say that this value is altered
unless you assume that before the alteration it had a definite
value. Thus the uncertainty would be perfectly clear, but the indeterminacy would be lost. The whole sequel confirms me in this
impression. I was astounded by the beauty and ingenuity of your
various applications of the principle. But philosophically it puzzled me tremendously how it could be possible to infer existences
from mere lack of knowledge, uncertainty. I believe that I have
found a solution of this paradox: the Heisenberg principle [3], by
saying something about the quantitative uncertainty of our
knowledge, $\sigma_p \sigma_q \geq h$, implies something very positive about the
nature of the universe of the atom. It is this *knowledge* which is

utilized in the inferences and not the lack of knowledge, the uncertainty. In other words: the principle of uncertainty seems to me to contain a definite *determination* of nature, a determination which is different in kind from that of the laws of classical physics [5], but which is a determination nevertheless. Connecting this idea with your text on p. 100 previously quoted, I am tempted to say: the principle of uncertainty says something about the simultaneous alterations of p and q. However this may be, I am not convinced that this principle instead of introducing freedom into the world, does not give us a new kind of determination of the world.

After this excursion into the meaning of the principle of uncertainty I return to the argument about organization which was interrupted. If I look at what you say on p. 271, it seems to me that here you are really dealing with organization, although you use the word "structure" in its place.

All this knowledge of structure can be expressed without specifying the nature of the operations. And it is through recognition of a structure of this kind that we can have knowledge of an external world which from an ordinary standpoint is essentially unknowable.

This structure is a set or group of operations which are not defined as such, but whose interconnectedness or structure is essential. If we say, this, then, it seems to me, structure has a very definite meaning with regard to reality. In sooth: since the operations per se are not defined, they contain no assertion about reality. Conversely since you say that "through recognition of a structure of this kind we can have knowledge of an external world," this *structure* must contain properties which its parts do not possess. In my terminology the structure would be a gestalt, and knowledge of the world would be in terms of gestalten. Not the fact that you can introduce this structure by defining certain arbitrary operations to be performed on arbitrary material makes this structure the powerful tool of knowledge it is, but the *whole-character* of the set. I do not know Dirac's wave equation [3] of

an electron nor how he discovered the set of E operations, but I
feel reasonably sure that he did not do it by starting, say, from
the operation which on p. 267 you call Sα and then adding Sβ to
it in a random or trial and error way. What he must have found
first is, unless I am very much mistaken, the structure, not the
individual operators; the whole, not the parts of which it is composed. Therefore I conclude that the essential characteristic of
the external world, as far as the physicist knows it, is structure
or organization. But a world which is essentially organized is
not a world in which each particle can do what it likes, nor is it
a world whose features can be discovered by what you call the
inventory method, i.e., by studying each particle for itself, because structure or organization is not a feature belonging to a
particle per se. I believe that you will agree to this statement. I
have formulated it, not because I think it in conflict with your
view, but because I should give more emphasis to it than you
seem to do. As a matter of fact statements on p. 234 and p. 313
seem to support my belief.

> . . . for my own part I can say unhesitatingly that in the struc-
> ture of the universe as known to present day physics where is
> at most one arbitrary constant . . . It may be that the one re-
> maining constant is not arbitrary, but that I have no knowl-
> edge. (p. 234)
> What we are dragging to light as the basis of all phenomena
> is a scheme of symbols connected by mathematical equations.
> That is what physical reality boils down to when probed by the
> methods which a physicist can apply. (p. 313)

If physical reality "boils down" to a scheme of symbols, then
inasmuch as this scheme is not a random agglomeration of equations but a consistent and coherent whole, the world has whole-
character, it consists of parts which are not independent elementary particles but large organized systems with their laws of
organization. Whether all these subsystems together form an
all-comprising large system, whether the whole world is a gestalt, is a different question. What you say on p. 234 seems to

indicate that it probably is; for otherwise it would be hard to
understand why all, or all but one, constants are not-arbitrary.
In this connection I must also refer to another paragraph on
p. 322:

> Whilst therefore I contemplate a spiritual domain underlying
> the physical world as a whole, I do not think of it as distrib-
> uted so that to each element of time and space there is a corre-
> sponding portion of the spiritual background. My conclusion is
> that, although for the most part our inquiry into the problem of
> experience ends in a veil of symbols, there is an immediate
> knowledge in the minds of conscious beings which lifts the veil
> in places; and what we discern through these openings is of
> mental and spiritual nature. Elsewhere we see no more than
> the veil.

Your metaphysical hypothesis that a spiritual domain underlies
the physical world is specified to maintain not a point to point
but a whole to whole correspondence. This again, unless I misin-
terpret your text, seems to imply that physical reality is composed of wholes and may be a large whole in its entirety.

    There is, however, one passage in your book which, while it
seems to me particularly important, causes me great difficulty. I
mean your conjecture about the physical events underlying volition. You write (p. 88) "My own tentative view is that this 'conscious unit' does, in fact, differ from an inorganic system in having a much higher indeterminacy of behaviour—simply because
of the unitary nature of that which in reality it represents,
namely the Ego." I find it hard to connect this sentence with the
rest of your system. In the first place it introduces a very definite
dualism, whereas ultimately you reject a body-mind dualism.
But if a "conscious unit" differs from an inorganic unit, then
physical nature itself falls into two parts, "conscious units" and
the inorganic units. In the second place I fail to see why, on
premises stated by you, the unitary nature of the "conscious
unit" should provide it with greater indeterminacy. Have I over-

looked a part of your argument, or have you omitted it? Or do
you introduce this whole explanation as a mere assumption in
which the "because" does not refer to any recognized reasons?
Not knowing the answer to these questions I shall formulate my
own conclusions: that the physiological processes underlying
acts of volition are unitary in nature is as much my conviction
as it is yours, a conviction moreover which is supported by my
knowledge of other parts of psychology which I shall discuss
later. From this conviction I should draw conclusions different
from yours. Instead of affirming that therefore some parts of
physical reality are different (in an absolute sense) from all
inorganic systems I should say: we find parts of the external
world—for you as well as I must call the physiological processes
in the brain part of the external world—unitary. Have we sufficient reason to believe that these unitary parts are in this respect different from the rest of the world? My answer would be
negative just because of the general nature of the physical world
which I have discussed in the preceding pages. If structure is the
main characteristic of the physical world, then the unitariness
which some parts of it possess does not for this reason distin-
guish them from the rest. They may still be different by the kind
and degree of unitariness, but such distinctions apply to the
whole universe and do not justify a radical dualism. Lastly: why
does this unitariness imply indeterminacy of a higher degree? I
have tried to show that organization limits the freedom of each
particle in what it can do. The more highly organized a system
is, the less its particles can do what they like. I return once more
to the quotation from which my whole discussion started. The
physiological processes which underlie the finding of a mathematical solution—or any logical thought-process—must also be
unitary; this in accordance with your statement: "It seems to me
that we must attribute some kind of unitary behaviour to the
physical terminal of consciousness" (p. 89), a quotation which I
shall refer to again. And yet the outstanding characteristic
of this system is, not that it is indeterminate, but that it must
reach the true solution. Of course, I can lie. But if I do so I know

that I am in conflict with the logical system which demands the proper solution. Thus indeterminacy would be based on the possibility of my lying whereas you build your whole spiritual solution on the will for truth. Of course I would not really argue this way; my explanation of lying would be that in such cases the behaviour of the organism would be under the influence of many systems, of which the "solution system" is only a part; and the same argument would apply to "error." I cannot in this letter write a treatise on psychology, and therefore I must drop this matter. But my point is that great unitariness is not only compatible with, but demands determinacy. However, I have to add one important clause to this statement: the determinacy demanded by unitariness is not *blind* determinacy, not the blind causality of classical physics [5], not the causality which you rightly want to eliminate from the conception of the universe. The determinacy demanded by unitariness is *intelligible* or rational determinacy. It is therefore my belief that one can hope to reconcile physics and ethics, not by introducing indeterminacy, but by changing the meaning of determinacy.

I may express my meaning also by saying: the dilemma between classical determinism and your indeterminism may be the result of a wrong interpretation of the cryptogram. Indeed it seems to me, as I have indicated at the beginning, that you do not treat the story teller's story quite adequately. This leads to a discussion of three more of your propositions, which I epitomize here:

(1) Finally we have to remember that physical law is arrived at from the analysis of conscious experience; it is the solution of the cryptogram contained in the story of consciousness. How then can we represent consciousness as being not only outside it but inimical to it? (p. 87) and again,

It seems to me that we must attribute some kind of unitary behaviour to the physical terminal of consciousness, otherwise the physical symbolism is not an appropriate representation of the mental unit which is being symbolised. (p. 4)

(2) The making of the story from the wire messages transmitted by the nerves. (pp. 3, 4)

(3) A fanciful story based on these signals. Metaphor: mistranslation of a cipher. (pp. 6, 7)

With the first I am, of course, in full accord. Difficulties crop up with (2) and (3). According to (1) conscious experience is our ultimate datum, but according to (2) a complete record of the impulses transmitted along the nerves is all the material we need. Much as I grant the first statement I have to criticize the second. I admit for the sake of argument that independent impulses travel along the nerves without influencing each other. Would the knowledge of these impulses really give us all the material we need for deciphering the cryptogram? Would the nerve-impulse cryptogram be a better, i.e., more adequate, starting point for the scientist than the story teller's story? On p. 13 you describe the observer as he is constituted after relativity theory [5]: he "could no longer recognize form or extension in the external world, but he could tell whether two things were in apparent coincidence or not." This, then, is the minimum of material you demand for the task of deciphering. Is this minimum contained in the nerve impulses? Certainly not. Since according to our assumption each nerve carries its own excitation independently of all other excitations, the sum of all nerve impulses does not contain anything like "two things," and therefore of course nothing like "a coincidence." To use your terminology: the nerve impulses have (geometrical) arrangement, but they are not organized according to our assumption, and they are not a picture. "Two things": coincidence, on the other hand are *pictorial* aspects. Inasmuch as these are necessary, the knowledge of all the nerve impulses is not sufficient for the physicist's task; rather, the physicist needs, even for his simplest tasks like the observation of a pointer, the contribution of the story teller. As these contributions are in a vast number of cases not so bad as you imply in proposition (3) I need only elaborate my remarks about the observation of a pointer. For the physicist the pointer is *one* thing, the scale *another*, whatever his theory about the nature of things—for microscopic theories have to conform to macroscopic facts.

Between the instrument and the eye, however, this distinction is completely lost. In the light that reaches our eye from the instrument there is nothing in any way similar to the distinction of two things, and since it is the light and not the instrument which affects our eye and sends impulses along the nerves these impulses cannot possibly contain anything like the distinction in the external world. Our direct experience on the other hand does contain it, and therefore the sum of the nervous impulses is something very different from the physical terminal of conscious experience. This point has been overlooked in practically all discussions of this problem and similar ones. It was explained with great clearness and all appropriate emphasis by Köhler in his *Gestalt Psychology*.

The psychologist has the task of explaining why so often the story teller's story contains more about reality than the sum of the nervous impulses, and the work of the last 25 years has contributed a considerable amount of material to the solution of this problem. This solution must not contain the real objects, because they are not in direct contact with the organism; the problem would be the same if it were stated: given a certain distribution of light on the retina, what shall I see? Of course often the story is quite wrong, and always it is partially so. But there is something in the story which the physicist cannot do without and which is not in the sum of the nerve impulses.

You acknowledge this fact again and again, it is indeed the cornerstone on which you build your metaphysics. But you will utilize these parts of the story—responsibility, will for truth— only for the purpose of discovering the spiritual matter of the world; you reject it as an indication of the nature of the physical world. In this attitude you seem to have been misled by a one-sided selection of your material, a selection which seems to me also arbitrary. You reject on p. 4 conceptions of colour spaciousness, substance, because "the transmitting mechanism is by its very nature incapable of conveying such forms of conception."

But you overlook that this last statement could not be made without accepting some such aspects. How could we have discovered the facts of nervous transmission, which, as you say yourself (on p. 3) "no scientific-minded person disputes," without perceiving and acknowledging the nerves as things, i.e., under the category of substance. How can you, to return to a previous point, accept a scheme of symbols as truth about the external world, when this scheme is definitely such that "the transmitting mechanism is incapable of conveying it"? I believe that unwittingly you use far more contributions of the story teller for the construction of the universe than you admit. And therefore it seems to me arbitrary to single out certain ones which you use exclusively for the determination of spiritual matter.

Your selection leads you even to an illegitimate fiction. On p. 13 you say: "If he (Einstein) removed the retina of the eye except one small patch, the observer could no longer recognize form or extension in the external world, but he could tell whether two things are in apparent coincidence or not." But this contradicts the facts. If you make the patch small enough, then because of this smallness, the observer would be practically blind; he could no longer fulfill the task you set him. In order to do that he must be able to do more than that. I have said before that the "coincidence of two things" is part of the story, not of the nervous impulses. My point now is that this story cannot be told under the conditions you specify. The reason is very simple: the story presupposes a *physiological process in extension*, so that each part of the extended process depends on all other parts. If you remove too many of them, the rest will lose its articulation. This is but an application of your statement on p. 89, quoted above, that "we must attribute some kind of unitary behaviour to the physical terminal of consciousness."

What I am driving at is not a wholesale acceptance of conscious experience for the construction of the physical world; I said before that I agree completely with your criticism of so-called New Realism. I am only insisting that we are using more data of consciousness than we recognize, and that lack of recognition is responsible for a great many of the philosophical diffi-

culties which we encounter. The chief concept I have in mind is
the concept of organization in all its aspects; and as I have previously mentioned, causality may well be an aspect of organization. My argument is again similar in nature to one you employ.
You write: "The question 'It is true?' changes the complexion
of the world of experience—not because it is asked *about* the
world, but because it is asked *in* the world" (p. 310–311). Similarly I argue: organization in the story teller's story does not
only give a (right or wrong) report *about* the world, but it happens *in* the world, which therefore is such that stories can be
told in it. Therefore, the characteristics of the story are characteristics of at least some parts of the world.

A last word about your metaphysical solution as crystallized
in the following quotation: (pp. 319, 320)

> Interpreting the term material (or more strictly, physical)
> in the broadest sense as that with which we can become ac-
> quainted through sensory experience of the external world, we
> recognize now that it corresponds to the waves not to the water
> of the ocean of reality. My answer does not deny the existence
> of the physical world, any more than the answer that the ocean
> is made of water denies the existence of ocean waves; only we
> do not get down to the intrinsic nature of things that way. Like
> the symbolic world of physics, a wave is a conception which is
> hollow enough to hold almost anything; we can have waves of
> water, of air, or aether, and (in quantum theory) waves of prob-
> ability. So after physics has shown us the waves, we have still
> to determine the content of the waves by some other avenue of
> knowledge.

I was simply astounded when I read it by the boldness and origi-
nality of the conception. Of course since Aristotle we have been
accustomed to think in terms of the opposite analogy: nature =
matter and spirit = form. Therefore your complete reversal was
a real intellectual experience to me. But as you will know by
now, I cannot accept it. On the one hand it seems to me that you
say too much when you say that a wave like the symbolic world

of physics is a conception hollow enough to hold almost anything. By saying "almost" you protect yourself to some extent, but your statement certainly emphasizes the idea that form and content are practically independent of each other. This, of course, is not strictly true of waves. The kind of waves we observe presuppose very definite materials, different for transverse and longitudinal ones, to give but one example. And asphalt could not carry waves like those of the ocean. On the other hand, and more important, I cannot believe that the opposition of wave and water fits the pair physical and spiritual world. What you admire in the spiritual realm is *not* a material property, like fine silk vs. coarse cotton, but a type of form of behaviour. Wertheimer has pointed out that a spiritual world of ideas ruled by the blind laws of association would have less of the "spiritual" in your sense than a living tree. And he continues: "It cannot matter of what material the particles of the universe consist; what matters is the kind of whole, the significance of the whole." Therefore, instead of preserving the spirit in my picture of the universe by assigning to it the role of the matter which fills the whole skeleton, but excluding it from the physical world (see pp. 312, 313), I should retain it by keeping organization and with it rationality in my whole world picture. Organization will be more perfect in some places than in others—it will not disturb you that I introduce the value concept into the conception of the universe, since you are basing your own position on the recognition of value—and those places will therefore deserve the name spiritual more than others. It is however good not to forget that God and the devil live close together, and that such places of higher organization are also the only ones where radically evil and ethical behavior can occur.

What then about the determinism of Omar Khayyam? My answer is an uncertainty, because I see an alternative without any reason for choosing one of its sides; it is possible that a concept of causality based on organization and therefore different from blind causality does not contain Omar's creed as an implicit assumption. Before such a concept of causality has been worked out one cannot say whether it does or not. If it does, however, then a determination which is rational loses much of the odium which blind determination carries, particularly since in this causality rational beings with their responsibility are effective causes.

Please forgive the length of this letter. Of course I should be tremendously pleased to get some reaction from you to the ideas presented in these pages. But again I urge you not to let my will for truth interfere with your work.

Believe me yours sincerely,

[K.K.]

Explanatory Notes

Fredrik A. Lindholm
Professor of Electrical Engineering
University of Florida

1. *Maxwell's equations.* James Clerk Maxwell (1831–79), Scottish physicist and first professor of experimental physics at Cambridge University, is known today best for his studies in electromagnetism, which compacted the results of previous investigations into four simple equations that describe nearly all phenomena involving electricity and magnetism. These *Maxwell equations* treat the force that would act at each point in space on an electrical charge placed at that point. The resulting "*field* of force," and the related electric and magnetic *fields*, are to be conceived as existing even when no electrical charges are placed to test for their existence. How these fields are created in space by material objects and how they propagate is described by the Maxwell equations. So comprehensive is this description that it not only predicted the possibility of propagating electromagnetic waves—the basis of transmission of radio, radar, and television—but it also had a unifying influence on physical thought by showing that light itself could be considered as an electromagnetic effect.

2. *Conservation of energy.* The conservation laws are among the most basic of the laws of nature. In general, a conservation law states that, within a given physical system under specified condi-

tions, there is a measurable quantity that never changes. The *law of conservation of energy*, due to Hermann L. F. von Helmholtz in 1847, states that energy does not change (it cannot be created or destroyed), although it can be converted from one form to another (e.g., light energy into electrical energy). This is also known as the *first law of thermodynamics*.

3. *Uncertainty principle; Schrodinger, Heisenberg, Dirac; classical physics; quantum physics. Classical physics* is based on two assumptions that have been shown to conflict with the results of experiment. The first of these is that the magnitude of the interaction between two physical systems can be reduced to arbitrarily small values. (The second assumption will be discussed in note 5 below.) The overthrow of this assumption began in 1900, when Max Planck, a German physicist, suggested that any radiation, including light, came in finite (non-zero) bundles of energy, called *quanta*, the value of each of which was inversely proportional to the wavelength of the radiation. The overthrow was cemented by Albert Einstein's demonstration in 1905 that the previously unexplained photoelectric-effect experiment could be understood if radiation not only consisted of finite quanta of energy but also was absorbed by material objects in finite quanta. The recognition of the existence of a finite quantum of energy in any interaction between physical systems was incorporated into the *quantum (wave) mechanics,* or *quantum physics,* which replaced Newtonian (classical) mechanics as the tool needed to describe many of the observed properties of atoms, molecules and electrons.

Quantum mechanics was developed in the late 1920s and early 1930s by such physicists as Schrodinger, Heisenberg, and Dirac, all of whom received the Nobel Prize for this work. To incorporate the quantum nature of interactions, quantum mechanics is formulated on a probability (statistical) basis. Rather than asserting that an electron has a location and a velocity (or, more precisely, momentum) at a certain instant, as would be done in classical mechanics, quantum mechanics instead asserts only the probability that the electron is located in any specified volume and has a velocity in a specified range.

One outgrowth of quantum mechanics is the *Heisenberg Uncertainty Principle*, which states that any measurement made on a physical system (such as an electron) destroys some of the knowledge gained about that system from previous measurements. Thus, for example, there is always some uncertainty in knowledge about the position and velocity of an electron. Heisenberg stated this uncertainty quantitatively, showing that to gain more accurate knowledge of position creates more uncertainty in our knowledge of velocity. Qualitatively, one would anticipate the Uncertainty Principle just from the proposition that the interaction between two physical systems (the observed and the observer, in this case) involves non-zero quanta of energy; the energy required in the interaction changes the quantity being measured.

In symbols, if σ_p denotes the uncertainty in the momentum p and σ_q denotes the uncertainty in the position q, then the Uncertainty Principle can be written simply as, $\sigma_p \cdot \sigma_q \geq h/4\pi$. Here h stands for Planck's constant, which is a fundamental constant of nature (just as the speed of light and the charge on an electron are fundamental constants of nature) and $\geq$ means greater than or equal to.

4. *Second law of thermodynamics, entropy, Boltzmann's logarithmic law of entropy, arrow of time, phase space.* In any process involving the conversion of energy from one form to another (e.g., heat energy into energy of motion in a steam engine), a portion of the energy is wasted in the sense that it is lost as nonuseful heat energy, unable to perform work. This portion of the energy is reflected in the measurement of a physical quantity called the *entropy*. In a broader sense, the entropy can be regarded as a measure of the degree of disorder (or *random element*, in Eddington's words). The connection between heat and disorder comes from the kinetic theory of matter, which views a hotter body as being constituted of atoms and molecules in more agitated random motion than those in the same body when it is colder. The word *entropy* was borrowed from the Greek by the German physicist Rudolph Clausius, in 1850. It means transformation.

The *second law of thermodynamics* states that the entropy (the random element) of the universe is always increasing. (In symbols, if dS designates the change in entropy occurring in time interval dt, then the second law can be written simply as dS/dt $\geq$ 0.) That this is true is consistent with the observation that in any process involving a flow of energy there is always some loss to nonuseful heat. As Eddington emphasized in his writings, the second law is the only one of the physical laws that distinguishes past from future. Entropy is *time's arrow*, to use his words. It points in one direction—to the future—and in one direction only. Philosophical implications of the second law are important. From the law it follows that the farther back we go in time, the more organized the world must have been. Thus, Eddington argues in NPW, the universe must have had a beginning, and, then, it must be expected to have an end. The second law demands both.

Although the entropy of the universe always increases, a region of the universe can be so isolated that no net energy passes through its boundaries. For such a region, or physical system, the entropy stays constant, time has lost its arrow, past and future are indistinguishable. This is the condition of *thermodynamical equilibrium*, which occupies an important place in physics because it yields to calculation and displays many properties that help toward an understanding of the physical world.

Ludwig *Boltzmann* (1844–1906) of Vienna played a leading role in the nineteenth-century movement toward reducing the phenomena of heat, light, electricity and magnetism to atomic models based on Newtonian mechanics. He showed how mechanics, which is deterministic and reversible in time, could be used to describe the irreversible phenomena occurring in the real world that are governed by the second law of thermodynamics. In this demonstration, he dealt on a statistical basis with the multitude of atoms and molecules constituting matter. He introduced a *probability distribution function* that described how many atoms or molecules at any instant had such positions and velocities that they occupied a certain volume in a *phase space*—the coordinates of which are position and velocity. His work related probability and entropy in the *Boltzmann logarithmic law of entropy* referred to by Koffka in his letter.

5. *Relativity theory; classical physics.* Classical physics is based

on two assumptions that conflict with experimental results, as was stated in Note 3 above which discussed the first of these assumptions. The second assumption allows signals (information) to travel with infinite speed. The realization that the speed of propagation of signals has a non-infinite upper limit (the speed of light) led to the development of *relativity theory*.

Einstein's Special Relativity (1905) predicted as a natural consequence of its formulation that no body or physical effect can travel faster than the speed of light. Special Relativity predicts many other important results that conform to experiment, including the famous equivalence of mass and energy given by $E = mc^2$.

Special Relativity altered the previously held conception of space. To Maxwell, space was filled with an aether whose mechanical compressions and rarefactions produced the propagation of electromagnetic radiation, including light. Special relativity abolished this concept. To Newton, space served as the agent responsible for the resistance of a particle to acceleration. But Special Relativity did not deal with accelerated motion or gravitation. These were the subjects of Einstein's General Theory of Relativity of 1915, which abolished this Newtonian concept of space.

The General Theory completely alters the notion of gravitation by viewing it as a property of space, rather than as a force between bodies. The presence of matter curves space, and particles and light rays are postulated to move along certain preferred curves in space. In both Special and General Relativity, Einstein means by "space" a four-dimensional space-time continuum, in which time and the three space coordinates are treated equally.

References

Eddington, Arthur Stanley. 1929. *The nature of the physical world*. New York and Cambridge: The Macmillan Company and the University Press. Reprinted as an Ann Arbor paperback, University of Michigan Press, 1958.

———. 1935. *New pathways in science*. New York and Cambridge: The

Macmillan Company and the University Press. Reprinted as an Ann Arbor paperback, University of Michigan Press, 1959.

Koffka, Kurt. 1935. *The principles of Gestalt psychology*. New York: Harcourt Brace and Company. Paperback reprint, 1963.

Wertheimer, Max. 1925. *Über Gestalttheorie: Vortrag gehalten in der Kantgesselschaft Berlin am 17 Dez. 1924*, Sonderdrucke des Symposion 1. Erlangen. Translated by Kurt Riezler in *Social Research* 11 (February 1944): 78–99.

glossary of names

Edgar Douglas Adrian (1889–1977). British physiologist. Cambridge University (from 1920), professor of physiology (from 1937), master Trinity College (1951–65), vice-chancellor (1957–59), chancellor (1967). Royal Society of Medicine, president (1961–62). Research on functions of the heart and nervous system. Shared (with British physiologist Charles Scott Sherrington) the Nobel Prize in medicine (1932). Created 1st Baron Adrian in 1955. His writings include: *The Basis of Sensation* (1928), *The Mechanism of Nervous Action* (1932), and *The Physical Background of Perception* (1947).

Gordon Willard Allport (1897–1967). American psychologist. Assistant professor (1930–36), associate professor (1937–42), professor (from 1942), Harvard. Among his publications is *Personality: A Psychological Interpretation* (1937).

Sir Frederic Charles Bartlett (1886–1969). Leader in experimental psychology in England. Cambridge faculty (from 1914), director, Cambridge psychology laboratory (1922–52). Editor, *British Journal of Psychology* (1924–48). President, British Psychological Society, 1950. Devised numerous machines for testing servicemen during World War II. Among his publications are *Psychology and Primitive Culture* (1923), *Textbook of Experimental Psychology* (1925), *The Problem of Noise* (1934), *Political Propaganda* (1941).

Julien Benda (1867–1956). French philosopher and essayist. Advocated an uncompromising intellectual approach to life. Among his works are *Le Bergsonisme ou une Philosophie sur la Mobilité* (1912), *La Trahison des Clercs* (1927; *The Great Betrayal*, trans. R. Aldington, 1928), *La Fin de l'Eternel* (1929).

Madison Bentley (1870–1955). American psychologist. Cornell psychology department (1898–1912); University of Illinois psychology professor and director of psychology laboratory (1912–28), Sage professor of psychology at Cornell (1928–36), lecturer and consultant in psychology (from 1936). Experimentalists member. American Psychology Association president (1925). Editor, *American Journal of Psychology* (1903–51). Among his works are *Critical and Experimental Studies in Psychology* (1921), *The Field of Psychology* (1924), *Cornell Studies in Dynasomatic Psychology* (1938).

Alfred Binet (1857–1911). Most prominent French psychologist of his time. Promoted interest in human intellectual capacities and developed with T. Simon the Binet-Simon test (now the Stanford-Binet) and other tests to measure intelligence. Founded first French psychology laboratory at the Sorbonne (1889), director (from 1894). Founded first French psychology journal, *L'année psychologique* (1895).

Edwin Garrigues Boring (1886–1968). American psychologist known for his contributions in theoretical psychology, psychophysics, sensation, and the history of psychology. Psychology faculty, Clark University (1919–22); associate professor (1922–28), professor (1928–56), director of psychological laboratory (1924–49), Edgar Pierce professor of psychology emeritus (1957–68), Harvard. American Psychology Association president, 1928. Editor, *Contemporary Psychology* (1956–61). American Psychological Foundation Gold medal (1959). Honorary president, International Congress of Psychology (1963). Publications include *A History of Experimental Psychology* (1929; 2d edition, 1950), *The Physical Dimensions of Consciousness* (1933), *Sensation and Perception in the History of Experimental Psychology* (1942), *Psychologist at Large* (1961), *Source Book in the History of Psychology* (1965).

Sir Edward Farquar Buzzard (1871–1945). Physician, National Hospital for Nervous Diseases, London (1897–1922); consulting physician for numerous hospitals (from 1922); regius professor of medicine, Oxford University (1928–43). Leader in founding the Nuffield Institute for Medical Research (1935), Oxford; influenced the direction of its activities toward social medicine.

Sir Hugh William Bell Cairns (1896–1952). British neurosurgeon at the Nuffield Institute at Oxford. During World War II helped organize a special hospital for head injuries on the premises of St. Hugh's College, Oxford.

Leonard Carmichael (1898–1973). American psychologist with special interest in early developmental behavior, fatigue, and efficiency. Psychology faculty, Princeton (1924–27); associate professor and professor (1927–36), director of psychology laboratory (1927–36), director of Laboratory of Sensory Physiology (1934–36), Brown University; director of Laboratory of Sensory Psychology and Physiology, Tufts University (1938–52); secretary, Smithsonian Institution (1953–64); vice-president for research and exploration, National Geographic Society (from 1964). American Psychological Association president (1939). Editor, *Manual of Child Psychology*, 2d ed. (1954). Associate editor, *Journal of Genetic Psychology*.

Margaret Wooster Curti (1891–1961). American psychologist interested in space perception, child thought, and general theory. Assistant professor, Beloit College (1920–22); psychology department, Smith College (1922–37); research associate, Teachers College, Columbia (1937–42); lecturer, University of Wisconsin (1943–44); writer (from 1944).

Harvey Williams Cushing (1869–1939). First American to devote full time to the development of neurological surgery. Moseley professor of surgery (from 1912), surgeon-in-chief, Peter Bent Brigham Hospital (1913–32); Sterling professor of neurology, Yale (1933–37). The Harvey Cushing Society, founded in 1932, became the American Association of Neurological Surgeons.

Karl M. Dallenbach (1887–1971). American psychologist with special interest in sensation, attention, forgetting, physiological psychology. Instructor, associate professor, Cornell (1916–30); visiting professor, Columbia (1930–32); professor (1932–45), Sage professor of psychology (1945–48), Cornell; distinguished professor (1948–58), emeritus (from 1958), University of Texas. Experimentalists member. Editor, *American Journal of Psychology* (from 1926).

Raymond Dodge (1871–1942). American experimental psychologist and editor. Psychology faculty (1899–1924), professor at Institute of Psychology (1924–29), professor at Institute of Human Relations (1929–36), professor emeritus (from 1936), Yale. Experimentalists member. American Psychological Association president (1916). Discovered fundamental law of visual perception in reading and developed eye-movement and eye-testing apparatus. Among his works are *Elementary Conditions of Human Variability* (1927) and *Sensorimotor Consequences of Passive Oscillation* (1928).

Alice Vibert Douglas (1894–). Canadian astronomist and astrophysicist. War Office, London (1916–18); Cavendish Laboratory and Cambridge Observatory (1921–23); lecturer in physics and astrophysics,

McGill University (1923–39); dean of women (1939–59), astronomy professor (1943–62), Queens University. President, Royal Astronomy Society (Canada) (1943–45).

Max Forrester Eastman (1883–1969). American editor and writer. Strong Marxian socialist who helped found *The Masses* (1911) and *The Liberator* (1918). Among his works: *Enjoyment of Poetry* (1913), *Kinds of Love* (verse, 1931), *The End of Socialism in Russia* (1937).

Sir Arthur Stanley Eddington (1882–1944). English astronomer. Professor, Cambridge (from 1913) and director of the observatory (1914). Known especially for researches on the motion, internal constitution, and evolution of stars. His books include *Internal Constitution of the Stars* (1926) and *The Nature of the Physical World* (1928).

Beatrice Edgell (1871–1948). First Englishwoman to take a Ph.D. in psychology (with Kulpe, in 1901). Lecturer in philosophy and department head (1898), reader in psychology (1918), professor of psychology (1927), emeritus professor (1933), Bedford College, University of London. President, British Psychological Society (1929–31). Among her publications: *Theories of Memory, Mental Life, Encyclopedia of Religion and Ethics.*

Erik Homburger Erikson (1902–). Graduate of Vienna Psychoanalytic Institute (1933); Boston psychoanalyst; researcher at Harvard and Yale medical schools (1933–39); long-range study of children (1939–50). Among his works: *Childhood and Society* (1940), *Identity, Youth and Crisis* (1968). Winner of Pulitzer Prize and National Book Award, 1970.

Frank Fremont-Smith (1895–1974). Neuropathology Department, Harvard Medical School (1925–36); medical director, Josiah Macy, Jr., Foundation (1936–60); visiting professor, clinical psychiatry, Temple University (1962–70); numerous consulting positions (1948–74).

Adhémar Maximilian Maurice Gelb (1887–1936). Russian psychologist. University of Frankfort faculty (1919–31); director, with Max Wertheimer, of the Psychological Institute, professor of philosophy and psychology (from 1929). Discovered Gelb phenomenon (space perception depends on time experienced) in 1914. Research and publications on analysis of disturbances in sense perception, color perception, speech, and recognition processes after brain damage.

Arnold L. Gesell (1880–1961). American psychologist and pediatrician. Founder (1911) and director, Yale Clinic of Child Development. Author of such works as *The First Five Years* (1940). Member of Harrower's Ph.D. examining board, 1932.

Morris Ginsburg (1889–1970). Lecturer in philosophy (1914–28), Martin White professor of sociology (1929–54), emeritus professor (from 1954), University of London, London School of Economics. Among his publications: *The Psychology of Society* (1921; revised edition, 1964), *Studies in Sociology* (1932), *Sociology* (1934).

Kurt Goldstein (1878–1965). German Gestalt psychologist and neuropsychiatrist. Professor, University of Konigsburg (1912); head, Department of Neurology, Neurological Institute, University of Frankfurt-am-Main (from 1915); among founders and original editors of *Psychologische Forschung* (1921); director, Institute for Brain-Injured Soldiers (1917–33); neurology professor, University of Berlin (1930); Rockefeller Fellow, Amsterdam (1933). Came to the United States with the Rockefeller Foundation (1936); clinical professor of neurology, Columbia University (1936–40); head, neurophysiological laboratory, Montefiore Hospital (1936–40); clinical professor of neurology, Tufts University Medical School (1940–45); visiting professor of psychology at City College of New York (1950–55), at the New School for Social Research (1955–65), at Brandeis University (1956–57). Goldstein's research focused on psychopathology, comparative normal and pathological anatomy, speech and optic sphere disorders, brain injuries and tumors, and schizophrenia. Among his many publications in German, French, and English: *The Organism: A Holistic Approach to Biology Derived from Pathological Data in Man* (1934), *Human Nature in the Light of Psychopathology* (1940), *Language and Language Disturbances* (1948).

Hans Walther Gruhle (1880–1958). German psychologist. University of Heidelberg faculty (from 1912), named provisional director of Bonn Neurological Clinic in 1934 but was rejected because of politics; director, Bonn Neurological and Psychological Clinic (from 1946), emeritus (1952), provisional director (1955). Research on psychopathology, psychiatry, criminal psychology. Member of original editorial board, *Psychologische Forschung* (1921).

Sir Henry Head (1861–1940). English neurologist known for classic work on nerve regeneration and aphasia. For many years a consulting physician associated with London Hospital. Editor *Brain* (neurological journal) (1905–21). Among his publications: co-author, *Studies in Neurology* (1920), *Aphasia and Kindred Disorders of Speech* (1926).

Charles William Hendel (1890–). Philosophy professor, Princeton University (1920–29); MacDonald professor of moral philosophy and department chairman (1929–40) and dean, Faculty of Arts and Science

(1937–40), McGill University; professor of moral philosophy and metaphysics and department chairman (1940–59), Clarke professor emeritus of moral philosophy and metaphysics, Yale (from 1959).

Clark Leonard Hull (1884–1952). Psychology faculty and director of psychology laboratory, University of Wisconsin (1916–29); psychology professor, Institute of Human Relations (1929–47), Sterling professor of psychology (from 1947), Yale University. Research interests included learning, thought, aptitude testing. Among his works: *Aptitude Testing* (1928), *Hypnosis and Suggestibility* (1933).

George Humphrey (1889–1966). English experimental psychologist. Charleton professor of psychology, Queens University (1924–47); experimental psychology professor, director of the Institute for Experimental Psychology, Oxford University fellow (1947–56), emeritus professor (from 1956), Magdalen College, Oxford. Research focused on the nature of learning and thinking. On Harrower's Ph.D. examining board, 1932.

Harold E. Israel (1899–1961). Psychology department faculty, Dartmouth College (1922–25); psychology department, Smith College (from 1927). Research dealt with transfer of training and interference in learning. On Harrower's Ph.D. examining board, 1932.

Erich R. Jaensch (1883–1940). German psychologist and philosopher. Credited with the discovery of eidetic imagery and the related classification of persons into physiological types. Sought to establish a closer relation between psychology and philosophy.

Herbert Henry Jasper (1906–). American neurophysiologist. Assistant professor, Brown University (1933–38); professor of experimental neurology, McGill University (1938–64); professor of neurophysiology, University of Montreal (from 1965). Pioneered studies of electrical activity of the brain and the development of electroencephalography. Co-author with Wilder Penfield* of *Epilepsy and the Functional Anatomy of the Human Brain* (1953).

Wolfgang Köhler (1887–1967). Laid the foundations of Gestalt psychology with Wertheimer* and Koffka. Privatdozent at University of Frankfurt; director of anthropoid research station of Prussian Academy of Sciences (1913–20); professor, University of Berlin until Nazi regime. Moved to United States in 1935; professor of psychology, Swarthmore College (1935–55). Member of original editorial board, *Psychologische Forschung* (1921). Among his publications: *The Place of Value in a World of Fact* (1938).

Oswald Külpe (1862–1915). Latvian-born German psychologist. Professor, University of Leipzig (1886–94), at University of Wurzburg (1894–1909), at University of Bonn (from 1909). Experimental studies on attention, abstraction, and psychophysics.

Herbert Sidney Langfeld (1879–1958). American psychologist. Professor and director of Princeton Psychological Laboratory (1924–47). Editor, *Psychological Review* (1934–47). American Psychological Association president (1930). Research on visual sensations and perceptual problems. Among his published works: *The Aesthetic Attitude* (1920); joint author and editor, with E. G. Boring* and Harry Weld,* *Psychology—A Factual Textbook* (1935), *A Manual of Psychological Experiments* (1937), and *An Introduction to Psychology* (1939).

Karl Spencer Lashley (1890–1958). American physiological psychologist. Psychology faculty, University of Minnesota (1917–26); research and psychology professor, University of Chicago (1929–34); research professor of neuropsychology, Harvard University (1935–55); director, Yerkes Laboratories of Primate Biology, Orange Park, Florida (1942–55). Research concerned with vision and learning, and animal brain function in relation to behavior. His major work: *Brain Mechanisms and Intelligence* (1964).

Harold J. Laski (1893–1950). English political scientist. Professor, University of London (1926–50). Labour party leader, executive committee member (1936–49). His books include *Communism* (1927), *Liberty in the Modern State* (1930), *Democracy in Crisis* (1933), *Parliamentary Government in England* (1940).

Kurt Lewin (1890–1947). German psychologist. Psychology and philosophy professor, Psychology Institute, University of Berlin until Nazi regime. Came to the United States in 1932; psychology professor at Stanford University, Cornell University, University of Iowa (1932–44); director, Research Center for Group Dynamics, Massachusetts Institute of Technology (from 1944). Researched problems of individual and group motivation, dynamics of group behavior. Among his works: *A Dynamic Theory of Personality* (1935), *Resolving Social Conflicts* (1947).

Arthur Oncken Lovejoy (1873–1962). German-born American philosopher. Philosophy professor, Johns Hopkins University (1910–38). Co-founder, *Journal of the History of Ideas* (1940). Publications include: *Revolt Against Dualism* (1930), *The Great Chain of Being* (1936).

Alexander Romanovich Luria (1902–1977). Russian psychologist. Institute of Psychology, Moscow (1923–36); professor and department head, Ukrainian Psychoneurological Academy (1933–36); professor and head of psychology department, Moscow University (from 1945). Major contributions in the areas of development of thinking in children, mental retardation, relation between language and thought, neuropsychology. Among his works: *Nature of Human Conflicts* (1932), *Traumatic Aphasia* (1947), *Human Brain and Psychological Processes* (1963).

William McDougall (1871–1938). British mechanistic experimental psychologist. Psychology professor, Harvard University (1920–27), Duke University (from 1927). Early research focused on physiological psychology and vision. Publications include: *Body and Mind* (1911), *Introduction to Social Psychology* (1908), *Outline of Psychology* (1923).

Robert Brodie MacLeod (1907–1972). Canadian-born; naturalized American, 1938. Psychology lecturer, McGill University (1927–28); psychology instructor, Cornell University (1930–33); psychology and education department chairman, Swarthmore College (1933–46); psychology professor and department chairman (1946–48), director of psychology laboratory, McGill University (from 1948); Sage professor of psychology (from 1948), psychology department chairman (1948–53, 1965–66), Cornell University. Research in psychology of perception, language, and thinking. Among his publications: *Improving Undergraduate Instruction in Psychology* (1952).

Karl Marbe (1869–1953). German psychologist and philosopher. Philosophy professor and director, Psychological Institute, Frankfort (Ger.) Academy (1905–9); professor, Psychological Institute, University of Wurzburg (from 1909). Experimental study of judgment.

Walter Richard Miles (1885–1978). American psychologist. Psychology faculty, Wesleyan University (1913–14); research psychologist, Carnegie Nutrition Laboratory, Boston (1914–22); professor of experimental psychology, Stanford University (1922–32); professor of psychology (1931–53), emeritus fellow (from 1954), Yale University. American Psychological Association president (1932). President, Psychological Corporation, New York City, 1939–44. Experimentalists member. Warren Gold medal in experimental psychology (1949). Research into the structure and function of the human fovea; inventor of psychological methods and apparatus.

Henry Alexander (Harry) Murray (1893–). American psychologist. Psychology faculty (from 1926), professor (1950–62), emeritus professor (from 1962), Harvard University. American Psychological Association award for distinguished scientific contribution (1961). Developed method for assessing personality, especially the Thematic Apperception Test (T.A.T.). Among his publications: editor and co-author, *Explorations in Personality* (1938); *Assessment of Men* (1948); *Personality in Nature, Society and Culture* (1950).

Charles Samuel Myers (1873–1946). British psychologist, Cambridge University. Editor, *British Journal of Psychology* (1911–24). President, International Congress of Psychology (1923). From 1922 to 1946, devoted to establishing and developing the National Institute of Industrial Psychology. Most influential publication: *Text-Book of Experimental Psychology* (1909).

William Allan Neilson (1869–1946). Scottish educator. English instructor, Bryn Mawr (1898–1900), Harvard University (1900–1904), Columbia (1904–6); English professor, Harvard (1906–17); president, Smith College (1917–39). Among publications: *Essentials of Poetry* (1912), *A History of English Literature* (1920). Editor in chief, *Webster's New International Dictionary*, 2d edition (1934).

Marjorie Hope Nicolson (1894–1981). American educator. English faculty, University of Minnesota (1922–23), Goucher College (1923–26); professor (1926–41), dean (1929–41), Smith College; professor, English graduate faculty (1941–62), Trent professor emeritus (from 1962), Columbia University. Editor, *American Scholar* (1940); first woman president of Phi Beta Kappa (1940–46). President, Modern Language Association (1963).

Richard Charles Oldfield (1909–72). British psychologist. Psychology lecturer, Oxford University (1946–50); professor of psychology, University of Reading (1950–56); psychology professor and director, Institute of Experimental Psychology, and Magdalen College fellow, Oxford University (1956–66); director, speech and communication research unit, Medical Research Council, Edinburgh University (from 1966). Research and publications in perception, and language and its disorders.

Wilder Graves Penfield (1891–1974). American surgeon. Assistant professor of surgery, Columbia University (1924–28); neurosurgeon, Royal Victoria and Montreal General hospitals, Montreal (1928–60); professor of neurology and neurosurgery, McGill University (1934–54); director, Montreal Neurological Institute (1934–60). President, Royal College of Physicians and Surgeons of Canada (1939–41). Publications include: *Cytology and Cellular Pathology of the Nervous System* (1932); *Epilepsy and Cerebral Localization*, with T. C. Erickson (chapters by

H. Jasper* and M. Harrower-Erickson) (1941); *Manual of Military Neurosurgery* (1941); *The Excitable Cortex in Conscious Man* (1958); *The Mystery of the Mind* (1975).

Jean Piaget (1896–1980). Swiss psychologist. Major writer in developmental psychology, especially child development.

Albert Theodore Poffenberger (1885–1977). American psychologist. Psychology faculty (1912–26), department head (1927–41), and emeritus professor (from 1950), Columbia University. President, Psychological Corporation (1938–39). President, American Psychological Association (1935). Experimentalists member. Research in applied and physiological psychology. Among his works: *Psychology in Advertising* (1932), *Principles of Applied Psychology* (1942).

Edward Stevens Robinson (1893–1937). American psychologist. Psychology faculty, University of Chicago (1920–27); professor of psychology, Yale University (from 1927). Experimentalists member. Editor, *Psychological Bulletin* (1930–34). Research in learning and memory, work and fatigue, applications of psychology to personal and social problems. A major publication was *Law and the Lawyers* (1935), an attempt to introduce a social psychology of the law.

Erwin Schroedinger (1887–1961). Austrian physicist known for his work on the wave theory of matter and quantum theory. Winner (with Paul Dirac) of Nobel prize for physics (1933).

Jan Christiaan Smuts (1870–1950). South African general and statesman. A Boer leader in the Boer War (1899–1902), instrumental in effecting the Union of South Africa. Prime minister (1919–24), minister of justice (1933–39). His philosophical theory of holism posits that whole entities, which are fundamental components of reality, exist other than as the mere sum of their parts.

Charles Edward Spearman (1863–1945). British psychologist. Professor of psychology, University College, London University (1907–31). British Psychological Society president, 1923–26. Identified a single general factor of intelligence; marked the inception of the modern school of factor analysis. Main contributions include: *The Nature of Intelligence* and the *Principles of Cognition* (1923), *The Abilities of Man* (1927), and *Human Ability*.

Susan Stebbing (1885–1943). English philosopher. Philosophy lecturer (1920–26), reader (1927–33), professor (from 1933), Bedford College, London University; visiting professor, Columbia University (1931). Notable contributions to philosophical analysis. Among her publications: *A Modern Introduction to Logic* (1930).

William Stern (1871–1938). German psychologist. A pioneer in differential psychology, his studies focused on psychology of youth and of talent. Among his works: *Person und Sache* (3 vols.), 1906–24.

Sir Charles Putnam Symonds (1890–1978). British neurologist. Radcliffe Traveling Fellow, Oxford University (from 1920); honorary visiting neurologist, Johns Hopkins University; consulting physician emeritus for nervous diseases, Guys Hospital and the National Hospital (from 1970).

Dorothy Thompson (1894–1961). American journalist. Married to author Sinclair Lewis (1928–42). Correspondent in Vienna (1920–24), in Berlin (1924–28). Syndicated columnist, New York *Herald-Tribune* (1936–41).

Edward Lee Thorndike (1874–1949). American psychologist. Psychology professor, Teachers College, Columbia University (from 1904). Research on intelligence. Among his works: *Animal Intelligence* (1911), *The Psychology of Learning* (1914), *The Measurement of Intelligence* (1926), *Fundamentals of Learning* (1932).

Robert Henry Thouless (1894–). Scottish psychologist. Psychology lecturer, Manchester University (1921–25), Glasgow University (1926–37), Cambridge University (from 1938); reader in educational psychology, Cambridge (1945–61). British Psychological Society president (1949). Among his publications: *An Introduction to the Psychology of Religion* (1923), *Social Psychology* (1925), *General and Social Psychology* (1937, 1951, 1957), *Authority and Freedom* (1954).

Edward Chace Tolman (1886–1959). American psychologist. Psychology instructor, Northwestern University (1915–1918); psychology department (1918–54), emeritus professor (from 1954), University of California. American Psychological Association president (1937). Among his works: *Purposive Behavior in Animals and Men* (1932), *Drives Toward War* (1932), *Comparative Psychology* (1934).

Lord Tweedsmuir (John Buchan) (1875–1940). Scottish novelist, biographer, historian, and diplomat. Governor-general of Canada (1935). Among his publications, *The Thirty-Nine Steps* (novel), *A History of the Great War* (4 vols.). (At Wilder Penfield's * request, Harrower wrote a poem for Tweedsmuir's funeral, at which she read it.)

Margaret Floy Washburn (1871–1939). American psychologist. Psychology faculty (from 1903), professor (1908–37), Vassar College. A major scientific contribution was *The Animal Mind* (1908; 4th ed., 1936), a handbook of research in animal psychology. *Movement and Mental Imagery* (1916) presented a motor theory of all mental functions.

318 *glossary of names*

Harry Porter Weld (1877–[?]). American psychologist. Psychology faculty, Clark University (1900–1912); psychology professor (1912–45), department chairman (1938–45), professor emeritus (from 1945), Cornell University. Experimentalists member. Research in general and legal psychology. Among publications: editor, with E. G. Boring* and H. S. Langfeld,* *Psychology—A Factual Textbook* (1935), *A Manual of Psychological Experiments* (1937), and *An Introduction to Psychology* (1939).

Max Wertheimer (1880–1943). Founder of Gestalt psychology with the 1912 publication of "Experimental Studies on the Seeing of Motion" in which the effect of so-called apparent motion (induced by stroboscopic presentation) is identified as the *phi phenomenon* to stress the psychological reality of the experience in contrast to the older practice of describing the effect as an illusion or mis-perception. Privatdozent, University of Berlin (1916–29). Founder of *Psychologische Forschung* (1921), editor (1922–35). Came to United States in 1933 and joined the faculty of the New School for Social Research, "The University in Exile," New York City. Among his publications: *Productive Thinking*.

William Wilson. Professor of physics, Bedford College, University of London (1921–44).

Robert Sessions Woodworth (1869–1962). American psychologist. Psychology faculty (1903–42), emeritus professor (from 1942), Columbia University. Experimentalists member. American Psychological Association president, 1914. Psychological Corporation president, 1929. Editor, *Archives of Psychology*, 1906–45. Research stressed importance of both physiology and mental activity. Among works: *Adjustment and Mastery* (1939), *Experimental Psychology* (1938), *Heredity and Environment* (1941).

works cited

Ellis, Willis. 1938. *A source book of Gestalt psychology*. Introduction by Kurt Koffka. London: Kegan Paul, Trench and Trubner and Co., Ltd.

Goldstein, Kurt. 1939. *The organism*. New York: American Book Company.

Harrower, M. R. 1932. Organization and higher mental processes. *Psychologische Forschung* 17:56–120.

———. 1933. *Spiral and other poems*. New York: Ellis Printing Company.

———. 1934. Social status and moral development of the child. *British Journal of Educational Psychology* 4:75–95.

———. 1936. Some factors determining figure-ground articulation. *British Journal of Psychology* 26:407–24.

———. 1937. *The psychologist at work*. London and New York: Kegan Paul, Trench and Trubner and Co., Ltd., and Harper Bros.

———. 1939. Changes in figure-ground perception in patients with cortical lesions. *British Journal of Psychology* 30:47–51.

———. 1940a. Brain lesions and mental functions. In *Thirty-ninth Yearbook of National Society for the Study of Education*.

———. 1940b. The contribution of the Rorschach method to wartime psychological problems. *Journal of Mental Sciences* 86:1–12.

———. 1946. *Time to squander, time to reap*. New Bedford: Reynolds.

———. 1971a. A note on the Koffka papers. *Journal of Behavioral Sciences* 43 (April):141–53.

———. 1971b. Koffka's Rorschach experiment. *Journal of Personality Assessment* 35 (1):103–21.

———. 1972. *The therapy of poetry*. Springfield, Ill.: Charles Thomas.

319

Harrower-Erickson, M. R. [M. R. Harrower]. 1940a. Personality changes accompanying cerebral lesions, I. Rorschach studies of patients with cerebral tumors. *Archives of Neurology and Psychiatry* 43:859–90.

————. 1940b. Personality changes accompanying cerebral lesions, II. Rorschach studies of patients with focal epilepsy. *Archives of Neurology and Psychiatry* 43:1081–1107.

————. 1941. Changes accompanying organic brain lesions, III. A study of preadolescent children. *Journal of Genetic Psychology* 58:391–405.

————. 1942. Kurt Koffka 1886–1941. *American Journal of Psychology* 55:278–81.

Hebb, Donald, and Penfield, Wilder. 1940. Human behavior after extensive bilateral removal from the frontal lobes. *Archives of Neurology and Psychiatry* 44:421–38.

Köhler, Wolfgang. 1938. *The place of value in a world of facts.* New York: Liveright.

Koffka, Kurt. 1922. Perception: an introduction to Gestalt theory. *Psychological Bulletin* 19 (10):531–81.

————. 1924. *Growth of the mind.* New York: Harcourt Brace and Company.

————. 1930. Some problems of space perception. In *Psychologies of 1930*, edited by Carl Murchinson. Worcester, Mass.: Clark University Press.

————. 1930–34. Smith College studies in psychology. From the William Allan Neilson research laboratory, K. Koffka, director. Northampton, Mass.: Smith College.

————. 1932. A new theory of brightness-constancy: a contribution to a general theory of vision. *The Physical and Optical Societies Report of a Joint Discussion of Vision.*

————. 1935a. The ontological status of value. In *American Philosophy Today and Tomorrow*, edited by S. Hook and H. Kallen. New York: Lee Furman.

————. 1935b. *The principles of Gestalt psychology.* New York: Harcourt Brace and Company. Paper reprint, 1963.

————. 1938. Purpose and Gestalt: a reply to Professor McDougall. *Character and Personality* 6:218–38.

————. 1940. Problems in the psychology of art. In *Art: A Bryn Mawr Symposium*, with Richard Bernheimer, Rhys Carpenter, and Milton C. Nahm. Bryn Mawr Notes and Monographs, 9. Bryn Mawr, Pa.: Bryn Mawr College.

———. 1954. The place of a psychologist among scientists. *Texas Reports on Biology and Medicine* 12(1):28–109.

Koffka, Kurt, and Harrower, M. R. 1931. Color and organization, parts 1 and 2. *Psychologische Forschung* 15:145–275.

Penfield, Wilder, and Erickson, T. C. 1941. *Epilepsy and cerebral localization.* Springfield, Ill.: Charles Thomas. (Chap. 9: M. R. Harrower. Psychological studies in patients with epileptic seizures.)

Piaget, Jean. 1932. *The moral judgment of the child.* London and New York: K. Paul, Trench, Trubner and Co., Ltd., and Harcourt, Brace and Co.

Tolman, Edward C. 1932. *Purposive behavior in animals and men.* New York: The Century Co.

index